# THE KING'S MOST LOYAL ENEMY ALIENS

'Freedom! Out of the clutches of the Nazis,
I might yet live to fight them.'
Peter Masters (originally Peter Arany), 1938

—..—..—

Dedicated to the men and women of German and Austrian
origin who sacrificed their new-found freedom to liberate
Europe from Nazism

# THE KING'S MOST LOYAL ENEMY ALIENS

## GERMANS WHO FOUGHT FOR BRITAIN IN THE SECOND WORLD WAR

### HELEN FRY

SUTTON PUBLISHING

First published in the United Kingdom in 2007 by
Sutton Publishing, an imprint of NPI Media Group Limited
Cirencester Road · Chalford · Stroud · Gloucestershire · GL6 8PE

British Library Cataloguing in Publication Data
A catalogue record for this book is available from the British Library.

Hardback ISBN 978-0-7509-4700-8
Paperback ISBN 978-0-7509-4701-5

Typeset in Goudy.
Typesetting and origination by
NPI Media Group Limited.
Printed and bound in England.

# CONTENTS

# PREFACE AND ACKNOWLEDGEMENTS

When I embarked on the research for this book, it soon became clear that the sheer volume of material emerging meant that it would not be possible to cover all aspects of 'enemy aliens' in the British Forces in the Second World War. I have therefore limited the material to German and Austrian refugees who enlisted in the British Forces, and with one or two exceptions, only those who fought in the European campaigns. I have not been able to go into any depth on overseas service in Africa, the Middle East or Far East. Neither could I extend this book to include the part played by Czech, Italian and Polish refugees, all of whom made their own special contribution to the British Forces during the war. Other individual profiles, photographs of the period, and appendices of official war diaries for the alien Pioneer Corps companies are contained in my previous book *Jews in North Devon during the Second World War*, and have not been duplicated in full here. Every endeavour has been made to ensure accuracy of information throughout the text.

I would like to pay special tribute to the veterans and their families who have given so much of their time to be interviewed and supply information. It has been a pleasure and huge privilege working with them. Many have shared experiences about which they have not previously spoken for fear of burdening their families with the past. Now their voices are heard here, some for the first time. They have ensured that their selfless contribution to the defeat of Nazism and that of their colleagues are remembered. My sincere thanks to Eric Sanders for extensive help on 12 Force/SOE; William Howard for the

Royal Navy; Colin Anson for material on 3 Troop of No. 10 Inter-Allied Commando; also Fritz Lustig and Michael Streat for the Entertainment Section of the Pioneer Corps and other related material. Each has spent many hours with me and helped enormously in the production of this book.

To the veterans of Harry Rossney's monthly coffee mornings, a special thank you for sharing your wartime experiences and supporting my research on many levels. Thanks especially to Harry Rossney, Geoffrey Perry and Willy Field.

This book would not have been possible without the enormous help of archivists and historians in specialist libraries, museums and archives. My thanks must go to Martin Sugarman of the Association of Jewish Ex-service Men and Women (AJEX); Howard Spier of the Association of Jewish Refugees; staff at the Imperial War Museum; David Fletcher, historian at the Tank Museum; staff at the Wiener Library and the Jewish Military Museum, and Dr Elisabeth Lebensaft and Christoph Mentschl at the Austrian Academy of Sciences in Vienna for material on Austrians in the British Forces in the Second World War.

I would also like to pay particular tribute to the late Captain Peter Leighton-Langer, who died earlier this year. An ex-Austrian refugee, he served first in the Pioneer Corps from 1941 until 1943 and then the Royal Artillery, seeing active service in India from January 1945. After his wartime service, he spent many decades researching, recording and accumulating a huge archive about fellow Germans and Austrians who enlisted in the British Forces during the Second World War. This extensive and encyclopedic research resulted in the publication of two books, the first of which was entitled X Steht für unbekannt: Deutsche und Österreicher in den Britischen Streitkräften im Zweiten Weltkrieg and was published by Verlag in Berlin in 1999. His translation of that book, The King's Own Loyal Enemy Aliens: German and Austrian Refugees in Britain's Armed Forces, 1938–1945, was published by Vallentine Mitchell in 2006. Without his unprecedented work in this field, so much about the refugees who served in the British Forces would now be lost to future generations.

Sincere thanks to Jonathan Falconer, my Commissioning Editor, and staff at Sutton Publishing for publishing the book and making it such an enjoyable experience.

I am fortunate to have a close circle of friends who support me during the writing of my books. To each of them goes my particular thanks: James Hamilton, Richard Bernstein Paul and Daphne Ruhleman, Karen Davy, Edith Palmer, Dorinda and Lorna. To Elkan Levy, former President of the United Synagogue and currently Director of Small Jewish Communities, I owe a huge debt of gratitude. He deserves a special mention for his tireless and enthusiastic support of my work and for spurring me on. Thanks to Mick Catmull, producer at BBC South-West, who has enthusiastically taken up this story and with whom it is a pleasure to work. Over the summer of 2006 he produced a short documentary about some of these veterans for BBC South-West's programme 'Inside Out' which he entitled *The King's Most Loyal Enemy Aliens*. It was broadcast on 16 October 2006 and then shown twice on Armistice Day, 11 November, across Britain.

My heartfelt thanks must go to my friend and mentor Mary Curry. For the last few years she has sent appropriate material my way and read the drafts of every chapter. Her comments and meticulous attention to detail are much appreciated and have enhanced the quality of my writing.

My love and thanks to my husband Martin and mother Sandra without whose practical help this book could not have been written. To my young boys Jonathan, David and Edward: thank you for being interested in my work and asking questions. May you continue to appreciate the significance of recording history for posterity.

# INTRODUCTION

This is the extraordinary story of the 10,000 Germans and Austrians who fought for Britain during the Second World War. Their particular contribution to the Allied victory over Hitler and Nazism is largely unknown. One in seven of the 75,000 German and Austrian refugees who came to Britain between 1933 and 1939 enlisted in the British Forces, a surprisingly high percentage. Under Nazi law they were stateless, but according to British law they were still Germans. They all took the unprecedented step of swearing allegiance to King George VI even though, with a few exceptions, they did not receive British nationality until after the war. The majority began their army life in the non-combatant Pioneer Corps, the pick and shovel on their cap badge emblematic of hard physical labour. They became affectionately known as 'the King's Most Loyal Enemy Aliens'.

They had come to Britain as victims of Nazi oppression, mainly the Jewish intellectuals of central Europe but also Aryan Socialists and 'degenerate artists'; the political opponents of Nazism. All had one thing in common – their lives and those of their families were at risk after the Nazis gained power in Germany in 1933 and Austria in 1938. Born and raised in those countries, the Jewish refugees saw themselves first and foremost as loyal German and Austrian citizens. Their Jewishness was secondary. A trace of Jewish ancestry or opposition to Nazism put thousands of ordinary German lives at risk. Many had relatives who had fought the British during the First World War or they themselves had done so and received the Iron Cross for bravery. All this counted for nothing. So, just twenty-one years later, they found themselves on the other side in British uniform fighting their fellow Germans. Their story is unique in British history and all the more extraordinary because none of them could be conscripted. All had to volunteer. Each wanted a hand in defeating Nazism and to repay the debt to Britain for saving their lives.

The exodus of Europe's most prominent intellectuals began when Hitler came to power in 1933. During the 1930s German society was gradually transformed into one of tyrannous fear and exclusion of anyone not considered a 'true Aryan'. Prominent Jewish scientists, professors, musicians, doctors, surgeons and other public figures left Germany to begin a new life in Britain and the United States. The Nuremberg Laws, passed in the summer of 1935, excluded Jews from public life and forced them on to a path that would eventually lead to the Holocaust and the Final Solution, although they could not have totally foreseen such a fate. By the late 1930s it became clear that Hitler had designs to incorporate neighbouring countries into a 'Greater Germany, a Third Reich. Austria was the first when German troops crossed the border on 12 March 1938 in what became known as the *Anschluss*. The face of Austria changed more dramatically than anywhere else. Just two days later, on 14 March, Hitler paraded through the streets of Vienna amid a rapturous welcome from the crowds. The anti-Jewish laws which had gradually defined and restricted the lives of Germany's Jews over a number of years since 1933, applied immediately to Austrian Jews. The cultural and social fabric of Austrian society crumbled as its Jewish population was denied its public appointments as lawyers, doctors, musicians, architects, teachers, dentists, scientists, bankers and businessmen. All found themselves without employment and many sought ways of leaving Austria, as intellectuals had done in Germany since 1933. Obtaining an exit visa was by no means straightforward. Britain had strict quotas for entry into Britain and Palestine. Even for those with an international reputation, such as Sigmund Freud (the founder of psychoanalysis), leaving Vienna was not easy. His family was fortunate in obtaining the financial and moral support of Princess Marie Bonaparte of Greece, but it still took two months to secure the necessary papers. The Freuds endured raids on their home and business, and a period of house-arrest before they came to Britain.

In the relative safety of Britain enemy aliens, including members of the Freud family, enlisted into the British Army's Pioneer Corps. However, it would be nearly two years before the government granted permission for them to fight in combatant units or offer their expertise and knowledge of German for intelligence operations. From 1943 they transferred in large numbers from the Pioneer Corps into fighting regiments and were at the forefront of every campaign of the war, especially after D-Day. With the Royal Armoured Corps, the infantry, the Commandos, the Royal Marine Commandos and the Parachute Regiment, they spearheaded the advance through Normandy and finally into Germany, often working behind enemy lines. Others trained for 'special duties' and were formed into German-speaking units for covert operations, either with raiding forces, the Commandos or Special Operations Executive (SOE). Their fluency in German was crucial for each regiment, especially once German prisoners were captured. They could interrogate prisoners and gain vital intelligence for the Allies. They also had to cope with the reality of losing their comrades in battle, whether fellow German refugees or British comrades. Their motivation was never in doubt. If it was anyone's war, it was certainly theirs. Some had already spent time in concentration camps and were lucky to survive the appalling conditions and brutality. For Willy Field (Willy Hirshfeld), born in Bonn and a survivor of Dachau concentration camp, his motivation for joining-up is clear:

> I volunteered for the British Forces because I wanted to give something back to Britain for saving my life. Without it I would have perished in the Holocaust alongside my parents and other family members. I could have stayed in Australia or the Pioneer Corps where in either case life would have been easy, but I didn't. I wanted to fight the Germans. It was my duty.

William Ashley Howard (Horst Adolf Herzberg), half-Jewish in the eyes of the Nazis, served first in the Pioneer Corps and then the Royal Navy and was involved in the height of action at sea:

Having been in Germany and lived through what was happening, every fibre of my body suggested that I had to do something. The regime was so evil. I was aware of the plight of the Jewish people and I considered it unquestionably my duty to fight at the highest level.

Max Dickson (Max Dobriner) of 3 Troop explains that from 1942/3 many German-speaking refugees were aware of what was going on in the concentration camps.

I knew then that I had to fight. I had tried to get my parents out of Germany but they were too far East. My eldest brother went to France where he was shot. Another brother went to Denmark and in 1942 was sent to Theresienstadt and Auschwitz. He was rescued by Count Bernadotte who exchanged German POWs for Jews in concentration camps, and survived.[1] My parents were sent to the Warsaw Ghetto and didn't survive. I had come to England in 1939 and knew that I had to fight in the British Forces.

How did it feel to be fighting fellow Germans? Ken Adam (Klaus Adam), the only known German fighter pilot in the RAF, comments:

Even Germans today often ask me did I feel any qualms when I attacked German soldiers during the war. I say, 'No, I didn't'. Apart from anything else, when you're flying in a single-seater fighter aircraft, you are not in contact with the death you create on the ground. You're very much in contact with the death of your friends who are shot down or crash in flames, but not with the people on the ground. By that, I mean the military. Obviously, we didn't attack any civilians. But having said that, even if I had been eye to eye with it, I decided that we had to win the war and we had to get rid of Hitler and the Nazis.

But the story of these remarkable men and women did not end with the silencing of the mortars and guns. When Germany signed the unconditional surrender and the European war was officially over in

May 1945, the enemy aliens in the British Forces were drafted in their thousands to begin the vital work of denazification and reconstruction in Germany and Austria. Their fluency in German and intimate knowledge of the towns and cities of their birth meant that they were an inestimable asset, and one that the Allies could ill afford to lose. They were assigned to the hunt for Nazi war criminals, compiling evidence of war crimes, interrogation of POWs, translation of key military and civic documents, and overseeing local government and translation work at the War Crimes Tribunals. How did it feel as victors? Walter Eberstadt, who served in the Oxfordshire and Buckinghamshire Light Infantry and worked for the British military authorities at Radio Hamburg at the end of the war, comments:

> I tried not to abuse my power. We had innumerable discussions, often late into the night, about the past and future. I tried not to impose my opinions, let alone bully, because of the authority vested in me by a British officer's uniform, because Britain had won the war, because my parents had been kicked out of Germany, my grandparents had died at Belsen, because Germany had been responsible for two world wars, for killing six million Jews. By setting myself strict standards, I hoped it would become self-evident to those with whom I was in contact that Jews were not what they had been made out to be by Hitler. I wanted to earn respect by what I did, not because I wore a uniform and we had won and they had lost. Personal example provides the only effective form of leadership.[2]

Failure to defeat Nazism was never an option in their minds. Many have since discussed how they did not expect to survive the war, especially those involved in frontline fighting and operations behind enemy lines. By the end of the war, they had distinguished themselves out of all proportion to their numbers. Without them, the war would have lasted longer and the task of reconstructing postwar Europe become impossible in such a short space of time. Postwar obligations lasted longer than the war itself. They remained loyal to Britain, were granted British citizenship and went on to distinguish themselves in public life.

*Chapter 1*

# THE PIONEER CORPS

War broke out on 3 September 1939, changing the status of Germans and Austrians living in Britain. They were immediately classified as enemy aliens even though they had been granted refuge as victims of Nazi oppression. Three and a half thousand refugees were living in Kitchener Camp, a transit camp on the Kent coast. The majority volunteered for the British Forces because they wanted a direct hand in defeating Nazism. They had seen too much in the countries of their birth to sit back and allow others to do the fighting. By the end of 1939 the British Government permitted enemy aliens to join the non-combatant Auxiliary Military Pioneer Corps (AMPC), the only unit open to them at that time. Those who enlisted took the momentous step of swearing allegiance to King George VI, donned British Army uniform and received the King's Shilling. They became affectionately known as 'The King's Most Loyal Enemy Aliens'.

The alien Pioneer companies were trained at No 3. Training Centre of the Pioneer Corps, initially based at Kitchener Camp under the command of Lord Reading (Lord Rufus Isaacs). A number of men of alien nationality living elsewhere in Britain, who had also volunteered for army service, were sent directly to the camp for training. Derelict since the First World War, it had been given by the British Government to Jewish relief organisations in 1938 to be rebuilt as a transit camp for men fleeing persecution. Reconstruction began after *Kristallnacht*, the Night of Broken Glass, when on 9 November 1938 the Nazis burned synagogues and smashed Jewish businesses throughout Germany and Austria. Kitchener Camp was rebuilt using the skills of 200 refugee craftsmen from Germany. The work was carried out under the supervision of British architect Ernest Joseph and aided by two refugee architects, Viennese-born Dr Walter Marmorek, and Berlin-born Dr Rudi Herz. Both enlisted in the Pioneer Corps. Walter Marmorek served with 74 Company and in 1943 transferred to the Royal Engineers, eventually posted to Italy and Austria. He attained the rank of major. Rudi Herz joined 220 Company and then 77 Company of the Pioneer Corps. In 1943 he also transferred to the Royal Engineers and in June 1944 embarked for service in India where he remained for a year as chief engineer in Bangalore. In October 1945 he was posted to Germany to work on designing buildings in army quarters and camps for the British Army of the Rhine (BAOR). He was demoblised in September 1947 with the rank of captain.

Six Pioneer Corps companies were raised at Kitchener Camp, each consisting of about 300 men. These were nos 69, 74, 77, 87, 88 and 93. Five of these companies were sent to France in early 1940 to join the British Expeditionary Force (BEF). Before they left, the men changed their names in case of capture and signed the following declaration:

> I certify that I understand the risks . . . to which I and my relatives may be exposed by my employment in the British Army outside the United Kingdom. Notwithstanding this, I certify that I am willing to be employed in any theatre of war.

The declaration is a poignant reminder of their commitment to the freedom of Europe and the personal risk that they were prepared to undertake to secure that freedom.

The first to be raised at Kitchener Camp was 69 Company which arrived in France on 23 January 1940. The men worked around Rennes in Brittany with a railway construction company. On 1 February, 74 Company landed and was stationed in Rennes and then Bruz (15km south of Rennes) working on roads. On 18 March, 87 Company landed and commenced work with the Royal Army Ordnance Corps at the port of Le Havre before moving to Harfleur. In April, 88 Company arrived and worked alongside 87 Company in guarding the docks at Harfleur. Finally, 93 Company arrived on

11 May 1940, the day after Holland had fallen to German forces. They worked initially on road construction at Bruz and then handled stores at a railway dump and road construction at Château Bray. The companies were essentially an unarmed manual labour force, supporting the BEF, and remained in France until their evacuation in mid-June 1940. Only 77 Company remained in England, stationed from February at the Royal Engineers Stores Depot at Donnington.

Back in England, men of German and Austrian nationality continued to enlist at Kitchener Camp and train for the Pioneer Corps. Alfred Perlés, the metaphysical writer and friend of Henry Miller and Lawrence Durrell, who was training for the Pioneer Corps contrasted the mood of the refugees with that of the nation:

The fears that obscured the minds of the Pioneers were well founded in fact. These men were desperate because they knew from their own experience all the atrocities of which the Nazis, unloosed, were capable. Nearly every one of them had been subjected to the cruelty and brutality of the Hitlerites. The English, on the other hand, had never experienced this fear. They were apprehensive, of course, of the war situation in general but they were not really afraid. Their very ignorance of the thoroughness of German native brutality, which none of them had experienced in the flesh, saved them from the panic with which the victims of Nazi oppression seemed to be seized. Had the English actually known, as the refugees did, the terrible tortures and ordeals in store for them should the Germans be able to get a foothold in these islands, they too might have lost their heads and given in before the struggle for life and death was actually to take place. It so happened that their ignorance of the true danger, coupled with their nerve, saved the world from the terror of Nazi domination. England could resist only because the English had no idea what they were resisting, nor how heavily the dice were loaded against them.[1]

For Harry Rossney (Helmuth Rosettenstein), one of the 200 craftsmen reconstructing Kitchener Camp, all hope lay in Britain:

'England, at that hour, was the hope of the world, of freedom and tolerance. We clung to its apron, blessing the day we were allowed to set foot on it, albeit originally on a temporary visa.'[2]

When in the late spring of 1940 Belgium, Holland and France was overrun by Nazi forces, panic struck the British Government. There was the very real possibility and fear that Hitler would parachute German spies in British uniforms, 'Fifth Columnists', into Kent and infiltrate the refugees. As a result, the remaining refugees at Kitchener Camp were moved overnight with No. 3 Training Centre to Willsworthy Camp near Lydford on Dartmoor in the heart of Devon. Morale was low and the weather on the moor was terrible. For several weeks, the men camped in tents in dense fog and heavy rain. Nicolai Poliakoff, more famously known as Coco the Clown of Bertram Mills Circus, had also enlisted in their ranks and entertained the men with his comedy sketches in the NAAFI tent. In his autobiography *Behind My Greasepaint*, he writes:

> The weather was very bad, pouring with rain. It was not enough that the weather was wet but I had to pour buckets of water all over myself and get wetter still; but I didn't mind that as long as I could make the boys laugh.

Alfred Perlés, who served with 137 and 249 Companies, describes the depressing conditions on Dartmoor, interspersing his memories with no small amount of humour:

> The camp proper – a tent camp – was reached after half an hour's cross-country march from the village [of Lydford]. It was a most desolate place. We lived in a meadow like cattle. None of us was used to living under canvas, and we all felt highly uncomfortable. The tents seemed too small, yet eight men had to find accommodation in one tent, together with their full equipment. . . . The weather too changed overnight and the first morning we woke up in the tents it was raining outside. Rain is always depressing at the best; but when your abode is a tent it is tragic. We did have floorboards – not all the tents had them – but they did protect us

from the chilly damp. . . . There was a wash-place in the open: cold water and a few washbasins, hopelessly inadequate for the whole company. Only the inveterate cleanliness fiends went out in the rain for a wash. The latrine was an abominable contraption, seemingly conceived and constructed by a paranoiac corporal. It was no longer the lack of privacy that bothered us, but the total absence of any minimum of comfort. At night it was quite a hazardous matter to venture to leave the tent, as all the tents looked alike in the rigorously enforced blackout. Yet blackout or no blackout, a man has to get out of his tent once in a while when the cold and damp begin to have their effect on the bladder. Gorloff [a colleague] had marked our tent 'Ritz Hotel' with a piece of white chalk.[3]

Frankfurt-born Edgar Bender was assigned as army cook on Dartmoor. From there he was sent on detachment to a quarry near Mary Tavy, again as cook but also on general work including loading and unloading goods trains. He writes in *Reminiscences of the Pioneer Corps: 1940–1942*:

On one occasion I unhooked a goods wagon to push it into a more convenient position for unloading and stacking the contents and on hooking it up again I must have fixed it wrongly. It came away later. As the railway line from the quarry to Plymouth station was downhill all the way, we had a telephone call from the station to say that a lonely goods truck had just rolled into the station![4]

With no washing facilities at Willsworthy Camp, the men bathed in the fast-flowing River Tavy. Complaints about the conditions were finally heeded and the men were moved to Hilltop Holiday Camp at Westward Ho! on the North Devon coast. Edgar Bender was responsible once again for cooking duties:

From our detachment in the quarry we were sent to a former holiday camp by the sea near Bideford. I had to cook again, at first in the field. I had to send out a 'fatigue party' every day to collect drift wood for my Aldershot oven. This was a mud tunnel built over corrugated iron sheets in a trench. The meals were cooked in large oval pots. It was all very primitive. Breakfast for 200 men had to be ready by 8 a.m. As well as cooking, I helped in our work of building large rectangular pits in the local golf course for storing high octane aircraft fuel.[5]

Westward Ho! with its miles of sandy beach and pebble ridge was an idyllic setting, seemingly remote from the realities of war. It was a secluded haven where the men could enjoy the delights of a Devonshire cream tea, rationing not yet having taken hold. Training continued in anticipation of forming more alien Pioneer companies. It was a tense time with fears of an imminent German invasion. Harry Rossney writes:

We were training hard, but still without weapons. Only non-commissioned officers and officers were armed, most of these were British. We were also guarding the area against agents being dropped, or invasion forces taking advantage of good landing beaches. Bideford Bay was one. I remember one dark stormy night being alerted to rush to my post overlooking the bay. My weapon a pickaxe handle. With tin-hat, gas mask and gas cape, I flew as fast as my legs would carry me. Running up the dunes at 3 a.m., pitch-dark, I was challenged: 'Halt, who goes there?' Breathless and with a strong German accent I tried to explain who I was and what I was doing there. I did not get very far before I heard a rifle being cocked nearby by an English soldier behind bushes. My heart stopped beating. In those fearful days it was 'shoot first, ask questions later'. Then another command: 'Hold your fire! Raise your arms! Advance to be recognised!' A sergeant approached cautiously and asked me a question. I could breathe again. It would appear that they had moved another Regular Army unit in to guard the area. They did not know that a group of friendly aliens were billeted not far away. We were then confined to camp for 7 days to give the local people a chance to get used to the idea of foreigners with German accents running around in British Army uniform.[6]

Meanwhile the Germans were advancing through Western Europe at alarming speed. By May 1940 Belgium, Holland and Denmark had fallen. German troops finally swept into France and broke through the Allied lines cutting off Dunkirk and trapping the British Expeditionary Force. Paris was declared an open city. The British Government ordered the immediate evacuation of some 300,000 troops from the beaches around Dunkirk in an epic rescue operation. It was to be another month before the alien Pioneer companies were also evacuated. In the intervening period there was great anxiety and uncertainty with rumours abounding that they might be left behind. William Ashley Howard (Horst Adolf Herzberg), who was later in the Royal Navy, was stationed in France with 88 Company:

We had been billeted in a camp on a hilltop overlooking the docks of Le Havre. During the day we were assigned to loading and unloading freight in those docks. During the night we were bombarded by the Luftwaffe. On 19 May our daily routine was abruptly interrupted by Jeeps patrolling up and down the sea front hollering instructions to return to our units. Having clambered up the hill to our base, we reported to our section sergeant. We were told that we were on standby because the Germans had swept through Belgium overnight and had moved into French territory. We stood patiently in our huts, gas masks on because we expected an attack. We were told to have an early night.

At about 1.a.m, our agitated sergeant shouted instructions in his German accent that we must prepare to leave at once and only take essentials – a toothbrush and aftershave. We were marched down the hill on that starlit night to waiting lorries. We clambered aboard in a state of unease and foreboding. Where were we going? We soon had our answer. One of our learned members looked up at the night sky and exclaimed in his thick German accent, 'Looking at ze stars, I can tell ve are going to ze frontline'. There was great consternation all around. The general consensus was that this was impossible – we were unarmed. We were moving along, mostly in silence, and after about two hours we arrived in a sleepy village. It was about 4 a.m. and most of the houses surrounding the village square still had their shutters closed. We were told not to make a noise or speak German. At around 8 a.m. a staff car swept into the square and out stepped a brigadier. His gloved hands tightly grasped around his swagger stick. He mounted his soap box and called us to attention and then instructed us to stand easy. His plum, lisp voice declared words along these lines: 'Men of 88 Company, as you are probably aware, the enemy has broken through on several fronts and is heading in this direction. I therefore call on you to fight side by side with your British comrades. You will be given arms and ammunition with appropriate training. May God bless you all.'

We were stunned. Within the next two hours we were issued with Lee Enfield rifles. Most of us had never seen a rifle before. That afternoon we were marched to a field, each carrying a rifle. We assumed that we were about to receive instruction on how to use it. No. Our florid-faced sergeant major of Irish descent decided that first we must be able to handle the rifle like a soldier on parade. We were shown how to slope arms, order arms and present arms. We practiced incessantly whilst the enemy was closing in. The following morning we were each given five rounds of ammunition and shown how to load, aim and fire. Shooting was prohibited unless we saw the whites of the enemy eyes. We were moved closer to the frontline, on guard at all times, even through the night. During the third night I was on guard duty for four hours, marching up and down the highway with my rifle in the slope arm position. I had five rounds of ammunition in my pocket. Halfway through the watch the duty officer carried out his rounds and asked me whether there was anything to report. I replied, 'Yes, see over there at the foot of the valley. A flashing light is going on and off.' 'Well,' he replied. 'We'll investigate in the morning.' So much for reassurance.

Over the following two days the advancing German Army swung towards Paris and away from us. Once the immediate crisis had been averted we were rapidly disarmed and once again became non-combatant, digging trenches near Rennes.[7]

The five alien Pioneer companies were finally evacuated from St Malo in June, the sound of German gunfire clearly audible in the background. One of William Howard's lasting memories of that day was the sight of French citizens lining the streets and jeering at them for abandoning them to the incoming German forces: 'they called us all the names under the sun for walking out on them, but we walked to fight another day.'

Once back on British soil, the Pioneer companies were taken to Westward Ho! to re-group, with the exception of 88 and 93 Companies which went first to Alexandra Palace in London. After re-grouping they were sent all around the country on vital construction work, guarding strategic depots, fire-watch duties and clearing up after bombing raids on London, Plymouth and Exeter. Others were involved in constructing civil defences around the south coast.

## COLLAR THE LOT – MASS INTERNMENT OF ENEMY ALIENS

After the fall of Dunkirk, the government began the full-scale internment of enemy aliens. Those men who had already enlisted in the Pioneer Corps were not interned, but nearly 30,000 other Germans, Austrians and Italians were interned behind barbed wire under Churchill's policy of 'collar the lot'. Many were working in academic institutions and businesses, but in the early hours of the morning received a visit from a local policeman and were taken from their homes into custody. They remained in internment for several months, sometimes longer, while parliament debated their situation. The majority were interned on the Isle of Man, living in requisitioned hotels and boarding houses behind barbed wire. The camps became a microcosm of Central European intellect with the formation of a mini-university, an orchestra and the Amadeus Quartet. Artists, sculptors, scientists, musicians, doctors, surgeons and professors organised lectures and cultural activities.

About 1,500 internees were boarded onto the SS *Arandora Star* bound for Canada. On 2 July the ship was torpedoed by a German U-boat off the coast of Ireland, resulting in huge loss of life. The survivors were pulled from the freezing waters and taken back to internment camps. A few days later they joined 2,000 other internees on the troopship *Dunera* at Liverpool, bound for Australia. The

*Dunera* sailed on 10 July 1940, also carrying 251 Nazi POWs and 200 Italian Fascists, both Category A prisoners and deemed a threat to national security. The internees suffered a nine-week journey to Sydney amid appalling conditions on board. Many likened the *Dunera* to a floating concentration camp. Overcrowding was the main problem with internees sleeping on three levels below deck. One group slept on the iron floor, another on long tables or benches, and the third on hammocks strung above the tables. Most suffered terrible sea-sickness. The sanitary arrangements were spartan with only ten toilets for 2,000 men. Walter Freud, grandson of Sigmund Freud, was one of the *Dunera* internees. His mathematical brain calculated that if all ten toilets were in use all the time, then each internee would have just seven minutes a day for their requirements. Such a situation necessitated major organisational creativity. He writes in his unpublished memoirs *Before the Anticlimax*:

> The organisational talent of some of our co-internees, genuine German-Prussian merchant seamen and similar prisoners, came in very useful. They formed the toilet police, calling up people as vacancies arose. The shout '*Drei Mann rechts ran zum pinkel*' (three men to the right for peeing) is still clearly audible in my ears.

Not only were conditions severely cramped, but internees were confined below deck for 23 hours a day with a maximum of one hour's exercise above deck. Most passed the time playing bridge and chess, but for many of the older internees, the conditions were insufferable. In spite of the conditions, Freud comments philosophically:

> With hindsight, to transport us away from England was an act of mercy. If Britain had been invaded in the autumn of 1940, as many people anticipated, the Jews, particularly the German and Austrian Jews, could not have expected an easy time. Alternatively, if Britain had been forced to make a dishonourable peace, she might well have been asked to extradite all the immigrant Jews back to Germany. Far away, in Canada or Australia, outside British jurisdiction, we would be safe from such a fate.[8]

Occasionally they were permitted above deck, a luxury not afforded to other internees for more than an hour a day. Another internee Willy Field (Willy Hirschfeld) comments:

> I had survived Dachau concentration camp to be subjected to this horrifying experience. Where was my freedom? We were very badly treated aboard ship and not as refugees from Nazi oppression. England saved my life, but what happened to us on the *Dunera* was a grave injustice. We were not safe on board. We were torpedoed by a German submarine, the ship was overcrowded and people were sick. We never saw the light of day. The officer-in-charge was later court-marshalled for this.[9]

The internees remained in Australia and Canada until 1941 when government officials were sent out there to recruit men for the Pioneer Corps. In each case, several hundred internees enlisted and were sent back to England. The majority from Australia sailed back to England on the SS *Stirling Castle*, arriving in Liverpool in November 1941. They were sent to Ilfracombe and were among the last to be trained through No. 3 Training Centre of the Pioneer Corps.

## THE PIONEER CORPS AND ILFRACOMBE

The government authorised the gradual release of internees from camps around Britain as early as August 1940. One of the few ways to secure a speedy release was to volunteer for the British Army. Over 3,000 enlisted, swore allegiance to the king and were drafted into the Pioneer Corps. With the expected arrival of so many new recruits, the site at Westward Ho! was clearly inadequate to accommodate their numbers. At the end of September 1940 No. 3 AMPC Training Centre moved from Westward Ho! to requisitioned hotels in Ilfracombe, further around the North Devon coast. Karl Ruge, a refugee from Berlin and active Socialist in Germany, joined the Pioneer Corps at Ilfracombe in September 1940 and became one of the training instructors for eighteen months:

Ilfracombe was well-organised and we were allocated hotels around the town. I was billeted in the Britannia Hotel on the harbour. I became a corporal, providing instruction to new recruits on the use of rifles and machine guns. The training schools were based a few miles along the coast at Morthoe and Woolacombe. We were allowed a maximum of 2% fatal casualties during training exercises, but fortunately there were no such casualties whilst I was there. We used the long sandy beaches as assault courses and set up obstacles and gun positions.'[10]

Harry Rossney, a signwriter by trade and one of the craftsmen at Kitchener Camp, worked for nearly eighteen months in the Quartermaster Store in Wilder Road in Ilfracombe, kitting out every soldier who passed through the door:

The internees were a sad, disappointed and frustrated bunch. We kitted them out in minutes with great efficiency and eye-measurements. We still issued them with boots from the First World War. The rifles issued to the NCOs were of equal vintage (Ross rifles instead of Lee Enfields). Several thousand apprehensive internees of all ages came through the open doors of our store and left clutching their kit, more bewildered than ever. Not an easy time for anyone because many of them were highly educated from universities or businesses originally, but many turned themselves not only into smart soldiers but also very useful ones as their individual war records show later on.[11]

Ilfracombe marked a turning point in the people who enlisted in the Pioneer Corps. Those who had joined at Kitchener Camp, and by and large in Westward Ho!, were taken from among the newly arrived refugees. Those who joined in Ilfracombe were taken from internees who had already had a life in Britain, living and working here for a number of years; some as early as 1933. They had acquired a better command of English than the refugees from Kitchener Camp. Some, like Berlin-born brothers Peter and Geoffrey Perry (originally Pinschewer), had received a public school education.[12] They had become accustomed to English life and had acquired a good knowledge of the language. As with the internment camps, Ilfracombe became a microcosm of German and Austrian intellectual and cultural life as professionals were drafted into its ranks: lawyers, doctors, surgeons, architects, businessesmen, bankers, artists, dentists, musicians and scientists. Among them were the author and journalist Arthur Koestler; business and newspaper tycoon Robert Maxwell; artist Walter Nessler; Ken Adam, later production designer for over seventy films, including seven James Bond movies; artist Johannes Mattheus Koelz; and actor Peter Ustinov. Martin Freud, a lawyer and eldest son of Sigmund Freud, volunteered for the Pioneer Corps from the Isle of Man. He spent most of his army career in Ilfracombe in endless rounds of washing-up duties. He wrote:

> My chief occupation was peeling potatoes when I was not scrubbing the kitchen floor. One day, through some kind of disorganisation, the trays filled with sizzling sausages and onions were ready to be carried to the mess-room, but there was no one to carry them. Trying to be helpful, I took up one of the trays and made my way to the door. Here I was met by an indignant corporal who, taking the tray from my hands, barked, 'Who do you think you are to serve in the Sergeants' Mess?'[13]

Ken Adam (Klaus Adam), who later became the only German fighter pilot in the RAF, describes his time in the Pioneers in Ilfracombe:

> You could not carry any arms. Because of my OTC background, I became a corporal, having to escort units of the French Foreign Legion down to Ilfracombe, which was not an easy task for me. These units were escorted by train to Ilfracombe. They had just been evacuated from Norway and they were really tough because they had been in the army for twenty years and were professional soldiers. Somehow I was bright enough to have certain leadership qualities without bullying. I was philosophical in a way about it and compromised with them. It was an amazing time in Ilfracombe because of the nationalities – Italians, Czechs,

Austrians, Germans, French – all were there. I spent about nine months in Ilfracombe. The officers' staff were normally recruited from the ex-diplomatic service – people who had been Governor of Bermuda and so on. They were on a very high intellectual level. You had professors, lawyers and surgeons at the age of 60 or 55 in uniform who were all grouped in and around Ilfracombe. You had one of the best classical orchestras and singers (Italian tenors and so on). The cultural level was extremely high, certainly during the time that I was there. The more sad or amusing things that happened: since I was a training staff NCO, I found people that I vaguely remembered, or didn't, from my father's generation who came to me in uniform in their mid-50s or 60s saying, 'Corporal Adam, I knew your father. My wife is in London. Can you give me a weekend pass to go to London?' As a boy of 18, I realised the sadness in a way and the irony of it. These were people who had achieved success in their civilian professions. It was probably the most highly intellectualised unit in the British Army. We used to teach basic military training, equip Pioneer battalions with picks and shovels, but no arms. I was one of the younger and so I was used for the training and the drilling, which didn't really appeal to me.[14]

During the period in Ilfracombe, the Pioneer Corps became the Royal Pioneer Corps in an attempt to boost its image among the soldiers. However, even a name change could not disguise the reality of boredom and frustration felt from digging trenches, mixing concrete, constructing Nissen huts and carrying out other laborious tasks. Many had high hopes of fighting on the frontline, but would have to wait two years to fulfill that ambition.

In total eight alien Pioneer companies were raised in Ilfracombe between September 1940 and February 1942. In November 1941, several hundred internees returned from Australia aboard the SS *Stirling Castle*. Many, including the artists Hans Jackson and Johannes Koelz, enlisted in the army in Ilfracombe. They were among the last to be drafted into the alien Pioneer Corps as No. 3 Training Centre closed in February 1942.

## THE PIONEER CORPS AND ENTERTAINMENT

The army orchestra and entertainment section of the alien Pioneer Corps was originally formed at Kitchener Camp. Coco the Clown organised their talents and they regularly entertained fellow refugees and the local people of Kent. They too were evacuated from the Kent coast to Dartmoor in May 1940. A few weeks later they transferred to Westward Ho! with No. 3 Training Centre and then to Ilfracombe in September 1940. Their numbers swelled as new musicians, actors and professional singers joined their ranks, mainly from the internment camps.

In Ilfracombe professional Berliner and Viennese musicians, actors and tenors graced the stage to entertain the troops and local population.[15] Breslau-born violinist Sgt Max Strietzel, a survivor of Buchenwald concentration camp, conducted the orchestra. Unlike their comrades who were in Ilfracombe for a short time, the entertainment section remained in the town until the early spring of 1942 when No. 3 Training Centre was dissolved. It boasted the talents of singers Rudolf Jess (tenor) and H. Karg-Bebenburg (baritone); Cecil Aronowitz, later professor of viola at the Royal College of Music and renowned chamber music viola player; and pianist Walter Stiasny who had been a singer's coach at the Vienna State Opera. Classical concerts and plays became a regular feature in the life of the town for nearly two years, often performed in aid of local charities. Shows and concerts included *Almost a Honeymoon*, *White Cargo*, *Gypsy Life*, *Murder on the Second Floor*, and *Babes in the Wood*. Christmas 1940 saw a performance of the popular pantomime *Cinderella*. Berliner Fritz Lustig was a cellist in the orchestra and remembers it well:

We performed *Cinderella*, the title part of which was taken by the daughter of the Second-in-Command, Major Coles. Buttons was played by Coco (Nicolai Poliakoff) and Prince Charming by Coco's elder daughter. The orchestra had a supporting role to play, but it was my first experience of having to juggle with innumerable separate pieces of sheet music – taking a few bars out of here, another few bars out of there, waiting to be 'brought in' or 'cut off', and reading badly written manuscript music. The dress rehearsal seemed to be complete chaos and I just could not imagine how it would all come together eventually. The tenor Rudolf Jess was the producer, and miraculously, when it came to the first performance, it worked.[16]

In March 1941 the orchestra conducted an eight-day tour of Devon and Cornwall. The performance at the Globe Theatre in Plymouth was interrupted by the Luftwaffe blitz on the city. The *Ilfracombe Chronicle* reported:

From the Globe at Plymouth, part two of the programme was broadcast, special arrangements being made for this purpose by the BBC. Their careful presentation was well rewarded, as will be agreed by those who heard this magnificent programme on that night. Tribute must be paid to Pte. Rudolf Jess for his rendering of 'You are my heart's delight', ever popular, his fan mail has benefited already. The *Swing Trio* had an almost riotous reception and, of course, a word of very real appreciation must be said to Sgt. M. Strietzel for his conducting of the unit's orchestra. During the evening performance, just after the National Anthem, there were some unwelcome visitors to Plymouth [the German bombers] . . . a successful week that even the heavy blitz could not mar.[17]

The *Swing Trio* which was part of the entertainment section consisted of Pte Fred Leeding (drums), Pte Jack Norman (banjo), and Pte Herbert Kruh (piano). German prima ballerina Hanne Musch, wife of the stage manager Pte P. Wiesner, took part in the army performances alongside Coco the Clown's two daughters, Helen and Tamara. She delighted many an audience. The *Ilfracombe Chronicle* wrote in June 1941: 'That personification of all that is beautiful in the rhythm of the body, Hanne Musch, received one of the most enthusiastic ovations of the show with her ballet dance *Russian Waltz* and burlesque dance *The Street Urchin*. Her flexibility of movement was happily allied with a captivating stage personality.'[18] In July 1941, the entertainment section performed *Bal Tabarin*, colourfully described in the *Ilfracombe Chronicle* a week later:

They re-created some of the atmosphere of Montmartre, complete with underground sewers and a gangster second only to Hitler, in their presentation of an extremely entertaining variety show . . . The stage show window was attractively arrayed by Rudolf Jess who, as producer, gave evidence of his ability to display his goods to advantage, and great credit must also go to Pte P. Wiesner who, in addition to discharging a responsible task as stage manager, earned full marks for the dialogue and sketch of 'Taverne Rouge' which constituted the first part of the show. Indeed the gay atmosphere of 'Taverne Rouge', with its songs, surprises and delightful comedy, was an exceedingly palatable aperitif for the next part of the entertainment which took the form of cabaret.[19]

Fritz Lustig had a double role as cellist and actor in many of the performances, including *White Cargo*:

At the end of February a play called *White Cargo* was produced, the action of which took place in Africa and depicted the problems faced by a white settler who fell in love with a half-caste woman. I was to take the part of an African (according to the programme 'Jim Fish', a native), appearing briefly in a few scenes, in one of which I had to sing what I imagined was an African song and allow myself to be beaten by the half-caste woman, played by Hanne Musch. The part required that I was completely blacked-up (apart from my middle section which was covered by a loin-cloth) and that was a lengthy procedure which I was unable to carry out on my own. Proper black make-up was not available and so I was literally painted with a paintbrush and black watercolour by the man who also designed and painted the scenery, H. Gurschner.[20]

During a two-year period, it is estimated that the entertainment section of the Pioneer Corps raised nearly £3,000 for local charities, a substantial sum of money at that time. Their efforts enabled refurbishment at Ilfracombe's Tyrrell Hospital and cleared the hospital's four-year debts. When No. 3 Training Centre closed in 1942, the entertainment section (with the exception of a few members who were absorbed into ENSA) was transferred to Bulford Camp on Salisbury Plain and put under the direct authority of Southern Command Entertainment. The orchestra formed part of the much larger Southern Command Symphony Orchestra on several occasions, and on one occasion gave a concert at the National Gallery in London.

## DIGGING FOR VICTORY

After Ilfracombe, the Pioneer soldiers served for nearly two years in their respective companies, stationed all over the country, engaged in the construction of roads, camps and Nissen huts, loading and unloading supplies, mixing concrete and general manual labour. During the summer of 1940, 69 Company was working in Somerset constructing tank stops, laying mines, erecting miles of wire defences and digging tank trenches as part of the protection against an invading force. In November the company moved to Bexley, south London, clearing bomb debris and pulling survivors from the blitzed buildings. On 29 December five Pioneers from the company were killed when a bomb hit the bus on which they were travelling. Four are known to have been Heinz Goldstein, Emil Mesner, Gerhard Neuman and Solomon Buchsbaum and are buried in London's East Ham Jewish Cemetery in Marlow Road. In March 1941 the Official War Diary notes that men of 69 Company were supplying strategic information to Royal Air Force Intelligence from their personal knowledge of Germany, mainly about sites around Dresden. This included the location of manufacturing plants, power stations, petrol supply depots and airfields. During 1942 the company was engaged in work at the Royal Engineers stores and Royal Army Ordnance Corps dumps. In 1943 and 1944 the company moved around Yorkshire constructing Nissen huts and camps.

In early August 1940, 74 Company left Bideford for Llanvaches to carry out camp construction and forestry work. In January 1941 it moved to London to clear bomb damage and carry out demolition work. During most of 1942 the men were engaged in camp construction around Weymouth on the south coast and it was here that they featured in a Ministry of Information film, *Lift up your Head, Comrade*, scripted by ex-Pioneer and author Arthur Koestler. In May 1941, 77 Company, which had worked in Donnington for most of the time since its formation, moved to Long Marston near Stratford-on-Avon, employed in the Royal Engineers stores depot. It remained there until July 1943 when it changed its status from an alien to British company.

After leaving Bideford in July 1940, 87 Company moved to Somerset, engaged in defence work and bomb disposal. In January 1941 the company moved to Blackheath, clearing the bombed area in Woolwich. Two months later it was sent to Wales and then Liverpool on fire-watch duties. The remainder of 1941 was spent laying minefields and working on a pipeline. On 2 October the company moved to the Defensible Barracks at Pembroke Dock, a large Victorian moated fortification. Garry Rogers (Günther Baumgart) of 87 Company and later of the 1st Battalion Royal Tank Regiment, writes:

> We were now issued with Lee Enfield rifles and received training in the use of weapons. One such training session led to a disaster. The cause was never discovered, but during a training lecture on grenades, a live grenade exploded and caused a major accident in which five soldiers were killed and a number badly injured. The force of the explosion was so severe that it blew out windows and even damaged thick walls. One soldier was blown clear out of the window and into the moat.[21]

From Pembroke Dock the company moved to Long Marsden where it remained until the summer of 1943, working at a Royal Engineers railway siding loading and unloading trucks and packing cases for shipment. It was disbanded on 30 September 1943 because so many of the company had transferred to fighting units.

On 20 June 1940, 88 Company left Westward Ho! and moved to Berrington, working on defence posts in the Wye Valley. In October the company moved to east London clearing bomb damage around Bow and Poplar. In January 1941 it moved to Penlow in Monmouthshire, commencing forestry work with 129 Forestry Company. A year later, in

January 1942, it was stationed in South Wales on camp construction at Penclawdd and Carmarthen. During that year it was visited by a Swiss man, Mr Hartmann, who began asking the men whether they would volunteer for 'special duties'. Men from 87 and 88 Companies were eventually trained for one of two special German-speaking groups: a Commando unit known as 3 Troop, and Special Operations Executive (SOE). In December, 88 Company moved to Sennybridge, still in Wales, to work on the artillery ranges. During the summer of 1943 men from the company transferred in large numbers to fighting units. Those who remained in 88 Company moved to Denbigh in North Wales to load and unload stores. In April 1944 the company moved to Oswestry where it was disbanded on 11 May.

In July 1940, 93 Company moved from Westward Ho! and Bideford to Newbury to work at the Main Supply Depot handling food and petrol. In January 1941 the men were dispatched to Cirencester for forestry work. The official War Diaries note that the company has 'excellent camouflage expert in Sgt. Russ'. The following month, sixty-nine Austrians were transferred from the company to 229 Company and sixty-eight Germans received in their place. In July 1941 the War Diaries note that the company was armed up to 100 per cent. The remainder of that year was spent near Watchet in Somerset before moving to Redruth in Cornwall with detachments posted to Bodmin, Okehampton, Par, Truro, Redruth and Salcombe. In April 1942 the company moved to Weymouth with three sections working on the breakwater and the rest on camp construction. Having moved around the south coast during 1942, the men were sent to Southampton at the end of May 1943 to carry out miscellaneous construction work. Shortly after D-Day, some of 93 Company were deployed to Littlehampton, loading bombs onto ships. The company returned to the Continent, landing in Normandy in July 1944.

After its formation in June 1940, 137 Company moved to Yeovil in Somerset for work at the aerodrome at Yeovilton. Three sections were sent to Newport, Isle of Wight for camp construction, remaining there until July. In October the company moved to London on demolition and debris clearance in the bombed area of Deptford and Bermondsey. The War Diaries record that Pte Redlich was killed by enemy action on 11 January 1941. During 1941 the company was based at various locations around Somerset working for a time on construction at Yeovilton for the Fleet Air Arm. Alfred Perlés, who began his army career with 137 Company, writes:

> Breakfast was at 06.45 hours. We had three-quarters of an hour to wash, shave ourselves and make our palliasses. All this had to be done before breakfast for there was no time afterwards, working parade being at 07.15 hours. In fine weather the kit had to be laid out outside the company lines and tent flaps turned up. Rain being not an uncommon phenomenon in Somerset, it often happened that the sun was shining when we carried our kits outside, and a little while afterwards the sky darkened and the rain came pouring down in torrents. For work we paraded in fatigue dress. Every morning it was the same. The 'right markers' of the ten sections fell in. 'Right markers . . . attention! . . . Left turn! . . . Nine paces interval . . . quick march! . . . Markers steady! . . . Company fall in!
>
> One might think that any idiot can work with pick and shovel, but that is not so. Simple as the thing seems, it has to be learned all the same. There is a technique of using a pick and shovel – as there is a technique to riding a horse or doing everything – which has to be mastered. To avoid excessive fatigue or blisters on the hands when using a pick is to a large extent a matter of technique.[22]

After Somerset, 137 Company moved to Dumfries on camp construction and quarrying. During 1942 and 1943 it was engaged in erecting camps around Scotland. On 29 July 1944 the men were moved south to Fareham and landed at Arromanches in Normandy on 2 August.

After being formed at Bideford in July 1940, 165 Company moved to Cirencester on forestry duties and work at the saw mills. In January 1941 the men were sent to Newbury where they constructed pill-boxes. Later that year a number of sections were posted to Devon to construct camps. In February 1942 the company moved to Arncott near Bicester to help the Royal Engineers. The remainder of the year was spent concreting roads, excavating trenches, and laying railway track and drainage. The company was disbanded on 20 February 1943. The Official War Diaries note that the newly formed 219 Company consisted of twenty-one different nationalities. From Ilfracombe they spent time on forestry work and camp construction at Chathill, Darlington and Long Eaton in Derbyshire. In July 1941 it moved to Northampton and was dispatched to different locations to carry out miscellaneous duties. By the end of January 1944 all enemy aliens had been transferred out of the company.

After its formation, 220 Company moved from Ilfracombe to Gloucestershire and in February 1941 became 'an Austrian only' company. During 1942 the men carried out forestry work in the Forest of Dean. On 6 August 1943, 220 Company moved to Tewkesbury for training and then to Gloucester where the nature of the work is not stated. Further training continued in June 1944 before the company landed at Arromanches in August. The diary entries for 248 Company are sparse because the company was based for a long period at the Royal Engineers depot at Catterick Camp in Yorkshire. On 26 April 1943 it changed from an alien to British company. Likewise after its formation, 249 Company worked at Catterick Camp and during 1941 was engaged on camp construction, first at Hawick and then in Glasgow. In August 1943 it changed to a British-only company.

The final alien company to be raised at Ilfracombe (with the exception of the Italian 271 Company) was 251 Company. In March 1941 it moved to Shirehampton to work at Avonmouth Docks. By June the men were dispatched to Cheltenham to construct roads and defences and erect electricity pylons. On 4 July 1942 the company moved to Arncott, erecting and painting huts and unloading supplies. Rolf Holden (Rolf Hirtz) recalls the 'Porridge Incident' at Arncott. In the mess hall the men sat twelve to a table with the man on the end responsible for representing the others in any complaints. He explains:

> One morning when I was occupying this seat of honour, I was instructed by my fellow diners to complain about the quality of the porridge: it was too salty and allegedly contained not a trace of sugar. When the orderly officer and the sergeant major made their

rounds, I duly complained to them. They asked for a spoon, tasted the porridge and pronounced it was perfectly in order. Then they asked the other eleven diners if they had any complaint about the porridge: there was silence. I was put on a charge for making wilful complaints and was punished by being confined to barracks for seven days, told to clean pots and pans in the cook-house and to perform one hour's pack-drill very night. That evening I presented myself in full battle kit, which included a thirty-pound shoulder pack and steel helmet. The show started with the drill sergeant shouting 'left-turn, right-turn, about-turn – everything at the double'. At every turn, I had to shout 'remember porridge'. I survived that hour, just about, but realized that six more sessions like that would do me serious harm. I consulted the medical orderly. He smiled and said, 'Well, this is not too complicated. Tomorrow night, you just collapse.' He explained briefly what that meant and what I had to do, and his parting words were, 'You will collapse as near as possible to the drill sergeant because that will give you the opportunity to throw your rifle on his feet. He'll remember you for quite a while to come.' The following night, I did just what I had been told to do. My performance must have been convincing because it started a dreadful commotion. The medical orderly, who had been waiting in the background, rushed over and stripped me of my battledress top. An ambulance appeared and I was taken to the medical emergency hut. I felt a bit of a fraud but I had to keep my mouth shut.[23]

After Arncott Camp, the company moved to Thame. In June 1943, it ceased to be an alien company.

During 1942, the most significant development occurred for enemy aliens in the British Forces when the government permitted them to transfer to fighting regiments. Most could not wait to leave the Pioneer Corps where they considered their efforts wasted. They transferred in their thousands, which explains why after 1943 most of the original alien Pioneer companies were disbanded or became British-only personnel. The potential asset of German-speaking refugees in the British Forces became a reality and they made a substantial mark on the future course of the war. The first units open to them were those designated for 'special duties': the Small Scale Raiding Force (SSRF), Special Air Service (SAS), Commandos and SOE (Special Operations Executive). Others transferred to technical units: Royal Electrical & Mechanical Engineers, Royal Engineers, the Royal Army Medical Corps and Royal Army Service Corps. From 1943 enemy aliens transferred to the Royal Navy, Royal Armoured Corps, Royal Artillery, Parachute Regiment, the infantry, and the Glider Pilot Regiment. Some were among the first wave of parachutists to be dropped into Normandy on D-Day and others were involved in intelligence operations, including interpreting duties and the interrogation of German prisoners. Their knowledge of German came to the fore and they were assigned to key roles in intelligence across the various regiments. A handful successfully transferred to the RAF which, alongside the Royal Navy, was the hardest for enemy aliens to join. Once they had transferred and were preparing and training for action overseas, they were advised to change their name in case of capture. It was of paramount importance that their German origins should not be discovered because they would have been treated as traitors by the Nazis and killed, rather than as POWs.

PIONEERS AFTER D-DAY

Only five of the original fifteen alien companies saw service overseas after D-Day. These were nos 69, 74, 93, 137 and 220. The first of the alien companies to land in Normandy on 4 August 1944 was 69 Company, which proceeded to Caen where the men worked on Caen Bridge. For the remainder of 1944 they carried out miscellaneous labour duties and were disbanded on 12 December 1944. On 6 August 1944, 74 Company landed in Normandy and started building a hospital. During September they were involved in camp construction, clearance of mines, unloading ships and handling ammunition in Royal Engineers stores. In February 1945 they moved into Belgium where they worked at the stores of the Royal Army Ordnance Corps. The last entry in their diary is recorded on 30 September 1945.

On 20 July 1944, 93 Company landed in Normandy and proceeded towards St Martins-des-Entrees. Harry Rossney, first of 249 Company and then 93 Company, writes:

> We walked ashore at St Come des Fresne near Arromanches on the famous Mulberry Harbour which had been towed across the Channel from Richborough in Kent. When we landed, I felt gratitude that the frontline had already advanced several miles inland; immense awe at the power and size of the war-machine in action and shock at all the dead bodies wrapped in blankets and the sight of make-shift graves. Finally fatigue. A never-ending tiredness, dust, dirt, sweat and foxholes. We saw no bread for nine days. Water was in short supply. Our first stop was near Ryes a few miles inland. That night a batch of POWs, all German officers, had to be guarded in a field. There was no barbed wire, only white anti-mine ribbons between trees forming the boundaries. Volunteers were called for as guards for four-hour shifts. I volunteered. It was the first time I came face-to-face with German soldiers since I had left Berlin five years previously. They were fit, arrogant Nazis strutting about, not realising that we understood everything they said. Word got around that they were planning an escape that night. One of our men said, 'I hope they do. I'll shoot every one of them!' To my great surprise I felt a really deep hatred welling up in me after all the years in England. Those faces, uniforms, jackboots and arrogant tones – I would have pulled the trigger at that moment, I believe. But I am relieved that I was spared that situation.[24]

In September, 93 Company moved to Dieppe on dock clearance. On 26 November the men were stationed in Brussels on guard duties until March 1945. On 21 May 1945 orders were given for it to become a British company and all alien personnel were assigned to the interpreter's school in anticipation of intelligence and interrogation duties in postwar Germany.

After 137 Company landed at Arromanches in August 1944, it proceeded to Caen to begin reconstruction of the bomb-damaged roads. During the remainder of 1944 the men were moved to various locations in Normandy unloading RAF stores, construction of roads and other miscellaneous duties. On 22 November they left for Antwerp. In April 1945, twenty-five of the men were posted to 21st Army Group Interpreters Pool and a further twenty-nine at the end of the month. In June the remaining soldiers awaited postings to interpreter's duties. Having landed at Arromanches on 4 August 1944, 220 Company moved to Ryes and Montiquet on camp construction. In mid-August the men worked with the Canadian Forestry Company and on 21 October 1944 crossed the border into Belgium engaged in camp construction at Hal. They worked at various locations in Belgium for a year, primarily on construction. In May 1945 sixty-eight men were transferred to the Interpreters Pool. On 3 September 1945 the remainder of the company moved into Germany and it was disbanded at Kellen in February 1945.

The alien Pioneer companies had formed over half of the 10,000 refugee contribution to the British Forces, not including those employed in Palestine. The total number who had enlisted through No. 3 Training Centre of the Pioneer Corps numbered 5,840 with at least 3,500 training in North Devon. They were a highly unusual bunch who formed the most intellectualised unit of the British Army, the like of which had never been seen before or experienced since. Many began their unglamorous army career 'digging for victory' at a time when the rest of Europe was succumbing to the advancing Nazi forces. It was a frustrating and boring experience, but during 1942 and 1943, their time had come when they transferred to fighting regiments. The following pages chart their contribution to the Allied Victory in Europe.

*Chapter 2*

# ROYAL ARMOURED CORPS

In total, over 216 refugees joined the Royal Armoured Corps (RAC), many of them drafted into the 8th Kings Royal Irish Hussars (8th Hussars) and the 1st Royal Tank Regiment (1st RTR).[1] They were part of the 7th Armoured Division, famously named the Desert Rats after the divisional emblem of the desert rat portrayed on their shoulder flash.[2] The RAC had suffered heavy casualties while fighting in the North African desert. The British forces were engaged in fierce fighting against Rommel in Egypt and Tripoli. Eventually Montgomery was appointed by Churchill and brought the first victory at El Alamein, Tripoli and Benghazi. The Germans had pushed the British forces back to Cairo. Morale was low and news of a victory was desperately needed to boost fighting spirits once again. After Egypt, the Desert Rats invaded Sicily and Italy before they returned to England heavily depleted and in need of reinforcements for the next campaign. This may explain why so many German and Austrian refugees were assigned to the RAC regiments. German-born Geoffrey Stuart (Gerd Stein) of the 8th Hussars comments:

The men of the Desert Rats were professional soldiers who had signed up and made the army their life and career. They were the backbone and elite of the British Army. When we came firstly we were not British-born and secondly we were Jewish but we were very quickly accepted. We were so different from them, and yet when the time came for Sgt Constable to choose a radio operator to go into action with him, he chose me because of my fluent German and I had passed an advanced radio operator's course.[3]

Rigorous training took place at the 55th Training Regiment, Farnborough, consisting of 'square bashing', radio operating, weaponry, driving tanks and map reading. To be accepted, each recruit was expected to complete a 10-mile route march in under two hours carrying full kit. Once attached to a squadron, each tank crew consisted of a commander, driver and co-driver, a gunner and wireless operator. During the spring of 1944 the tank units prepared for the D-Day landings. They were inspected by King George VI and Field Marshal Montgomery. Ken Ward (Karl Würzburger) recalls Montgomery's visit and rallying speech:

We had all been irritated when our leave had been stopped because the invasion was imminent. The night before Monty arrived we painted in large white letters on the tanks, parked in the field in which we were going to be inspected, the words NO LEAVE – NO SECOND FRONT. The officers were not pleased when they saw this in the morning but it was too late to clean off the tanks before his arrival. The whole regiment had assembled in the field when Monty arrived in his Jeep. He got out, jumped on the bonnet and slid off his jeep coat, revealing row and rows of medals to approving sounds from the whole of the crowd. He addressed us in a very loud voice, 'Alright boys, sit down. It's good to see you all again, and I am proud to be fighting the Boche with you now in Europe. There is one thing I am going to tell you right now and that is you will not be getting any leave but you will be getting a second front. The second front is imminent. You will be expected to fight at your best and there will be casualties but we will succeed, and we will defeat and destroy the enemy. We will give no quarter and we will only accept unconditional surrender. You will be given your orders when you have embarked. Good luck boys and I will see you over there.'[4]

Before the inspection, the 1st RTR moved to the extensive grounds of Orwell Park School between Brandon and Felixstowe for water-proofing the tanks. Squadrons of the 8th Hussars moved from West Tofts in Norfolk to Bognor Regis on the south coast to carry out the same task in anticipation of the seaborne invasion. Willy Field (Willy Hirschfeld) was assigned to waterproofing:

> The inspection plates under the tank had to be waterproofed with special black glue. That was my job. We also fitted an extension onto our exhaust so that no water could get into it. Once on dry land, the extension could be discarded. Just before D-Day, our regiment was on the move. At that time we had a feeling that we were going somewhere, probably France, but no one told us exactly. At last, I felt that I had achieved something – I could take an active part in the war. I was doing something worthwhile.[5]

The signal went up for the start of D-Day and elements of the invasion force moved in large heavy convoys towards their ports of embarkation. The air was full of anticipation, excitement and fear. Women waved from windows and cheered them on their way. Ken Ward describes that day:

> I realised that I might not be coming back and would not need the money I had in my pocket and threw it down to the children who whooped with joy when they saw the coins spilling on the pavement. I called out to the other members of my crew, 'Come on, throw your money to the kids, we won't need it when we land over there.' The boys on the other tanks realised what we were doing and joined us in throwing money to the waving crowd.
>
> The harbour was black with landing craft right on the quay, with others waiting further out to berth with destroyers and different types of warships laying offshore, protecting the invasion fleet with hundreds of barrage balloons floating in the air. There was a huge traffic jam which the harbour master and his officers were frantically trying to sort out. The squadron kept very closely together and we followed our troop, which was finally directed onto an LST [Landing Ship Tank]. We drove up the ramp straight into the hold and were directed by a member of the ship's crew to the other end, parking right against the closed ramp at the far end of the ship. It was very dark, smelt of fumes, and there was a lot of

clanging of chains as the crew secured the tanks to heavy metal
rings let into the floor.[6]

The various tank regiments landed in a continuous stream from
D-Day onto the Normandy beaches in a massive operation. The 1st
RTR and A Squadron of 8th Hussars landed on D-Day+1. Much of
the bloodshed and ferocious fighting had occurred the previous day,
but they still encountered resistance and sniping. C Squadron of
8th Hussars landed a few days later. The fiercest and most hazardous
battles were yet to come around Villers-Bocage and during the
advance on Caen, Lisieux and finally into Belgium and Holland. The
8th Hussars and 1st RTR played a leading role in spearheading
the advance through Normandy into Holland and Germany. The
following profiles provide eyewitness accounts from German veterans
who fought in the Royal Armoured Corps.

### KEN WARD

Ken Ward (Karl Robert Würzburger, born Frankfurt-am-Main, 1922)
served with A Squadron of the 1st RTR.[7] He had arrived in England
on one of the last Kindertransport on 25 August 1939. During the
early part of the war he had worked as an Eastman cutter producing
uniforms for the army, a reserved occupation. In May 1942 he
successfully enlisted into the Pioneer Corps and served with
87 Company. In September 1943 he transferred to 55th Training
Regiment RAC at Farnborough and in January 1944 joined the 1st
RTR in Brandon near Thetford. He landed with his squadron on Gold
Beach on 7 June 1944, D-Day+1. He recalls that tense day:

> The sea was quite rough as we approached the beach. There was a
> lot of shelling from the shore batteries and the big battleships lying
> off the beach. There were thousands of ships on the channel
> opposite the Normandy coast with each ship carrying barrage
> balloons so that the channel now looked like the defences of
> London. Flights of bombers were continuously droning overhead
> towards the French coast, with Spitfires flying in and around the

ships defending us from the Messerschmitts and the individual German Dornier bombers that were trying to have a go at the battleships. We were all told to be ready to land after lunch. We strapped all our bedding and equipment on the back of the tank and rushed up to the canteen for a quick last lunch. We were all quite tense but I tried not to show it as I was the only one in the crew who had not yet been in battle. As the LST slowly approached the beach we went into the hold and mounted our tank. There was a smell of oil and fumes in the air and we could hear the shelling, with shells landing on the beach from inside the hull. . . . Suddenly there was a lot of clanging and chain rattling as the front of the LST opened up and the front ramp came down. The ferry was already there, the plate appeared to clang on to it and as we were first in line, we drove on to the flat ferry which shuddered under our weight, and drove as far forward as we could to allow another tank to get on. We then closed in on the beach and had to drive through about five feet of water before getting the tracks onto dry land . . . As we moved up the beach the troop leader came up on the B set (which is short range only to speak to the troop commander) telling us to quickly move towards the right where there was a small lane leading off it and to drive up to the end until he had caught up. The beach was littered with knocked out tanks and vehicles. There was a first aid station at the side with medics moving the wounded on stretchers. The houses on the cliffs above were already flying French flags.[8]

The regiment proceeded towards the village of Villers-Bocage where Germans were dug in and hiding in the hedgerows. The battalion suffered heavy losses in a surprise attack by German armour and Ken lost the first of his comrades, Albala, in action. It was here that the crew came under direct fire from the 88mm guns of superior German Tiger tanks. They were forced into retreat and in so doing their own gun barrel hit a tree causing irreparable damage to their tank. They continued to move back at speed until cover was found behind a copse. Having returned safely to the regiment, they awaited a replacement tank. On 17 July 1944 the regiment moved from the orchards surrounding the small village of Jerusalem en route to their major target – the city of Caen. The city was heavily defended and subsequently came under sustained and heavy fire from Allied war planes.[9] Caen was devastated and flattened by the operation:

> We moved on and ended up on a hillside overlooking Caen. We had a clear view of the town spreading out in front of us. There was a lot of shelling going on from both sides. The Germans using their Nebelwerfer which fired a large number of shells, all hitting the ground practically at the same time. We stayed well inside the tank, just occasionally jumping out to brew up a cup of tea behind the tank, making do with our hard dog biscuits, tinned butter and some tinned Spam, which we made up inside the tank. We waited for the early hours of the morning when the air attack started. Hundreds of planes came over, flying in formation bombing the town. In practically no time Caen was flattened and I could not see how anybody could have possibly survived.
>
> We moved in with our tanks, accompanied by infantry and found that a large number of Germans had survived the bombing and artillery barrage, which was now laying down a barrage further ahead of us. We drew a lot of fire from the infantry who knocked out some of our tanks with their bazookas. The German SS Panzer Lehr Division had withdrawn behind the hills at the other side of the town. We followed and left the infantry to clear Caen of the remaining German pockets, pulling up in some of the fields the other side of Caen, knowing that the German tanks were not far in front of us, being heavily shelled by our artillery. We managed to cook a meal behind the tank, but took it inside to eat . . . The battle continued for a few days with us advancing slowly, losing a few tanks when we were positioned on top of a hill with the sun setting behind us making us a clear target. But we got our own back when the sun rose in the morning behind a row of German tanks, clearly illuminating them against the skyline. We opened up and knocked out four tanks before they could move back behind cover. By now our division was considerably below strength, the infantry and the tanks having had a trying time

taking Caen and we went for a rest and re-fitment back into the nearby Caumont area.[10]

After a period of respite, the regiment was on the move again to rejoin the front line. They moved through the Falaise gap into Lisieux where they encountered widespread devastation – dead soldiers and cattle everywhere. They advanced towards the Seine and eventually entered Holland on 10 November 1944. By Christmas they were stationed at Sittard:

We dug the tanks in as we expected a counter attack by the Germans. It was so cold that you could not touch the outside of the tank without gloves on as it would have burnt your skin off. The Germans were east of us, just the other side of Tüddern. As we were short of infantry we had to man foxholes on guard in the forward area. On Christmas Day I could hear the Germans singing Christmas carols in a house across the field from where I was in a foxhole. No shots were fired that day.

On the 18 January 1945 we advanced into Echt and subsequently Schilberg and were straddled down the main street. Our troop advanced to a crossroad and turned right, moving up about three hundred yards. We were told to stop at a junction while the rest of the troop advanced further. Our infantry boys occupied the houses on either side of the road. The radio crackled, telling us of fighting in close proximity. Suddenly the three tanks of our troops returned at great speed, driving past us without stopping. The troop leader ordering us to stay and shoot up any enemy tanks that might be following. The infantry boys who had been occupying the houses on either side withdrew leaving us on our own. The shelling and small arms fire we had been hearing grew louder and closer. German troops started firing on us from the houses on either side of us, which they had now occupied . . . I looked to my right as we turned left into the main road taking in at a glance the German SP [self-propelled] gun, about 30 yards away on the left hand side of the road, with its vicious 88mm gun pointing directly at us with a Churchill flame thrower immediately on the right hand corner, well alight. For a moment the world stood still. Then everything erupted at the same moment. The turret of the Churchill lifted straight up in the air with a terrific roar and came down next to the tank. The German SP gun fired at us at the same time, the armour-piercing shot passing inches in front of our tank. Within seconds our Sherman tank was in top gear racing down the road at a speed Shermans were never built for. By the time the German loaders had had time to put the second round into the breech of their gun, the aim of the gunner had been put out by the speed at which we were racing away from him, the shell going past us. We pulled in next to the squadron leader, reported back and rejoined our troop.[11]

By the 18 March the regiment had advanced deep inside Germany. They were on the edge of an impenetrable forest where three attempts had already been made to push through the German defences, resulting in heavy losses. Ken's troop was given the orders to try one last push with some of the infantry through the forest. The thick undergrowth obscured the German troops which began to open fire. The regiment returned fire with a barrage of bullets. The pockets of German resistance did not survive the counter-attack.

On 3 May 1945 the Divisional Commander of the 7th Armoured Division accepted the surrender of Hamburg.[12] The 1st RTR was in the vicinity and then moved to the village of Meldorf. Ken was transferred from the RAC to the Military Police where he worked as an interpreter. He had come through the war without injury, a rare situation for tank personnel involved in frontline fighting. He had survived the loss of four tanks and still mourns the loss of his comrades. He comments that 'changing tanks is very much like moving home. You get so attached to it, you know every nook and cranny, you know the sound of the engine and you hear and feel how the tracks move. You get to love it. It becomes part of you.' He reflects on his own survival:

Albala had been the first of my friends to be killed at Villers-Bocage shortly after landing. Then Ralph Parker was injured at Ellon, near Jerusalem in Normandy at the end of June and was evacuated back to England. Then Jimmy Hague was killed at Shilberg, which was to be followed soon by Jimmy Gibson's death near Oosterhout in Holland. I often wonder why I am still alive? If the gun barrel had not hit the tree and ruined the traversing gear we would have had to stay and battle it out with the two Tigers. We would have been well out-gunned and not stood a chance. If the turret of the Churchill had not blown up just at the right moment, the SP gun could not have missed our tank. If Jimmy's tank had not shed a track, we would have been in the exact position where Jimmy was killed. If the gun had not misfired, something which had never happened before in either mine or my friends experience with a 17-pounder gun, we would not have reversed, and the second AP shot would have gone clean through the turret. Statistically I should have been dead, so who had been watching over me? Why? Was it in order that my children and grandchildren could be born?[13]


## GEOFFREY STUART

Geoffrey Stuart (Gerd Werner Stein, born August 1922) served with A Squadron of the 8th Hussars.[14] Born in Frankfurt-an-der-Oder, some 100km from Berlin on the current German-Polish border (with a population of about 100,000), his family lived an affluent life, employing a chauffeur, cook and a nanny. Their home was fitted with central heating, an unusual luxury in those days. Geoffrey's father had served in the First World War and had been awarded the Iron Cross. His father had a well-established fashion business which included three workshops selling clothing and underwear and making furs, men's suits and ladies' costumes. The shop was smashed on *Kristallnacht*. Georg Stein, Geoffrey's father, was arrested after *Kristallnacht*, although his final whereabouts were unknown at the time. He was released after a time and went to live in Palestine where he started a small business. His wife Ella did not manage to escape Germany and died in Ravensbrück concentration camp during the war. In December 1938 Geoffrey boarded a train in Berlin with the Kindertransport. He was just sixteen years old. Once in England, Geoffrey was taken to Dovercourt holiday camp where he stayed for three months. It was a particularly harsh winter and there was no heating at the camp. He remembers being given a hot water bottle at night and in the morning it had turned to solid ice, giving an indication of the severity of the winter conditions there. Of his early time in England, Geoffrey recalls:

> My father used to import cloth from Savile Row in London. He wrote to the firm explaining that I was coming to England and could they find employment for me as a tailor. This is exactly what happened. After three months at Dovercourt, I left to begin work in Savile Row. I still had a lot to learn. I first worked in men's tailoring, and later ladies' tailoring. Because of this job I could support myself financially. When I left the men's tailoring business in February 1940, I worked for a ladies' tailoring firm Messrs Charles Ruperstein in Poland Street, off Oxford Street. Then on 8 July 1940, I was interned at Kempton Park racecourse. I volunteered to cook, something which, I believe, saved me from internment in Canada or Australia.

Geoffrey was released from internment on 10 October 1940 and granted permission to return to his lodgings at 3 Guilford Street, London. He continued his work with Messrs Charles Ruperstein. In January 1941 the firm was evacuated to Long Eaton in Nottinghamshire and Geoffrey volunteered for the British Forces. He had ambitions to be a pilot but it was difficult for enemy aliens to be accepted into the RAF. He volunteered for the Royal Armoured Corps (RAC), primarily because, as he himself admits, 'there was no walking involved and no digging of foxholes. Your tank provided everything.' Before joining the RAC he was required to train for a month with the Pioneer Corps. On 17 September 1942 he began his initial training with 87 Company of the Pioneers, at that time based in Denbigh, North Wales.[15] He then transferred to RAC at Farnborough, during which time he changed his name from Gerd Stein to Geoffrey Stuart. In the spring of 1944 preparations were made for the invasion of Normandy. The D-Day landings were postponed because of bad weather and over a million troops were crammed into holding camps. He recalls:

On the southern coast, the British Army had to hide a million men so the Germans did not know what was happening. If the Luftwaffe had flown overhead and seen large troop movements, they would have been alerted. Eisenhower's greatest problem was how to hide all these troops. We were taken to holding camps not far from the coast which were hidden in woods and camouflaged. We were ready to go at a moment's notice. We didn't know exactly what was happening and all leave was cancelled. We were given strict orders not to make telephone calls or write letters. The Military Police enforced strict security in the holding camps. We then left the camps on D-Day and travelled overnight to somewhere near Gosport, ready for embarkation the following day. It was midnight when the heavy tanks started rolling towards their destination. The noise must have been deafening because women in their night wear opened their windows and waved us on. They realised that we were part of the invasion force and cheered us on our way. It was very exciting for us driving through the night and having these women waving us on. It gave us a huge boost.

We headed for an embarkation port near Gosport. When we arrived there, having driven all night, we were so tired that we just slept on the pavements. Are these the invasion troops? These tired worn-out soldiers? Early that morning the army officers came around with tinned peaches and cream for breakfast. No one had seen tinned peaches since the start of the war. I thought, 'this is feeding the pigs before the slaughter.' We set off on D-Day+1 very early in the morning, landing on the same day at Gold Beach. There was no resistance because the Germans had evacuated the area. We headed for Bayeux, where we were stationed in readiness for the advance on Caen. I was the radio operator for our tank crew. Our tank commander, Sergeant Constable, was an excellent tank commander who had a great deal of experience gained from the Middle East.

We made for Caen, pushing through the dangerous area of Villers-Bocage where we suffered casualties. Around Villers-Bocage there was a narrow road with enormous hedges on either side with only room for one tank to pass between them. When our HQ did not know where the Germans were positioned, they sent a couple of our tanks along the narrow road between the high hedgerows. Hidden in the hedges were German anti-tank guns. As we were travelling along, the only way we could tell where the Germans were, was to wait for them to fire at us. The Germans had 88mm guns and were camouflaged. The leading tank worked at the front for only 6–8 minutes at a time because of the stress and nerves. The person in the front tank knew that he had a high chance of being shot and killed, so it was nerve-shattering. After 5–6 minutes the first tank would drop back to allow the next tank to move forward. Once the Germans had knocked out our front and rear tanks, that narrow road was a death trap for the rest of us. We could not move. But this strategy was the only way that HQ could find out the German positions. We radioed back and gave the position of the Germans. The artillery then came in and bombarded them, supported by the infantry. We stayed put until the infantry knocked out the German positions.

At one point, we were shot at in the Bocage region with artillery fire with such accuracy that someone had to be telling the Germans of our positions. We received a radio message that a nearby tower overlooked the area where we attacked. A Frenchman was directing the German artillery. To kill him, we drove through the farm building and came out the other side with bricks covering our tank. We certainly dislodged him as the tower came crashing down and prevented any more German artillery fire.

Our biggest battle was in Caen. We were there for two weeks on the outskirts, waiting. Caen was subjected to heavy bombardment from the air. Montgomery refused to attack Caen unless he could take it without too many casualties. We were stationed so close to the Germans, yet they could not shoot us for fear of killing their own people. One night, I recall, that I was looking out of my tank, reading a newspaper. Caen was burning so brightly from the bombing that I could see the small print on my newspaper. After two weeks we entered Caen on 10 July 1944. The city lay in ruins. From there my regiment was dispatched back to woods between Aunay and Villers-Bocage to assist the 1/7th Queens in clearing the area of Germans.[16]

One incident I recall from July/August 1944. We were held up in the forward lines for our tanks to be serviced. Only qualified Rolls-Royce engineers were allowed to work on our tank engines. During that time, I heard an animated discussion amongst two soldiers. When I joined them, I listened. I overheard an argument by one soldier who had worked for a Jewish firm and was exceedingly well treated. The other soldier, who was obviously anti-semitic, ran all the Jews down irrespectively. At the end of the argument, that soldier said in a triumphant voice, 'Have you ever seen a Jew with dirty hands?' I couldn't help myself. I went to the front and showed my hands which were quite filthy. I only had to say, 'Have a look at my hands,' and the crowd disappeared within seconds and the argument was won.

During August we advanced towards Lisieux. We were all overwhelmed by the stench of death emanating from slaughtered cattle lying dead (killed by air onslaught and artillery fire). The carcasses were left in the heat, rotting.

We were amongst the first tank units to liberate Brussels. The welcome we received was overwhelming. We then advanced into Holland and were stationed at the Philips factory in Eindhoven. We carried out mopping-up operations after the disaster at Arnhem. Our tanks were sent in to clear out the Germans from their dug-outs. We were cleaning up the area and looking for Germans when a German soldier came out of a dug-out with an anti-tank gun pointing at us which, if he had fired, would have killed all of us. I tried to shoot at him with my Bren gun but it jammed. He was more scared than me. I could have used my pistol. He jumped back into the dug-out and I shouted 'advance' to our tank driver and we ran over him. I radioed back to the infantry and told them that we had buried a German alive and dig him out if they can. They dug him out. As he came out, his defiance was unbelievable. He saluted and said, 'Heil Hitler. We are going to win the war.' He was quite fanatical, but that's the kind of thing the Allied troops faced at that time.

In January 1945 Geoffrey's unit was stationed in the tiny Dutch village of Echt, on the Dutch-German border. It was a particularly cold winter:

There was snow on the ground, it was foggy, and very poor visibility. The tank driver was making a cup of tea because our crew had been standing in their tank in the snow right through the night. We were cold and tired. From nowhere in the fog, a couple of German tanks surprised us and opened fire. One shell exploded right next to the tank. I was hit by shrapnel, the only one of my crew to be hit. The soldier who took my place when I was wounded, shortly afterwards was killed by a sniper. That could so easily have been me. Strange as it may seem, I didn't know I had been wounded. I had great difficulty breathing, which gave me the idea that something wasn't right. I could feel nothing to start with, but the shrapnel had shot through my uniform, through my Army Pay book in the breast pocket and lodged between my heart and lungs. All at once, even though it was bitterly cold, I started to perspire. I was getting very hot and uncomfortable. I unzipped my tank suit and saw blood pouring from my chest near my heart. I radioed to HQ and decided to abandon the tank. To this day, the shrapnel is still there because it was too tricky to remove it.

As I jumped off the tank, a minor battle took place between my crew and the German tanks. Tanks were moving everywhere and I could see that I was about to be run over. I jumped into a ditch just as a tank rolled over the top of the ditch; something which I remember to this day as a terrifying experience. In the heat of the battle, the crew could not concern themselves with me. I was left entirely to my own devices. After a short time the battle subsided and I crawled out of the ditch. I managed to find my way to the Forward Dressing Station.

On the 'blood wagon' back to the field hospital, I asked what had happened to the trooper who had also been wounded with me. The reply came, 'He has been shot in the foot.' When I asked the doctor later how the trooper was progressing, he told me that he had lost his foot. People who are wounded often don't know how badly they are wounded. The trooper felt he was wounded in the foot but in fact he had lost a foot.

I was taken to a Regimental Dressing Station and eventually to a Military Hospital in Brussels. I was kept alive by one thing –

penicillin. In those days it was comparatively new and cost £5 a shot. This was a lot of money in those days when one considers that we earned between £3 and £6 a week. I had a shot every three hours for quite some time. I had served on the front line from D-Day+1 until I was wounded in January 1945. This was quite remarkable because the average time before injury or fatality for a member of a tank crew was 3 months. From Brussels I was transferred to Derby Infirmary in the north of England for recovery. I was in hospital for a total of 3 months.

During 1945, after the Russians had beaten the Germans, Geoffrey was asked whether he would be prepared to be dropped behind enemy lines in civilian clothing to spy on the Russian troop movements in his home town, Frankfurt-an-der-Oder. If caught, the British government would disavow any knowledge of him. He declined.

Once Geoffrey was discharged from Derby Infirmary, he was sent to Catterick Camp, the largest base in Yorkshire. Due to his wound he was downgraded from A1 to B1. Following an interview, the army officer informed him that he could be useful because of his knowledge of German.

Subsequently he was sent to Brussels on an interpreters' refresher course and from there posted to Iserlohn in Westphalia. He served as personal interpreter to Brigadier Bordass and was then promoted to the rank of sergeant. Once this work was completed, he was posted to the Control Commission and involved with the denazification process in Brunswick. His primary duty was to ascertain whether any of the local people had committed war crimes. These people needed official clearance to enable them to work in the new Germany.

Geoffrey was demobbed on 18 February 1947. He left the army with the rank of war substantive sergeant. He was naturalised as a British citizen on 29 March 1947. To test his loyalty, during the naturalisation interview he was asked what he would do if war broke out between Palestine and Britain. He replied, 'I would be with the British Army.'

DENNIS GOODMAN

Dennis Goodman (Hermann Gutmann, born Frankfurt, February 1923) escaped Nazi Germany in October 1936 and attended school in England. His parents escaped Germany for Holland the following year. In December 1939 he passed his matriculation, by which time he felt more English than German. There was no question of continuing his studies because funds had run out and he took up work in a factory in Lancashire, before returning to London. On 2 July 1940 he was interned at Kempton Park racecourse, outside London, and sent two days later to Huyton near Liverpool. He was ordered aboard the *Dunera* for Australia. After a year of internment there, he volunteered for the British Army and arrived back in Liverpool on 28 November 1941. On 9 December he reported to No. 3 Training Centre at Ilfracombe in North Devon. After training, he was posted first to 251 Company and then 74 Company. He had been pressing for a transfer to a fighting unit and in August 1943 was posted to the 55th Training Regiment RAC. On 15 January 1944 he was posted to the 8th Hussars. He landed in Normandy with his section of A Squadron 8th Hussars on 9 June 1944 (D+3) after about twenty-eight hours aboard the LCT in rough weather:[17]

A Squadron manoeuvered ashore in their water-proofed Cromwell tanks onto the sandy beach at Port-en-Bassin and promptly proceeded north of Bayeux. The following day, we moved to Jerusalem, a tiny Normandy village. On D+6, we advanced towards Livry taking the village, but in the process lost three tanks with only four survivors out of 15 men. The following day, we lost a further three tanks. In human terms, our squadron lost fourteen comrades in the first four days ashore, not mentioning those wounded. The next couple of days were spent in replacing tanks and personnel. A Squadron consisted of 20 tanks with 5 men to each tank, namely a total of 100. And of these only 10 were still with the squadron at the end of the war and I was one of those fortunate ones.

Our section of A Squadron then advanced towards Villers-Bocage without further losses. I had a lucky escape on 25 July in the proximity of Caen, when our tanks were positioned between knocked-out Canadian tanks. I was sitting on the ground at the back of my tank poring over maps with the Squadron Leader, Major Threlfall MC. He asked me to go and retrieve another map out of the turret. When I returned a few minutes later, jumping down from the tank to sit next to him, I was horrified to find that shrapnel from a shell-burst had killed him.

On 8 August A Squadron carried out a reconnaissance mission in the Mont Pinçon area where we broke through the German lines. We advanced until there was resistance from heavy armour-piercing guns just north of Cauville. Within minutes of each other, three tanks were knocked out including mine. I was the co-driver and gunner. The driver escaped unhurt but ran into German hands from which he was liberated in a subsequent engagement. I set off a smoke screen under the cover of which I escaped from the tank into a trench, sheltered by a hedge and then crept back to the tank to find that Sergeant Webber and Trooper Sowray had been killed. I helped the wounded wireless operator out of the turret and into the trench. The two of us were then joined by five men from the other two knocked-out tanks. Seven of us crept along the hedges into a nearby forest where in a clearing we by-passed a group of conferring German officers. Since we only had one pistol between us, we thought it better not to tackle them. Once we reached the echelon (supply division), I was allocated to another tank. On 16 August we crossed the River Orne and I counted fifteen knocked-out Sherman tanks (mostly Canadian, I believe) along the near bank. It brought home to me the fierceness of the enemy's resistance. Around this time we were strafed by our own fighter planes as the frontline was fluid.

The second half of September 1944 brought Operation Market Garden, the airborne drop and battle of Arnhem which, if successful, would have brought about the liberation of the north of the Netherlands much sooner and brought the war to a close by the end of the year. We were leaguering in Veghel in the corridor leading up to Arnhem but we had to satisfy ourselves in clearing the south of the Netherlands. This was of course also a terrible personal disappointment as I had wanted to get to Amsterdam as quickly as ever possible, hoping against hope that my parents were somewhere safe. January and February 1945 were spent in southern Holland and then Germany. We crossed the Rhine around 20 March and continued fighting, resulting in tragic casualties caused by the fanaticism of Nazi indoctrinated units. The war for the Germans was lost, but many thousands still had to lose their lives in the final advance. One of my comrades Lutz Saunders (born Salinger), a gifted violinist, was killed on 30 March. The official War Diaries of the 8th Hussars records:

*Gt. Burlo to Oding : A Squadron attacked – Leading troop A Squadron virtually written off. Lt. Anstey being killed, Sgt.Constable wounded but continued to fight until his was the only tank remaining in action. Enemy Battle Group PRIMUS, Hermann Goering Troop of 7th Paratroop Division. Sgt. Taylor captured 50 German Paratroopers. A Squadron lost 4 tanks (Cromwells),1 tank (Challenger) damaged, Lt. Anstey killed and 6 other ranks killed, 3 other ranks wounded, 6 other ranks missing believed Prisoners of War.*

On 4 May 1945 we entered the ruins of Hamburg. I have very little recollection of my time in northern Germany prior to the regiment moving to Berlin because it was overshadowed by efforts to obtain compassionate leave to travel to the Netherlands in search of my parents. When I reached Holland, I learned of their ghastly fate. In 1943 they had been rounded up in Amsterdam, taken to Westerbork Camp and from there transported to Sobibor in Poland where they were gassed on arrival. I also discovered that my aunt on my father's side and her two children were transported from the Netherlands to Auschwitz and were also murdered. My grandmother survived the war in Holland having been introduced to the Dutch Resistance, hidden by farmers in the north of the country. It is indescribable how we both felt when I found her there shortly after the war. On 7 July 1945 the regiment moved to Berlin and was quartered in the Olympic Stadium. There I discovered an untouched card-indexed library of thousands of naked athletes, with body measurements from head to toes collected to prove the superiority of the 'pure Aryans' – the Master Race. Shortly thereafter I was seconded to the British Delegation Area of the Potsdam Conference, attended by Prime Ministers Winston Churchill and then Clement Attlee. My duties entailed walking casually in the grounds with a pistol concealed in my pocket to guard against possible intruders.

On 21 July Dennis took part in the Victory Parade in Berlin when the 8th Hussars made an impressive showing, driving tanks past the Prime Minister, Commander-in-Chief and guests on the *Siegesallee* (Mall of Victory). On 21 August the regiment returned to the north of Hamburg and Dennis was asked to attend a course at No. 1 Interpreters' School in Brussels. In mid-September 1945 he was seconded to VIII Corps Intelligence Office in Hamburg and allocated to the Review and Interrogation staff at No. 6 Civilian Internment Camp at the former Neuengamme concentration camp near Bergedorf, a suburb of Hamburg.

### WILLY FIELD

Willy Field (Willy Hirschfeld) served with C Squadron 8th Hussars. Born in Bonn on 17 August 1920, one of twins, his father owned a men's clothing shop there and had fought in the German forces in the First World War.[18] The morning after *Kristallnacht* Willy was arrested outside the factory where he worked and taken to a prison in Cologne where he was kept in isolation:

Prison was the worst experience. I was thrown into a cell and the door was locked. It was an extremely frightening experience. I knew nothing. Why had I been arrested? What had I done? The cell was small and dingy. Then 2 or 3 more Jews arrived. We had no idea what was going to happen to us. I was interrogated by the Gestapo. They wanted to know about things which I didn't know. They asked me lots of questions about my boss and of course I knew nothing of his whereabouts. I suffered some brutality at the hands of the Gestapo when I was in prison.[19]

A few days later on 15 November 1938 he was moved by cattle train during the night to Dachau concentration camp. For him it was the beginning of a three-month nightmare:

We arrived at 2am. There were searchlights. We were driven like cattle onto the parade ground. I was beaten by an SS guard with the back of his rifle. There was no choice – one had to carry on, otherwise there would be more beatings. We all had to undress. It was the middle of winter. We stood naked in the parade ground while we were hosed down with ice cold water. Eventually we were given the concentration camp clothing: blue and white striped pyjamas. We were each given a number. Mine was 28411. In Dachau, all the inmates were counted every morning and evening. It was a dreadful place. I saw lots of things happen. Elderly people would walk into the electric wire that surrounded the camp. In that way they took their own lives before the Nazis did. People were shot just because they did not do as they were ordered by the guards. In the overcrowded huts where we slept, we had to hang our towels next to our beds. The towel was no more than a scrappy piece of rag, but if it was not neatly folded, you were beaten. I was given the job of cleaning the windows of the hut. If there was one spot of dirt on the windows, you were beaten. There were no toilets, just holes in the ground. The fear that was instilled into us was chilling. We were too frightened to talk to each other. One of the roll-calls stays in my mind. It was found that one man was missing. He was eventually found, but until then we were forced to stand in the parade ground for between 48–60 hours in the freezing cold. At least 40–50 people died as a result. I survived that terrifying ordeal. I was 18 years of age. My parents eventually found out where I was. I was the only member of my family to be arrested and taken to a concentration camp at that time. I was allowed to write a letter to them. My parents and friends tried every effort to secure my release. The only way out was to produce papers for emigration.

Willy's release from Dachau was eventually secured by his former employer who had by that time emigrated to England. His parents presented the papers to the Gestapo in Bonn and the relevant documents for his release were signed. It was April 1939 and the day of his release had arrived. Even at the last minute, freedom was not inevitable:

When I came to be released, the SS asked me if I had any money to pay for my fare home. I had no money whatsoever. The guards replied, 'then you can't go. We are not paying.' To my amazement a fellow Jewish inmate who was being released at the same time, looked up and said, 'I'll pay.' And he paid my fare. But for him, I would have remained in the camp. As we arrived on the train through Munich station, there were 3 or 4 Jews with trilby hats standing on the platform. They were waiting for any people being released from the camp. We looked like convicts with our shaven hair. They gave us their hats so that people would not know that we had just been released from Dachau. I arrived in Bonn early in the morning. I didn't want to wake my parents because a knock at the door in the early hours of the morning could be an SS raid. I waited for several hours outside the door until I felt able to ring the bell.

Willy left for England in May 1939. His departure at Bonn railway station was the last time he saw his parents and other members of his family. Later after the war he found out through the Red Cross that his father had died while in Cologne awaiting transportation to a concentration camp. His mother Regina and brother Manfred, aunt Henriette Moses and uncle Markus Moses were all taken to Minsk on 20 July 1942 and murdered in the concentration camp.

Once in England Willy worked on various farms, often in harsh conditions. He was so unhappy that he ran away to London where he began work in the City filling up sandbags to protect banks and businesses. He then took up employment with a Jewish firm, Rose & Company in Whitechapel, which fitted sewing machines for factories manufacturing khaki uniforms for the army. In May 1940 he was arrested and taken to Kempton Park racecourse to join other German and Austrian internees under canvas. He was transferred to Huyton, Liverpool and put on the troopship *Dunera*, bound for internment camps in Australia. He remained there for a year, enlisted in the British Army while still in Australia and was sent back to England aboard the SS *Stirling Castle*. In November 1941 he was sent to Ilfracombe to train in the Pioneer Corps, serving in 165 Company, 248 Company and then 88 Company.

On 26 August 1943 Willy transferred from the Pioneer Corps to the Royal Armoured Corps, changing his name from Willy Hirschfeld to William Field.[20] He was assigned as a tank driver to C Squadron 8th Hussars. While stationed in West Tofts Camp near King's Lynn in Norfolk the squadron was inspected by King George VI on 24 February 1944.[21] The squadron landed near Arromanches on 9 June 1944 (D-Day+3):[22]

> During the first night in France to protect ourselves from the bombs we slept under the tanks. This was soon forbidden because the ground could be so muddy that a tank could sink and this could have been fatal. While in France, I was called upon to interpret for the POWs because my native tongue was German. When I spoke to the first German prisoners, it was exciting in a way. I was not angry in spite of all that I had been through. It's not in my nature to harbour resentment or anger. Winning the war was good enough for me.

The 8th Hussars advanced through Normandy and came under intense fire at Villers-Bocage on the way to Caen. The official War Diaries record that on 15 June 1944 C Squadron moved to the Briquessard area where they were involved in 'close and confused fighting but all attacks were beaten off. Lt H.R.D. Pegler was killed during the night.' The following day was spent repairing damaged vehicles and recovering two tanks of A Squadron. During that time, C Squadron suffered numerous attacks but managed to beat off the enemy fighting. The War Diary entry for 17 June states that 'C Squadron was attacked almost continuously during the night of 16/17 and by the morning of the 17th was very tired having been in their tanks for three days'. It was during this period that the squadron lost five tanks with eight personnel killed or missing.[23] It was not long before Willy's tank received a direct hit:

During September 1944, we were on our way to Nijmegen in Holland. My tank was attacked by a German anti-tank gun near the railway and we suffered a direct hit. I managed to climb out of the driver's seat. The tank was full of smoke. I noticed that the gunner (Albert Parfitt) and commander (John Sutherland) were dead. I managed to pull the wireless operator (John Gardner) out of the burning tank, placed him behind the tank and eventually struggled for help. He was badly wounded and died on the way to the medical station. I was wounded in the leg and was eventually sent to a field hospital for treatment. I was the only survivor of my tank crew that day. I later learned that all my comrades were buried at the British military cemetery at Eindhoven. It was a shock to see one's mates killed. In fact the trauma of the experience hit me when my colonel took me back to see the burned-out tank a few weeks later.

In October 1944 Willy received a moving letter from the parents of John Gardner, of his tank crew, who had been killed:

Major Huth has written to us telling us how our son Trooper J.A. Gardner met his death. He tells us that you got him out of the tank and went back for assistance. All I wish to do is to thank you on behalf of my wife and myself for all that you did for our son in his hour of great need. We are most grateful to you. We know you by name, for in some of his letters, John referred to your excellent powers of cooking. I need not say that this has been a crushing blow for us. We had hoped that our son would have been spared to the end and it is desolating to know that he is not coming back. We must bear our sorrow with the same courage and fortitude that he showed amid all the horrors of war . . .[24]

Once he had recovered from his wounds, Willy returned to frontline fighting in a new tank, this time as driver for an officer who was second-in-command of the squadron. The regiment headed through Belgium and Holland towards Germany. In January 1945 amid thick fog, reduced visibility and snow-covered ground, he was involved in the intense battle of Linne and St Joost in Holland. He recalls:

> We had to white-wash our tanks because it was winter and there was heavy snow on the ground. Just outside Linne we met with British commandos and made a commando charge through the village. It was the first time that a commando raid of this kind had taken place so successfully. We charged our tanks, 10 or 12 in a row, towards the village with the commandos sat on the back. It was very exciting. It was a successful campaign. We encountered stiff resistance at St Joost. It was a long straggling village which had to be cleared house by house. We spent several weeks in Holland during the winter of 1944.

Bill Bellamy, B Squadron Troop Leader (not a German-Jewish refugee) of the 8th Hussars, provides an eye-witness account of the assault on St Joost from a farm building nearby:

> I had an extraordinary view of St Joost from this angle and dimly in the foggy air could see, and of course hear, the noise of the battle going on there. It sounded and looked terrifying – flames, smoke, continuous machine-gun and rifle fire, the crack of tank guns and the whistle and crump of artillery shells which were landing towards the rear of the village. I was glad to be on my own in relative peace. It was nearly dark by this time, the snow was falling in big soft flakes and the atmosphere was heavy with cold.[25]

The *Illustrated London News* reported on the final clearing of the Roer Triangle, January 1945:

> The capture of Linne by a famous commando (which previously led the invasion into Sicily and Italy) – riding on tanks of an armoured division charging across the snow-bound plain and crashing right

into the village and hurling out the defenders – a most spectacular and successful action completely surprising the enemy and crushing the last strong point between Maas and Roer.

Willy moved with his squadron into Germany, heading for Hamburg. It was the first time he had set foot on German soil since his departure six years earlier:

We took part in the capture of Hamburg. There was little resistance. The Germans were in disarray. The city had been completely destroyed. I was busy interrogating POWs who had marched towards us in their thousands to surrender. I remember one experience. I was in my tank and heard someone crying. I got out of the tank. Behind the bush was a young German soldier, not more than aged 16, shouting 'don't shoot me. I'm going to give up.' I felt sorry for him – he was only a young kid. He was so surprised when I spoke to him in German. I even gave him a cigarette. He told me that he had been told by his CO that if he surrendered, they would shoot him. I assured him that there was nothing to worry about.

Most poignantly, considering all that he had been through and still as a German national, Willy took part in the Victory Parade in Berlin on 21 July 1945. He proudly drove his tank crew past Churchill and the Allied leaders for the victory salute. He was promoted to the rank of sergeant and as such was one of the few Jewish sergeants in the 8th Hussars. After the war he was stationed in Lingen near Munster in Westphalia overseeing the transport troop and training new recruits as tank drivers. He was demobilised in December 1946 and returned to England.

In December 2001 he courageously returned to Dachau with his wife Judy and a group of school children from Bonn:

It was a lousy day. The parade ground was there – bringing back floods of memories. There is a museum at the concentration camp now. The lady attending the museum brought out the original ledger which showed the hand-written entry with my name and the date that I was taken into the concentration camp. It was eerie for my wife and I to see that original entry. But somehow it did not affect me that much. What affected me was the way that the huts had been re-created and sanitised. But how else could it be 60 years later?

Given his extraordinary survival against the odds, Willy is in no doubt that serving in the British Forces was the right action. He could have spent the duration of the war in the relative safety of England, but he chose a different path. He expresses the sentiments of so many refugees who joined the forces – this was *his* war:

I am very proud to have served in the 8th Kings Royal Irish Hussars. There was wonderful comradeship which is something I will always remember. As a refugee from Nazi oppression, I am happy that I served England which had, after all, given me my freedom. For this I am very grateful. I feel absolutely British, even though I was born and raised in Germany for the first 18 years of my life. I have no difficulty with going back to Germany, but my motto is '*you should be able to forgive, but you should not forget*'.

*Chapter 3*

# THE SMALL-SCALE RAIDING FORCE

A most closely guarded secret of the war was the formation of units of elite fighters and raiders who could carry out clandestine operations and night raids into German-controlled coastal areas of Europe, Norway, France, and islands off North Africa and Italy. The purpose of the raids included the gathering of vital intelligence, destroying radio stations and capturing German POWs for interrogation. The Small Scale Raiding Force (SSRF) was one of the earliest units to be raised during 1942 and formed under the codename of 62 Commando. The German-speaking refugees had a central role to play because of their fluency in German and other European languages. Training for the SSRF was carried out at Anderson Manor near Blandford in Dorset. These groups carried out a number of covert operations during 1942 and 1943. However piecing together exactly who was in the SSRF is much harder as names are rarely mentioned in official diaries and papers. Nevertheless, a number of German-speaking refugees are known to have taken part in raids, including Peter Terry (Peter Tischler) and Ernest Webster (Ernst Weinberger) and also Corporals Patrick Miles (Hubertus Levin) and Frederick Bentley (Frederic Bierer) who undertook Operation Huckaback, a raid on Herm, Channel Islands, in February 1943.[1] Two other German-speaking refugees are also known to have been part of the SSRF: Richard Lehniger and Rudolf Friedlaender and their profiles are examined in more detail here.

RICHARD LEHNIGER

Richard Lehniger was born in 1900 in Becov nad Teplou (Petschau) in Bohemia, then part of the Austro-Hungarian Empire. His father Gustav fought in the First World War in the Austro-Hungarian Army and died of his wounds in 1916. From then Richard became the family breadwinner and at just seventeen followed in his father's footsteps by serving in the Austro-Hungarian Army. He fought in the trenches in Belgium and France against the British. Ironically, just twenty-five years later he was fighting on the other side, this time as a member of the British Army.

After the First World War, Richard earned a living as a roofer, tiler and steeple-jack. Because of the Great Depression in the 1930s he could no longer find work and support the family. He studied Economics at Charles University in Prague where he met his future wife Julia (Lilly) Dorfler who held the Chair of the Student Social Democrat Party at the university. When Nazi forces overran the Sudetenland and Czechoslovakia in March 1939, they were both at risk as political dissidents. On 17 March 1939 Richard fled to Norway. In May 1939 Julia was aided by the National Union of Students in England and received a visa for entry into Britain which she used two months later in August 1939. Richard landed at Harwich without permission on 29 August but because of Julia's political links, a local MP supported his entry which was granted for one month. They looked for a passage to Canada, but less than a week later the borders of Europe were closed and so they had to remain in Britain.[2]

In March 1940 Richard enlisted in the Pioneer Corps at Kitchener Camp and joined 93 Company.[3] As Private Lehniger, he remained with 93 Company until May 1942 when he was drafted into the newly formed SSRF, receiving his training at Anderson Manor. Before going into action, he was required to change his name in case of capture. Thus Richard Lehniger became Richard Leonard. The first operations began in August 1942, and he carried out a number of raids, although it is not known for certain whether he was involved in the Dieppe Raid or St Nazaire Raid.[4]

On 12 September 1942 a group of eleven men of the SSRF set off for the Normandy coast in Operation Aquatint.[5] It included a Free Frenchman (André Desgrange), an English aristocrat (Lord Francis Howard of Penrith), a German-speaker (Richard Lehniger/Leonard) and a Jewish Pole (Abraham Opoczynski). The purpose of the raid was to take German POWs and interrogate them for intelligence. Arriving after midnight at the wrong place, possibly because of fog, the raid was disturbed by a German patrol. Three of the raiding force, including Richard, died. Lord Howard was seriously wounded and two others were captured. One evaded capture and was taken up by the French Resistance where he remained until he was betrayed by a double agent. The boat crew that brought them managed to return to England safely. Gérard Fournier and André Heintz write in their extensive history of the raid:

At 00.17 hours the motor boat was anchored in three fathoms of water to the north west of the dry valley which led down to the sea, approximately 350 yards from the beach, not, as they thought, at Sainte-Honorine but at Saint-Laurent-sur-Mer. The Goatley (a collapsible boat used by commandos) was launched from the rear of the MTB. Eleven men climbed onboard . . . The light vessel cast off from the MTB at 00.20 hours and headed straight for the dry valley. It reached the beach five minutes later. But the major decided that the landing could not take place at this precise location which he considered to be too close to a group of houses. He therefore ordered for the Goatley to be moved farther east and the small craft was finally drawn onto the sand approximately 220 yards along the beach. The group left Captain Howard in charge of the Goatley. For 50 minutes, the ten men explored the surrounding beach and the foot of the cliff. In total darkness they could see no farther than five steps ahead. None of them were aware that they were in between two German 'resistance nests'.[6]

At 01.05 hours a German guard dog began to bark. The men were discovered and several rounds of gunfire and grenades were fired between the SSRF and the German patrol. Private Lehniger and

Sergeant Williams managed to get back to the shore and swim to the Goatley which was being showered by bullets from the German patrol. The Goatley began to fill up with water and subsequently sank. It is thought that both men were severely injured and drowned after the Goatley sank, although some mystery still surrounds the cause of their deaths. What is known is that during that fateful raid, Private Lehniger died with Major G.H. March-Philipps and Sergeant Allen Williams on 13 September 1942.[7] The three men were buried with full military honours by the Germans in the local Roman Catholic churchyard at St Laurent-sur-Mer.[8] Gérard Fournier and André Heintz write:

On Tuesday 15th September at 0.900 hours, and in the greatest solemnity, the Germans had the three British soldiers buried in the cemetery at Saint-Laurent-sur-Mer. Two inhabitants of Saint-Laurent, M. Jules Scelles and a WWI veteran, M. Henri Leroutier, watched the scene from behind a wall at the Hôtel du Carrefour. No inhabitants had been allowed to take part in the ceremony. The three coffins, covered with flowers and transported by three carts were preceded by a section of the 3rd Reserve Company stationed at Saint-Laurent and followed by German officers. The coffins were then lowered into the three graves that had been dug side by side. Then to close the ceremony, a guard of honour fired a three gun salute. The entire scene was filmed . . . the German propaganda services had decided to make maximum profit of the event.[9]

In the event of his death, Richard had entrusted a letter to his cousin Leo Felix to give to his wife Lilly. It was written originally in German from Anderson Manor dated 6 June 1942. In it he provides a rare insight into his motivation for being in the Special Forces:

This is not intended as a letter of farewell, just a reminder of me in case you do not hear from me anymore. It is possible that I could be taken prisoner in which case you would be able to find out my name and the address to which to write. It may be years before we both see each other again but I want you to know that I shall do my utmost to return to you both . . .

I cannot say that I am pleased to be going but I am proud that I was one of the ones selected to do something that might end the war sooner. And now darling, a very big request: if I should die – what a horrible word – do not change your demeanour in front of the child in any way. I believe a child understands far more of such things than we imagine. We are working for a better future for our child, a better life for mankind. Millions are dying in Russia, why should I be the exception. Please tell our child someday that I did what I thought was right.[10]


## RUDI FRIEDLAENDER

Rudi Friedlaender (born Munich, 15 August 1908) studied Law and Economics, graduating with a PhD in Economics.[11] In 1934 he went to Holland to train as a carpenter before travelling to England the following year where he worked as a carpenter until joining the Pioneer Corps at Bideford in 1940. He was posted with 137 Company of the Pioneer Corps. In August 1941 he transferred to the Royal Army Ordnance Corps (RAOC) and then the Royal Electrical and Mechanical Engineers (REME). In 1942 he volunteered for 'hazardous duties' and was sent for specialist training before being posted to North Africa on 5 March 1943, attached to No. 1 Small Scale Raiding Force. The purpose of No. 1 SSRF was to carry out amphibious and overland raids in North Africa. His first mission was to land with his group in Operation Spider, on one of the small islands off Bône, Algeria, then still in enemy hands. The purpose was to climb a gully, capture a listening station and if possible take prisoners for interrogation. In his diary he wrote:

We landed on the right spot; it really looked like the superimposed aerial photograph. We formed up and started our climb. We got to the plateau where it was planned that we should separate. There we hit barbed wire. The CO and the major halted us, with orders to wait. They went on reconnaissance. We waited for a while, then the order came to return to the boats as it was too late to undertake an attack, with a chance to get back to the beach in time. We went back, disembarked, paddled to the MTB [Motor Torpedo Boat] and made back for home. That was a great disappointment.'[12]

The second operation was carried out a few weeks later, again ending in disappointment. The raiders were discovered by Italian and German soldiers who fired shots in their direction. All managed to return safely to the MTB.[13] The men spent a few days in Malta before their next mission which was to land on the island of Lampedusa, halfway between Malta and the Tunisian coast. The aim of the raid was to destroy a wireless station and overwhelm a garrison on the west side of the island. They were trying to find a suitable landing place when shots were fired at them from two posts, one on the beach and the other on the cliff top. The entry in Rudi's diary reads:

Others opened up and then some heavier stuff – mortar shells, a small caliber cannon – came over the hills from the other side of the island. The three boats floated for a while aimlessly offshore, then the officer gave the order to retreat . . . Now once more we paddled for our lives. And this time we had tracers from several MG [machine guns] and some shells following us, and then came the first star shells lighting up the scene uncomfortably. The SM [sergeant major] grasped the Oerlikon, lifted it from its mounting in the bow and carried it back to the stern where he calmly exchanged magazines and began to fire once more, from the hip.

But we were paddling, with little hope ever to reach the MTB alive. The worst experience was to come. A searchlight suddenly sprang up out of the darkness to our left, sweeping across the water. Our first thought was a patrol boat, perhaps an E-boat. That would have been the end. We had about a mile to get back to the MTB which could not move nearer for fear of being caught in the searchlight. We paddled stubbornly, knowing that we might be picked up by the guns whenever the searchlight swept across our boat. We realised at last to our relief that the searchlight was mounted on the island, several miles to the east and that, although we seemed to be lit up from the coast, we could probably not be seen clearly. The searchlight seemed never to hold us in the beam. So we struggled for almost an hour, constantly fired at. But then we lay alongside our MTB once more. The searchlight had picked it up now and we had to move fast not to endanger the ship. We hauled our boat on deck and then the engines started . . . Shells splashed harmlessly in the water around and the ship began to put on speed. Under a slight smoke screen we raced around in a wide sweep to try and pick up the two missing canoe men. But then came the order from our flotilla leader that we would have to beat it, only the leader remaining on the island to continue the search. Still we were in range of the enemy shore batteries and the searchlight, but soon the powerful engines took us out of harm's way and we just all looked back into the far-off fireworks.[14]

In May 1943 Rudi transferred to the Special Air Service (SAS), changing his name to Robert Lodge in order not to betray his German background. He was issued a new service number, 5550151, because his original army number, 13801992, identified him as an 'enemy alien' of the Pioneer Corps. He was posted to 2 SAS Regiment under the command of Captain Bridgeman-Evans and in July he parachuted into Sicily on his first jump. He was captured and sent to a POW camp on the Italian mainland. Two months later he escaped, was recaptured, was moved from camp to camp and finally taken to Camp 66 a few miles from Capua near Naples.

We walked donkey-tired, sweating through this lovely, sunny stretch of country, our eyes resting longingly on the heavy bunches of grapes. But nobody offered us any. Then after an hour we turned and saw our camp: the squares of barbed wire, the bald long huts, red-roofed and bricked and obviously a brand new compound. We soon discovered that our compound was only a sector of a very large prison camp.[15]

Meanwhile the Allies were beginning their heavy RAF heavy bombing raids of Italy by the RAF and Rudi feared that he would be killed by his own side. He had been transferred from Camp 66 to

Camp 73, about 30 miles north of Modena, and began planning his escape, which became a compelling need when the Germans took charge of Camp 73. Soon the Germans decided to evacuate the camp and started to march the prisoners north. Rudi's chance came as the column of prisoners passed through a small town:

> Guards were driving the last men out of the huts as we moved off out to the road. It was about noon, a very hot day, and we soon felt the heavy burden of our load. The Germans had cars with machine guns mounted travelling ahead, in the centre, and the rear. Infantry marched either side at roughly 30 to 50 yard intervals. So we started what would be one of the most exhausting walks of my life. The heat was oppressive, and for about ten kilometres we struggled on, the Germans not once giving a halt. Many of the boys dropped their parcels; many more fell behind. I got so tired that I often thought I had to drop . . .
>
> We were by now marching in full disorder, as we entered the main street of the town, high buildings closing in on either side, the inhabitants looking out of windows or standing in open doorways. I walked on the pavement as near as possible to the houses, trying to keep an eye on the truck and to stay nearly half way between the nearest two German guards on this side of the column. Jimmy [fellow prisoner] was close behind me . . . A few yards in front of me I saw two women standing in or near an open door. From then onward I did everything almost automatically. I only remember the shape of the woman – large, erect, clothed in black. I shall never forget her, although I never saw her face. I dropped on hands and knees without looking round. Some of the boys must have understood my intention; they crowded nearer, forming a protective screen. And the guards did not see me. Jimmy must have followed my example. I crawled up to the woman, I touched her leg. She did not move, did not even look down. But somehow I felt that she knew and approved of my intention, and I quickly pushed through the door and found myself inside an hostelry, the bar being immediately near the door, I crawled behind the bar.[16]

Rudi and the British prisoners who had managed to escape with him began the long journey on foot trekking across Italy towards the Italian Alps, often aided en route by sympathetic farmers and shepherds. There was always the fear that they might be recaptured, especially if they crossed the wrong point of a mountain border-pass. Then began a period of hiding in a cave and slaughtering sheep for meat.

> So here was the cave, our home for four weeks. I cannot draw. It was a huge flat stone resting on two or three great pillar stones. The end of the flat stone hanging over formed the outer cave and we simply closed one side by resting young trees against it and bracing branches horizontally, closing the last gaps with large ferns which grew abundantly in the woods.[17]

After four weeks, Rudi decided to try and make his own way to the Allied lines without his companions. His military record shows that he finally arrived at Allied lines on 23 December 1943. He was flown back to England, and spent time in a military hospital being treated for jaundice and dysentery. On 9 May 1944 he returned to his Regiment, 2 SAS. A few days before his discharge from hospital, he wrote an extraordinary letter to his father, in which he speaks about his ambitions. As with most of the Germans fighting in the British Forces, he did not have British nationality:

> I am happy to be able to fight for my principles and for Britain, the nation which now champions these principles and has become a second home to me. If I survive there will be only one ambition left: to be able to continue to fight for freedom and peace as a British citizen.[18]

In August 1944, some two months after D-Day, he again parachuted with his comrades of 2 SAS under the command of Lieutenant-Colonel Brian Franks behind the German lines in the Vosges region of eastern France.[19] The objective of the operation in the Vosges was to establish a presence and set up bases from which to advance towards Germany; also to disrupt enemy communications and send back vital information.[20] The following months saw the largest and costliest operations undertaken by the SAS during the Second World War in that region. For his actions in the early phases of this operation, as Sergeant Lodge, Rudi was awarded the Distinguished Conduct Medal (DCM). The citation read:

> Sgt. Lodge was part of a small reconnaissance party which landed by parachute in the Eastern Vosges on the night of 12/13 August (1944). A large German force was sent to round up the party. On 19 August Sgt. Lodge found himself with a party of four surrounded by a large force of the enemy who gradually closed in on them. In the face of intense automatic and small arms fire, Sgt. Lodge stood up and fired a Bren magazine at the enemy at a range of about 30 yards. This allowed the rest of the detachment to escape to temporary safety and inflicted a considerable number of casualties on the enemy. Later the same day the same situation arose and Sgt. Lodge repeated the same courageous act. Finally the small party was extricated with only one casualty. Both on this occasion and on past operations which once included an escape from an enemy POW camp, this NCO has continually shown complete disregard for his personal safety, a fine offensive spirit and gifts of leadership much above the average.

Just a few days later while taking part in Operation Loyton, he was captured by the Germans in an ambush in the region.[21] The exact circumstances surrounding his death remain a mystery and were investigated by the official War Crimes Investigation Unit. His body was found to have a wound to the back of the head and bayonet marks in the stomach. The official enquiry stated that he had been murdered on or about 18 August, although no evidence of war crimes could be conclusively proved, so no further action was taken. The people of Moussey had provided support to the SAS men, including Rudi, an action that was to cost them dearly. On 24 September the Germans rounded up the entire male population and sent them to concentration camps.[22] The local priest Abbé Gassman offered his own life in exchange for the men of the village but this was refused. Of the 256 men taken, 144 did not return.

During his service with the SAS, Rudi had recorded his thoughts which provide a glimpse into his philosophy. It was a moment of self-knowledge and self examination when he came face-to-face with the reality of personal sacrifice:

First the struggle between life-serving and life-destroying philosophies must be decided by victory of the positive school; otherwise human beings would be conditioned to react in a destructive way. Examples are too painfully close at hand. An individualist must be essentially vulnerable against sudden changes of conditions. He may have had preconceived ideas [of] how to react to certain events, but when the actual experience is made, he may suddenly discover in himself entirely new qualities and the reaction will turn out to be more or less happy improvisation.

A man has decided to throw his life in for a cause. The sacrifice seems easy to him, his life is cheap to him compared with the result he hopes to achieve. Then comes the moment of the extreme test and trial. He suddenly discovers some new qualities in himself, he has a new vision of life, the new experience heightens the confidence in his powers, his own life becomes a higher value and the sacrifice suddenly seems entirely out of proportion to the result. If only he could live, how much more he could achieve for the cause with the strength of that new vision than by laying down his life.

He himself made the ultimate sacrifice. On 21 August 1944 he was buried in Moussey Churchyard in the Vosges. His grave lies on the south-western side of the cemetery close to the wall alongside nine other British soldiers killed in action in the region.

## Chapter 4

# THE COMMANDOS

The formation of the commandos was sanctioned by Prime Minister Winston Churchill in 1942. It was the brainchild of Lord Louis Mountbatten after he became Chief of Combined Operations that same year. The purpose was to train specialist fighters to carry out clandestine intelligence operations and raids, and where necessary be attached to other regiments. The German-speaking refugees had a central role to play with the creation of 3 Troop of No. 10 Inter-Allied Commando during the summer of 1942. A number of commando units were raised during the progress of the war but only 3 Troop, also known as X Troop, consisted solely of German-speaking refugees. They constituted different nationalities, primarily Germans and Austrians but also Hungarians and Czechs. It was an unlikely coalition but all were united by the fact that they spoke fluent German and had a common cause – to fight the evil regime that had ruined their lives and continued to threaten their families who were left behind in Nazi-occupied Europe. The troop was raised under the leadership of Captain Brian Hilton-Jones, originally of 4 Commando, who had taken part in the Dieppe Raid. Ian Harris (Hans Hajos), a former member of 3 Troop, describes him: 'He was a tough, wiry guy, could speak German and had been a junior official in the British Embassy in Berlin. He was a great example. He turned most of us into something quite formidable.'

The first two intakes of men began their training at Achnacarry between Loch Arkaig and the Great Glen in the Scottish Highlands before transferring to Aberdovey near Snowdonia in North Wales. Later units were sent directly to Aberdovey. In total over 100 men trained for 3 Troop. They received the most intensive and gruelling training that the British Army could offer, consisting of 8-mile jog-marches before breakfast, rock climbing, abseiling down sheer cliffs above rough seas, parachuting, mountaineering in Snowdonia, and armed and unarmed combat. Only live ammunition was used. The training was exacting and exerting, some of which was carried out at night time. Special exercises were created, such as penetrating an RAF base at Towyn, 6 miles from Aberdovey, to retrieve specific information without being detected. This particular operation was successful and the RAF authorities were none the wiser. The men were kept at the peak of fitness. Ian Harris recalls:

> We had equipment that no one else had. The purpose of our training was to train us as individual fighters rather than part of a unit. We were the first to be issued with the Dennison smock, later universally accepted as the uniform for parachutists; a camouflage jacket and green beret, boots with special grip, a tommy gun and a Colt pistol. We were given Shetland wool pullovers and special wearing apparel. I wrote to my parents: 'they are treating us like gentlemen here'. We were given double meat rations, private billets and not in Nissen huts. We were given a special allowance to pay for the private billets.

This troop brought specialist knowledge and skills to whichever unit they were seconded. Its members were able to crack open safes, pick locks, scale walls, kill a person silently with their bare hands, use explosives and assemble fuses and detonators. With an intimate knowledge of German military command structure, they were able to carry out night operations and raids effectively. For security purposes and their own protection, each man was required to change his name, which included creating a new family history. For those men who were later captured and interrogated as POWs it meant creating a cover story along the lines of having had a German education because their father was a businessman who travelled abroad, and so forth. Protecting their real identity as Germans or Austrians was paramount. An elaborate system was worked out for sending and receiving post. Colin Anson (Claus Ascher) explains:

We each had trusted British friends who would liaise with our relatives and friends from our former lives. They became our next of kin. They acted as intermediaries for our post and letters. Friends would write to us under our old name and the trusted family would then put it in another envelope with our new name on it. That security never broke down.

Once the training was completed, the men proudly wore the green beret with the badge of the Queen's Own Royal West Kents, Hampshire Regiment or General Service badge. They were the first servicemen to be issued with rubber-soled boots instead of the usual hob-nailed ones, enabling silent movement during operations. Members of 3 Troop were attached to different units and served in one of two major campaigns: the invasion of Italy and Sicily, and the D-Day landings in Normandy.

3 Troop suffered huge casualties and fatalities, mainly in Normandy after the invasion. Lance Corporal Peter Wells (Werner Auerhahn) was killed in action in Italy on 19 January 1944. Max Laddy (Max Lewinsky) and Webster (Weinberger) were killed on D-Day before they made it ashore on Sword Beach. George MacFranklyn (Max Frank), who had survived being wounded in action in Italy and posted with 4 Commando for the Normandy invasion, was killed by a mortar on the beach on D-Day. Eugene Fuller (Eugen Kagerer-Stein) was wounded on D-Day and died on 13 June. Ernest Lawrence (Ernst Lenel) was reported missing in action. His body was never recovered and he is commemorated on the Bayeux Memorial in Normandy. Richard Arlen (R. Abramovicz) was killed in action at Franceville-Plage on 7 June; Kenneth Graham (Kurt Gumpertz) on 12/13 June; Frederick Fletcher (F. Fleischer) at Le Plein on 11 June; Peter Moody (Kurt Meyer) died in Normandy on 13 June; Ernest Norton (Ernst Nathan), who was attached to 4 Commando, was also killed on 13 June; and Harry Andrews (Hans Arnstein) in August. Captain Robert Hamilton (Salo Reich) was killed at Walcheren on 1 November and Herbert Seymour (H. Sachs) crossing the Rhine on 23 March 1945. Eric Howard (Erich Nathan) was wounded in action on D-Day, commissioned in the field for bravery but was killed

at Osnabrück on 3 April 1945. Keith Griffith (Kurt Glaser) was killed in Germany on 11 April crossing the Aller River. Casualties were high in 3 Troop. Those wounded in action included Troop Sergeant Major Oscar O'Neill (Hentschel), Maurice Latimer (Levy), Tommy Swinton (Schwytzer) and Freddie Gray (Manfred Gans). Sergeant Brian Groves (Goldschmidt) was involved in Operation Partridge, a raid behind enemy lines in Italy over the River Garigliano during the Allied advance. He was wounded so badly that a foot had to be amputated. Steve Ross (Stephan Rosskamm) was wounded twice in Italy. Colin Anson (Claus Ascher) was seriously wounded just off the coast of Italy when shrapnel embedded in the base of his skull. Ian Harris was wounded three times in Normandy.

A number of 3 Troop were honoured for bravery. The troop commander Brian Hilton-Jones and George Lane (Georg Lanyi), a Hungarian, were both awarded the Military Cross. Ian Harris (Hans Hajos) was awarded the Military Medal; Robert Barnes (Gotthard Baumwollspinner) the Distinguished Conduct Medal; and Jack Davies (Hansen) Mentioned in Dispatches. The following profiles provide an insight into the cross-section of men who served with this highly specialised troop, each attached to different units for action overseas.

## COLIN ANSON

Colin Anson was born Claus Leopold Octavio Ascher in Berlin on 13 February 1922. He was raised as a Protestant, even though his father was originally from a Jewish family in Silesia.[1] His father Curt Ascher fought in an infantry regiment in the First World War and was badly wounded on the Western Front. After that war he joined the new *Reichswehrministerium* (of the government of the new Weimar Republic) in Berlin under the German Defence Minister Gustav Noske, a Socialist.[2] When he resigned as a result of the Kapp Putsch in 1920, Noske became Governor of Hanover, but was dismissed from his post by the Nazis in about 1935. Colin's father resigned his post at this time and became managing director of an industrial film company. For the young Colin the Nazi rise to power appeared exciting until one day his father urged him to 'have a closer look at what's happening'. After about a year, his father started to visit old friends in Berlin in the hope of mobilising some kind of opposition to the Nazi government, making no secret of his ideological views. This became an extremely dangerous position to hold and his business suffered. Colin comments:

> We knew war was coming. Goering had made the famous 'guns not butter' remark. My father refused to read German newspapers, disgusted by his German nationality. He was somewhat reckless in making his views known. When I asked him why he was so outspoken, he replied 'do you expect me to act like a coward?' My father was arrested in September 1937 and taken into police custody. He was then transported to Dachau concentration camp where he died on 15 October 1937.

Colin left Germany with the Kindertransport on 7 February 1939, a few days before his seventeenth birthday. Once in England, he was met by a Quaker lady and sent to an agricultural training centre at Wallingford in Berkshire to train as a market gardener. He recalls that he was 'greeted with enormous sympathy and warmth by the British people'. He was spared internment, but in the summer of 1940 became one of the welfare officers at Wallingford because of a shortage of staff. At the end of 1940 he travelled to Oxford to volunteer for the British Forces. He signed up, was given the King's shilling and awaited further instruction. In December 1940 he was instructed to report to Ilfracombe for training in the Pioneer Corps:

> I was excited about joining the army. After training in Ilfracombe, I was assigned to 87 Company who were in South London at the time, billeted in partially bombed property near Blackheath. We cleared bomb damage at the height of the blitz on London. I was mainly working with other German refugees. Most nights were spent in air raid shelters. We pulled people from the rubble after the heavy bombing raids. The local people appeared to have no hostility towards Germans, in spite of what they were going through. They didn't like Hitler but they were kind to us Germans.

We were then sent to Bootle, near Liverpool for fire-watch duty. Whilst we were in Liverpool a mysterious visitor by the name of Hartmann moved around the camp asking numerous questions about our motivation and attitude. Those with an Austrian background suddenly disappeared and we noticed that they did not return. It later turned out that they were accepted for Special Operations Executive.

After that we were billeted in an old woollen mill at Velindre in Wales, laying mines and barbed wire obstacle defences along the coast. It was here that the band and orchestra of 87 Company was formed by Lt. Wood, under the leadership of Karl Walter Billman (later Kenneth Bartlett). I played the double bass. The orchestra travelled around Wales giving concerts and playing at local dances. It meant that we were excused general duties and parades! Then in October 1941, 87 Company was sent to the ancient Defensible Barracks at Pembroke Docks which were over 100 years old, still with a moat and fixed, former drawbridge. There I stood, a German, on sentry duty at the barrack gates overlooking Milford Haven. It was a bizarre situation.

In 1942, Colin and his friend Karl Walter Billman received a rail warrant to travel to London to report at the Grand Central Hotel in Marylebone Road where they were interviewed. They were accepted for 'special forces' which turned out to be the commandos. Both were required to change their names and thus Claus Leopald Octavio Ascher became Colin Edward Anson.

Those of us who were accepted for special duties were sent to the Pioneer Corps depot at Bradford to await further instruction. Brian Hilton-Jones arrived at the mill where we were billeted with a stack of new pay books. It was at that point that we changed our names and were issued with new identities. My papers stated that I was part of the Royal Sussex Regiment. This was to mask the fact of having been in the Pioneer Corps which would give away our foreign origin. We piled into a train for Aberdovey, North Wales, where we were lodged in private billets. When we arrived in Wales we were a British commando troop waiting for training. We received a subsistence allowance and reported for parades when required. The first posting was to Achnacarry, the commando basic training depot in Scotland, in October or November 1942. It was very demanding, intended to weed out those whose heart was not in it. The course ended with a two-day exercise on half rations in freezing conditions. After this training, we were passed out and took the train back to Aberdovey where we were issued with green berets. We were kept at peak performance and fitness. In 1942/3, training consisted of expeditions to Snowdonia and mountaineering, and then to HMS *Tormentor* near Portsmouth on the south coast to undergo boat training on different kinds of landing craft. The troop went on parachute training, but I was no longer with them at that point. I was detached around May 1943 and attached to 40 (Royal Marine) Commando (A Troop of 40 Commando) with three other Germans. I joined 40 (RM) Commando for assault landing practice on the north-west coast of Scotland. It was an exceedingly wet time. We trained on enormous stretches of beach in the heavy rain. I stayed with them until embarkation onto a convoy on the Clyde, bound for action overseas. No one knew for certain what that would be or their intended destination.

We embarked circa May 1943 at Greenock onto the troopship *Devonshire*. We were issued with tropical kit. We thought this was to throw the scent and that we were bound for Norway. There was a huge convoy of ships with a piper playing as we passed through the Clyde. It was very impressive. Brigadier Laycock informed us that we were going to be part of what was then the biggest landing operation of all – the invasion of Sicily. In the Bay of Tunis we were joined by more ships. On the day before we landed, we joined a vast armada, stretching from horizon to horizon. We headed for the south-eastern corner of Sicily. The weather had taken a turn for the worse with enormous high seas. It was a dramatic journey – the sea was very rough and there was a danger of the landing craft capsizing. As we entered the bay, suddenly the sea went very calm. It was surreal. I can still remember the smell of warm tropical vegetation coming over the sea and the sound of Cicadas (grasshoppers).

On 10 July 1943 Colin landed with his unit in Sicily, making up part of a considerable landing force. They discovered that the Italians had constructed pill-boxes camouflaged as haystacks. They came under some fire but suffered few casualties. Most losses were experienced by the Italians. Grenades were thrown at the haystacks setting them on fire and making short work of the Italian defences. Concern that German Tiger tank units were operating in the vicinity were soon quashed as they had withdrawn, thinking that no landings were going to take place. Colin's force split into three columns – one went inland, the other two along the coast mopping up defences. Colin moved with the group probing inland, while larger forces landed. Eventually they advanced towards the town of Syracuse which was occupied. They suffered substantial air raids before proceeding to Augusta to embark on a fast assault ship the *Queen Emma*. Their brief was to land at the rear of the German positions in the plain overlooked by Mount Etna. While aboard, they came under an unexpected sustained air attack in which Colin was severely wounded, almost costing him his life. The ship's doctor and commando doctor were both killed. The ship was littered with the dead and injured. He recounts:

I had gone on the well-deck with my hammock because it was such a hot night. When the noise started, I rolled out of my hammock and lay on my stomach on the deck. When the hit occurred, a piece of shrapnel penetrated my helmet and into my skull. I remember the date clearly. It was 17 July 1943. I suffered a head wound which knocked me out. When I came around, I was aware of water as the ship was trying to right itself after the hit. Another marine had shrapnel wounds in his abdomen. I took off my helmet to hold over his face because another *Stuka* (dive-bomber) was coming. Blood dripped onto my arm. I was not actually aware that I had a head injury. I reported to the medical sergeant and asked for a bandage. He looked terribly serious and told me not to move. At that point

I began to feel queer. Someone wanted to give me some rum but the thought made me feel ill. I was then evacuated with the other wounded and it transpired that I wasn't expected to survive the night. My brain was exposed by the shrapnel which had smashed my skull and lodged in it. I was taken ashore to Sicily and transported to 151 Light Field Ambulance, a mobile hospital, staffed by Canadian nurses. It consisted of two 3-ton lorries with Red Crosses, one of which contained a complete operating theatre and a tent attached with about a dozen beds. In that mobile hospital the doctors carried out a very delicate brain operation, fishing out bone splinters and then sewing the skin back together. The shrapnel had lodged itself inside at the back of the skull. It remains in the base of my skull today! When I finally came around, I found that I was wearing a plaster cast helmet. I read the field card around my neck which said that I had been unconscious and had stopped breathing for half an hour. I was kept alive by 'heart massage', external pounding action of the heart. I was evacuated to Tripoli in North Africa for approx two weeks. I was then flown to Cairo to the 15th Scottish General Hospital. After that I was sent to an infantry-reinforcement training depot on the Suez Canal where I spent three tedious months, downgraded to B3. It was a very soul-destroying time.

In December 1943, when the medical team was sure that there were no tumours or infections on the brain, Colin returned to the 15th Scottish General Hospital to receive a bone graft and spend a further period of convalescence. He was determined to return to the commandos and eventually succeeded. He was sent to a transit camp south of Cairo to await posting. After some delay he rejoined 40 (RM) Commando in southern Italy, about to depart for Yugoslavia. For several months he served as part of the Intelligence Section of No. 2 Commando Brigade under Captain Jupp.

The summer of 1944 was idyllic. The main purpose of my work was to interrogate prisoners. I acted as the German speaker/translator on motor gunboat patrols along the coast. I was to shout the captain's orders to the German crew of any craft – but we didn't actually intercept any German craft at that time. Then came the raids on various islands, Brač and Hvar. We were stationed on the island of Vis. We were opposed by the 7th SS Panzer Division *Prinz Eugen*, largely made up of Balkan personnel, local Yugoslav Fascists and Austrian Nazi officers. They were a highly unpleasant group of individuals. The most spectacular raid in which I was involved was on the island of Brač. The aim of which was to raise as much noise and dust as possible to make it sound like a big operation. This was intended to draw German troops towards us and away from their hunt for Tito. We spun it out until we were sure that it had had some effect. We sat on the mountain tops with SS Panzers heading for us, a particularly hazardous time and yet this strategy was highly successful because it enabled Tito and his partisans to escape through the back of a cave in the Drvar region of Yugoslavia. Tito spent the rest of the war on the island of Vis under heavy Allied military protection.

We returned to Italy in the late summer of 1944 and were quartered in Monopoli. From there we travelled to Rimini to embark for Albania on what was supposed to be a short sharp action. After we landed, we were delayed because of the cold 'monsoon' rains which engulfed everything for 21 days, holding up our operations. The Germans were well ensconced. They showered us with shrapnel from 88mm guns from the northern tip of Corfu. Eventually the rain let up and we captured the small Albanian port of Sarande, even though it was heavily booby-trapped. We heard that there were still Germans remaining on Corfu, so a fellow marine and I boarded a motor gunboat to have a look. We entered the old harbour and jumped ashore. We were expecting the boat to tie up, but it didn't. It slid out and we were left stranded. Very quickly we were surrounded by Greeks who hadn't seen an Allied soldier in four years. We were given a tumultuous welcome and out came the ouzo. Eventually the rest of our brigade arrived on the island. We spent October 1944 in small hotels and then stationed for a while in the Summer Palace *Mon Repos*, the birthplace of Prince Philip. I helped with the evacuation of the German prisoners to Italy. In conjunction with the Chief of Police, I was then involved with the evacuation of the Italian civilian population and Fascist administrators who were not popular with the local Greeks. They were housed in a local prison for their own protection. We stayed in Corfu until approximately mid-November 1944 and then returned to the mainland. We saw Christmas 1944 in Monopoli. In the New Year, my friend Ken Bartlett (Karl Walter Billman), now a lieutenant commissioned in the field in Normandy, recruited a half-troop of German-speaking volunteers who were trained in south-central Italy by him, David Stewart (Strauss) and Alfred Shelley, with me as their sergeant.

We were sent to the north to take part in the last actions of the war in Italy. We went to Valli di Comacchio, north of Ravenna where we took 1,200 Russian-speaking POWs (Georgians who had been pressurised into the German Army). We saw the end of the war in Ravenna. It all ended quite suddenly. It was a huge anti-climax and we were all melancholic. We didn't feel like celebrating. I went for a long quiet walk through the streets of Ravenna. Then we were sent to Naples ready for re-embarkation to England. Once in England, we were stationed at Seaford in Sussex with Ken Bartlett as our commanding officer.

When the army commandos were disbanded, Colin was attached to the Control Commission for Germany. He requested to be sent to Frankfurt where he could search for his mother. His request was granted and he was stationed with Field Intelligence Agency Technical at the British enclave at Höchst near Frankfurt. He succeeded in finding his mother and they were reunited. His work was concerned with the background of scientific and industrial factories which involved translating documents and travelling all over Germany exchanging notes with doctors, visiting German generals in the Medical Corps, liaising with surgeons and industrial scientists. He was given the task of translating some of the documents of Albert Speer's Berlin-based Ministry of Weapons and Equipment. His emotional reaction to his return to Frankfurt shows how in the intervening years a 'brotherhood' had emerged from his training and combat in the commandos:

To walk these particular streets with the ghost of a German schoolboy walking ahead, with whom I had absolutely nothing in common anymore, was an almost schizophrenic psychological stress. To feel that I had to get back to my own people at the mess where I could relax again, showed me how I had changed. I hadn't really expected to survive the war in the commandos, but there was a job that had to be done. I wanted to repay the debt to Britain for saving my life.

Colin also visited the police headquarters in Frankfurt to look up his father's records and ascertain who had betrayed him. He stood at the crossroads of a moral decision:

I saw who had betrayed my father. I had a lot of discretion at that time and could have done something about it. I could have invited him for a walk and issued him with an invitation he couldn't refuse. I *was* tempted to pay him a visit, but I did nothing. Why? Because my religious upbringing reminded me that 'Revenge is mine,' says the Lord, 'I will repay'.[3] I hated the Nazis, but I could not exact revenge.

### PETER GILES

Peter Giles (Otto Hess) was among the first batch of recruits for 3 Troop. Born in Mainz in Germany in 1921, he spent much of his childhood in Wiesbaden on the Rhine. He came to England as a refugee on 20 August 1939. The following year he enlisted in the Auxiliary Military Pioneer Corps (AMPC) and was sent to North Devon for training. He was assigned to 165 Company and over the next two years carried out construction work, stationed for nearly a year near Tavistock in South Devon. He often visited the farm of the Giles family at Mary Tavy and because of the close friendship with them later changed his surname to Giles before departing on missions abroad.

Peter's official service record states that he was transferred from the Pioneer Corps to the Commando Depot as early as January 1942.[4] He was posted to Achnacarry and then Aberdovey for training with

3 Troop. He then spent a period in London, at which time he volunteered for special duties. After further training he was seconded to the Special Intelligence Service (SIS). In 1944 he was dropped behind enemy lines into Yugoslavia in Operation Beech, probably as part of SOE operations. The exact purpose of the mission remains unclear because MI6 has not declassified the files. A certain amount of information has been forthcoming from diverse sources, enabling a basic reconstruction of the events surrounding his mission.[5] Peter crossed into the area which is now Croatia to join with Tito's partisans. For some unknown reason he was unable to fulfil his mission and he contacted his emergency link. That link confirmed with London that he was who he claimed to be and escorted him towards Topolsica for evacuation to Italy. However he and his escort were ambushed by a German patrol on 1 October near Lekenik, south of Zagreb and killed. It is not certain whether Peter was captured, interrogated, tortured and then shot or killed in the ambush. German sources have suggested that he was taken to a nearby concentration camp, handed over to the SS where he was tortured and killed.[6] His body was never recovered. Since he has no known grave, he is commemorated on a plaque at the Groesbeek War Cemetery in Holland.[7] He was just twenty-three years old.

## PETER MASTERS

Peter Masters (Peter Arany), the Viennese pacifist who became a commando, fled Austria in August 1938. After a few weeks in England he worked on a farm in Hurley near Maidenhead in Berkshire before moving to London to attend art school. Internment followed in June 1940 at Lingfield racecourse and then the Isle of Man. Upon his release in August 1940 he volunteered for the British Forces and was sent to the Pioneer Corps. He served with 77 Company, before volunteering for special duties in 1943. Peter was among members of 3 Troop who were assigned to one of eight commando units for the Normandy landings on D-Day. He became second-in-command of 6 Commando detachment, a bicycle brigade, which used collapsible bicycles as their intended mode of transport through Normandy. His feelings as he crossed the English Channel for the assault on Normandy is poignantly described in his book *Striking Back*, a comprehensive history of 3 Troop:

> Towards evening (5 June) we boarded and sailed. One boat followed the other out of port, the men singing and cheering and waving to neighbouring craft. I wasn't really excited, and much as I tried to sense this momentous occasion, leaving English soil for who knew how long, perhaps forever, I just couldn't get worked up about it . . . The scene that presented itself [on] 6 June was dreary. There was no sun yet. The beach and sea were a drab, dull yellowish green. The houses on the model in the briefing tent no longer existed, so the beautiful model proved to be a wasted effort. I had the sudden realisation that this might be the last thing I would ever do. I tried to look back on my past life, and I recalled vividly all the girlfriends in my life, and my family paraded before my mind's eye in unprecedented peace. I concluded that at twenty-two I had had a rich, full life and therefore could not complain if it were to end then and there. But before that I, who had been harassed by the Nazis, intimidated and targeted for extermination, would at long last have the opportunity to strike back.[8]

Peter landed with 6 Commando on Sword Beach on D-Day. He and his colleagues made their way down the plank of the landing craft and waded ashore, tommy guns at the ready. Orders were shouted at them to 'get off the beach' as quickly as possible. He describes that long, momentous day:

> I remember the charged atmosphere, the noise, the smell of things burning, and few scenes in great detail. Some of the infantry that had preceded us were digging in behind some knocked-out, smouldering tanks. I even saw two men trying to dig in in the shallow water on the beach. Their sergeant yanked them out of their-water filled holes, yelling, 'Get off the beach!' Being a greenhorn, I did not know enough to be really frightened. The noise of the whistling shells didn't mean a thing to me. I had no idea whether they were coming or going; just as well I suppose . . .

When we were a few hundred yards inland, guns and mortars opened up on the beach again. What looked like balls of fire were sailing through the sky . . . No shells were exploding now in our path. Instead, riflemen sniped at us from the nearby woods as we were crossing the ploughed field. To make matters worse, several times we had to cross and recross a muddy creek. The bicycles proved difficult to grip while slipping in chest-deep brown water. A few of us managed to get across the field before the firing at us started. In front of me was a crowd of commandos using the only furrow worth mentioning as sparse cover. I had to join the queue, but it was hard to crawl with a bicycle . . . Just then some Sherman tanks came alongside us. The tank commanders were riding with their turrets open, exposing their heads and shoulders. That may have been all right in the wide no-man's-land of the African desert, but here in the Norman *bocage*, the hedge country, [it] was extremely risky . . . Behind the assembly area was a country road, where at long last we mounted our bikes for the first time and cycled west through Colleville-sur-Mer before veering southeast and making for Bénouville. There we hoped to find that the glider-borne Oxfordshire and Buckinghamshire Light Infantry of the British 6th Airborne Division had taken intact the two bridges over the river Orne and its parallel canal. I certainly hoped they had because it would save me swimming across with the rope and then having to help ferry the brigade across the two waterways. Once we were across the canal and river, we were to cycle on to Varaville to relieve the Canadian parachutists who were to have captured it by then . . . The smooth ride got tougher as we went along. Most of us were young men who had never seen action before, and the novel experience of death all around us was very personal; we died a little with each man who fell. We were shocked to see dead parachutists hanging in the trees. Even the sight of dead cattle in the fields adjacent to our route, belly up and bloated in rigor mortis, was upsetting.[9]

During their advance through Normandy, the commanding officer gave an order for Masters to go into a nearby village alone and draw out the enemy. As Peter walked brazenly down the open road towards the village, he contemplated that this might be the last walk of his life. It was risky and courageous. He writes:

I began to shout at the top of my voice [in German] – *'Surrender all of you! Come out! You are completely surrounded – you don't have a chance. Throw away your weapons and come out with your hands up if you want to go on living. The war is over for you!'* No one came out. It was silent. On the credit side of the ledger, nobody shot me either. With my finger on the trigger of my tommy gun, I concentrated as hard as I could on what might come to pass before me. There was some movement in one of the houses farther back on the right . . . I continued walking and yelling. Then it happened: a German popped up behind the parapet to my right front, firing a machine carbine at me from his midriff . . . I saw the German the instant he stood up. Instinctively, I went down on one knee as I pressed my trigger. He missed. I missed. My gun fired one shot – and jammed. He ducked for cover. I went through the 'immediate action' to clear my jammed weapon and then cocked it. He reappeared and missed with another burst. By this time I was lying flat in one inch of grass, trying to present the smallest possible target . . . Then I heard a noise from my right rear and turned my head. The entire troop was galloping down the road towards me. Apparently Robbo [Commanding Officer] had seen what he was looking for and had immediately ordered his men to fix bayonets and charge. In the lead was Cpl. George Thompson, a former Grenadier Guardsman, firing his Bren machine gun from the shoulder instead of from the hip – the usual method while running. He sprayed the low wall to discourage my personal enemy, or anyone else, from firing. For a few moments I just lay there, gratefully watching and reflecting on the miracle of still being among the living.[10]

Masters and his fellow commandos reached the first bridge where the gliders had crash-landed the previous day. Then came support at the rear for 45 (RM) Commando near Franceville-Plage, after which Masters was once again on the front line. Gradually they took POWs for interrogation and carried out reconnaissance missions. For the next two months, Masters was fighting on the front line with his unit and by the end of August they were mopping up resistance. No. 3 Troop had suffered so many losses and casualties that the men were recalled to England to replenish their numbers from new recruits, ready for the next stage of operations. On 1 November 1944 at least seven members of 3 Troop landed with 4 Commando on the island of Walcheren to ensure its surrender.[11] Having spent time at Eastbourne, Peter Masters landed in Holland with twelve other members of 3 Troop. Their task was to clear out the enemy between the Maas and the Rhine. There was a fear that the Germans were planning to recapture Antwerp. During the campaign in Holland 3 Troop linked up with the 7th Armoured Division to carry out a commando charge on the back of the tanks through the villages of Linne and St Joost (described in chapter two by Willy Field, tank driver of 8th Kings Royal Irish Hussars).

## JOHN WAXMAN

John Waxman (Wolfgang Wachsmann) was born on 1 May 1924 in Oppeln, near Breslau in Upper Silesia. He left Germany in August 1935 with his mother and brother Werner. Wolfgang was interned on the Isle of Man in the summer of 1940, just after his sixteenth birthday. From internment, he volunteered for the British Forces and was accepted for the AMPC, stationed for a time at Thame. During 1942 he was invited by his commanding officer to attend an interview at the War Office in London after he had won a boxing contest. He had learned boxing because he had been beaten up so many times as a boy growing up in Nazi Germany. After the interview he was transferred from the Pioneer Corps to the commandos for training. The army changed his name from Wolfgang Wachsmann to John Hayes, his papers stating his religion as Church of England.[12] He began his training at Achnacarry Castle:

It was hard, tough training. We had to climb Ben Nevis and back in a day with all our heavy gear. We trained for three months in unarmed combat. After 6 months I was transferred to Aberdovey in North Wales for further training. I was stationed there for sometime and went backwards and forwards on commando raids. I was a member of 3 Troop (also known as X-Troop), No. 10 Inter-Allied Commandos. Prior to D-Day, 3 Troop was involved in the overnight commando raids into Norway where they landed at Lofoten Island, off the coast of Norway. I was respected whilst in the commandos which was something that I had never experienced as a Jew in Germany or as a newly-arrived refugee in England. I became close friends with another refugee, Bernard Tuchmann, who came originally from Vienna (later Benny Taylor). We met in the Pioneer Corps and joined the commandos together. We became like brothers and my mother treated him like a son. He was killed on D-Day at Ouistreham, just north of Caen in Normandy.[13]

In late 1943 John was assigned to the 9th Battalion the Parachute Regiment, 6th Airborne Division. During this training at Ringway near Manchester, he carried out about forty-seven jumps. Due to the need for translators, he was then transferred to a Glider Battalion which was part of the 6th Airborne Division. He glided into Normandy on D-Day, along with the first few hundred other gliders. He landed at Ranville near Pegasus Bridge, which was named after the airborne forces' emblem of the winged horse. He vividly remembers that day:

I landed in a field where the Germans had put up wooden poles to stop the gliders landing. These had been chopped down by the paratroopers. Our gliders were made of plywood and had ski skids, not wheels for landing. The gliders were held together by three split pins which we pulled out on landing. We took out the two ramps so that the jeep and 2lb anti-tank gun could leave the glider. The glider was by that time full of bullet holes and we were lucky to land. I was fortunate to survive because the Germans were shooting at us as we were coming down to land. It was a close thing. My best friend Cliff Green (whose father was George Green, the cartoonist for the *Liverpool Echo*) was captured. Fortunately he was released because I met him again in London after I was demobbed. I was then involved in the Battle of St Honorine and Caen. Thirty-three days after D-Day, a tank shell or a mortar shell exploded a few feet from me and I was knocked unconscious. The fellow next to me had his lungs blown out. I was lucky to survive. I had been in a slight dip at the time and was sheltered from the worst of the blast. I was taken to 110th General Field Hospital, Bayeux, Normandy. After a few days there, I was taken back to England on a LC(T) Landing Craft (Tank) and was taken to a hospital in Sussex. From there I was transferred to Selly Oak Hospital in Birmingham where I celebrated my 21st birthday. It was a memorable occasion because the nurses baked a cake for me. It was also a very lonely time. I had a shrapnel wound on my temple which caused memory loss and speech difficulties. Because I was delirious and very noisy, I was given a sedative to keep me in a deep sleep for 10 days to recover. Due to my injury, I was eventually demobilised on the grounds that I ceased to fulfill the physical requirements for further duty.

After the war, he changed his name from John Hayes to John Waxman. He now lives in Australia.

### IAN HARRIS

Ian Harris (Hans Hajos) was born in Vienna on New Year's Day 1920 to a Jewish father and non-Jewish mother.[14] His father had served as a Captain in the Hungarian Horse Artillery in the First World War and was highly decorated for his service. Ian came to England in 1938 under the auspices of the Quakers, working for nearly two years on various farms. He volunteered for the British Forces and on 14 February 1940 joined the Pioneer Corps. In early March 1943 he successfully transferred to the commandos. Just before D-Day, training intensified and he was attached to 46 (RM) Commando with three other Germans:

Then came D-Day when we were supposed to land, attack and knock out the coastal battery at Franceville-Plage, to the east of the Orne. My job was to do with communications, making use of my German whenever I could and giving false messages. I spent the whole of D-Day on a cross-channel steamer called the *Prince Albert*. The battery had already been knocked out by the Air Force the day before. I recall standing on the side of ship facing the beach head and seeing the whole panorama of flames, explosions and infantry cheering as they went into action. These were the troopships of D-Day. The gliders of 6th Airborne Division were going over the top of us with their parachutists. We landed as reinforcements to either No. 1 or No. 4 Brigade on the beaches that had already been taken. It was still D-Day. Soon we were thrown into action. I dealt with the first lot of POWs. There was a German fortified radar station at Luc-sur-Mer and Douvres-la-Delivrande, north of Caen. There were skirmishes and nasty fighting along the main street between the churchyard and farm buildings. We had to fight our way up a slope. I finished in a farmhouse and herded in the POWs. A captured German doctor dressed some of our wounded men.

Ian crossed Pegasus Bridge to the other side of the River Orne with 46 (RM) Commando. They moved to the coast and dug in at St Arnoult, south of Trouville, where they formed the left end of the defences at the bridgehead. German troops were stationed opposite them, guns regularly firing at them. The brief for 46 (RM) Commando was to infiltrate German lines during the night. While in action in Normandy, Ian was wounded on three separate occasions. The first time was after crossing the River Dives where 46 (RM) Commando was to take a German hill position at Dozulé. It had been attacked by an Allied battalion the previous day with terrible casualties, most of which were still lying around the hill.

The colonel said to me: 'Harris, now you walk behind me. We're going to walk up this hill to start with in single file.' This went against all we had been taught. It was pitch dark. It was more or less a field with hedgerows on each side. We walked through the middle. The farm was burned out at the bottom. People were still moaning and screaming for help in German and English. It was terrible. At the top of the hill there was a hedge. We set off. I was behind the colonel who was taller than me. I said to him, 'There are Germans in the hedges at the sides.' He replied, 'We'll keep going.' Twenty yards from the top, the lights went up and it was just like day light. Machine guns fired at us from the left, the right and the top. We were in the open with no cover. I threw myself to the ground, I think, but I remember coming-to with a mouthful of earth. No recollection of events prior. I had been hit in the back. I felt my back and it was wet and damp. It was a splinter from a hand grenade. The colonel, being lucky, had walked on, straight into the trenches on top. He wasn't wounded at all and the operation was successfully completed. When I came to, I sat up. There was a dim light. I was facing down the slope and a second wave of chaps were coming up the hill. I still had a thick Austrian accent and thought, if I say anything, I'll be shot, but luckily someone recognised me. I got up and stumbled down the hill, got to a bomb crater and fell into it and rolled to the bottom and landed on something soft. As I looked, I was on top of a man in German uniform (he turned out not to be German but a Pole conscripted into the German Forces). My training came to the fore. Wounded or not, I reacted and took him by the throat and I was on top. He managed to say in German, 'Hans, is that you?' I realised that he'd been there all day and all night, waiting to give himself up. I said, 'alright, you're a prisoner'. He replied, 'thank you'. Then this man, my first personal prisoner, helped me up and took me to our lines. Once I had handed him over, my wound was dressed and I was in a jeep on the way to the field hospital. I then finished up in a field hospital in Bayeux.

When Ian had recovered, he reported back to 10 Inter-Allied Commando which was then stationed at Eastbourne, preparing for the Rhine crossings. He was determined to return to action and was attached to 45 (RM) Commando which landed at Ostende. During the Rhine crossing, one of the Buffaloes (armoured amphibious troop carriers) was hit and two of Ian's friends from 3 Troop were killed. Ian advanced with 45 (RM) Commando and witnessed Wesel being bombarded by over 300 Lancaster bombers. He comments that 'the ground was shaking beneath us as we lay flat on our stomachs. One believed that nothing could have lived through this bombardment. But when we entered Wesel there were Germans coming out of dug-outs. Many were shell-shocked, some were still fighting back.'[15] Then came Osnabrück where the fighting was not particularly heavy. Germans occupied one half of the town, the other was held by 45 (RM) Commando. Their colonel had been killed. The new commanding officer was Lieutenant-Colonel Alf Blake. Ian was wounded for a second time and it was his action at this time which won him the Military Medal:

> We moved up to the River Weser. By this time I had acquired some kind of fame. I had achieved all sorts of things. The colonel appreciated all that I had done. He made use of me whenever he could. When we crossed the river, the purpose of our mission was to relieve the Rifle Brigade who held a farm on the other side of the bridgehead. They needed replacing because they had come under heavy pressure from the German SS, Hitler's Youth divisional section. The bridge was being bombarded by artillery. Our engineers were trying to rebuild a replacement bridge and had lost a lot of men in the process. They were being shelled by the Germans and tried to rebuild in between the bombings. We crossed the river in dinghies and came under some fire but not much.
>
> A line of our marines was supposed to occupy a small provincial town on the Weser. There was fierce opposition by young well-trained SS troops. I saw the colonel and a few HQ staff in sheer danger, unable to cope quickly with the situation. We were standing on an extended piece of ground below the bank with a hedgerow on top of it and Germans dug in just behind it. The distance between the colonel and the Germans was about three yards. Both sides were petrified. One hand grenade from the Germans would have eliminated our HQ. The colonel gave me the signal to do something. Being a well trained commando, I climbed the bank with tommy gun ready. I saw that I was on top of a trench with four or five Germans in it. One of them ran, whilst I shot the

other two. Shooting the person from above was dreadful. I thought that I must kill them before they kill me. The third man crawled out of the trench backwards. I didn't shoot him. He got up and ran round the edge of the trench and his coat flew in the wind as he ran. At that point I was ready to shoot anything in field grey. I hated the bastards because they threw me out of my country. They denied me my birthright. That is the greatest crime someone could do. This was fulfillment. I did not give two hoots as to what would happen to me. Neither did I think about my own safety. This was perhaps the reason why I did crazy things then – a delight in being able to avenge all the injustices and unfair things they had perpetrated on me personally by denying me my rights as a human being; not that I had personally suffered a great deal physically but it was the intrinsic value of being able to more than pay back. I had no ammunition left. I had a clear idea what the Germans were doing on the top of the hedgerow – namely to cut our stretch of the line into several sections. This would isolate the marines from each other. I realised that we couldn't wait for them to attack and then react. I came across a Bren gunner in our ranks. I asked him, 'can I have your Bren gun?' He handed it to me. I went out in front and started firing at the Germans who were advancing towards us. They jumped into the trenches. Then No. 2 on the Bren gun came to support me. I had my beret shot off which should have been a signal. When a bullet is close, all you hear is the whip lash after it has passed. The thing that took my beret off was close. It flew a couple of yards. Picking up my beret, I put it back on my head. I kept on firing. The motivation in staying was the fact that I was hitting them.

A bullet then hit my Bren gun magazine which deflected the bullet. The magazine disintegrated and I got the full blast of the bits of the magazine all over my face, hands and neck. I managed to roll halfway down the bank. The No. 1 whose Bren gun I had, looked for morphine in my pocket and stuck it into me. The effect was immediate. I felt no pain, but there was an awful lot of blood. I couldn't see out of one eye, lots of blood over the other eye. I wasn't unconscious but I'd had an awful blow on the head. I had felt the main blow on the lower forehead. I thought, 'it's gone in here. It must be stuck in my head. How come I can think? So maybe it's not in my brain.' I was so fit. That fitness made it very difficult to destroy us until mortally wounded. My colleagues helped me up and put me on a stretcher. I couldn't see much. The Germans were still dive-bombing us. Planes were still trying to bomb the bridge. Whilst I was lying there, the colonel walked passed. The German advance had been stopped. He and I were close really. I heard him say, 'Who's this?' I thought, if he doesn't recognise me, I must be in a shocking state. I was given first aid and taken by ambulance to the Dutch-German border and flown to a military base, and then to a top military hospital in Brussels for one week of treatment. I was then flown to a hospital in Swindon where I had the rest of one eye removed.[16]

Ian was sent to a convalescent home in Stratford-on-Avon. Eventually he returned to his regiment, the Royal West Kents, as a colour-sergeant and was sent to a holding camp at Wrexham in charge of the Intelligence Section. It was now 1945 and interpreters were needed for the Allied Forces occupying Germany. Ian was transferred from Wrexham to the Control Commission Pool of Interpreters, returning to Germany. He was stationed at Brunswick where he was offered the post of chief ski instructor at the BAOR centre in Winterberg in charge of 50 German skiing instructors. That was his last position in the army. After his demobilisation he was offered employment as administrative assistant to the former commanding officer of French Troop, 10 Inter-Allied Commando, who knew him from his commando days. He worked as his assistant in an agency engaged in collecting valuables, assets, machinery, paintings and gold from the Germans and distributing them amongst the sixteen victorious nations. This included aiding the Chief of Mission in postwar Berlin and Brussels.

It was a very good job and highly paid but it ruined me for normal civilian life! I was driving Field Marshal Goering's convertible light blue Mercedes around Berlin; and from Berlin to the British Zone and through the Russian Zone. It was a job of a lifetime until I had an accident in it and wrote it off. It was a heavy vehicle but it just floated across the ice into a lorry on the autobahn!

Corporal Harris was decorated with the Military Medal. His citation was written by Lieutenant-Colonel Blake and signed by Field Marshal Montgomery, commanding 21st Army Group.

Having been engaged in some of the bloodiest and most difficult actions of the war, surviving members of 3 Troop were sent back to Germany to begin work for BAOR, some with Field Security, the section responsible for hunting Nazi war criminals. All had a vital role to play in rebuilding the new Germany because of their knowledge of the language. They spent at least a year fulfilling their final duties in British Army uniform.

## Chapter 5

# SPECIAL OPERATIONS EXECUTIVE

A German and Austrian contingent of Special Operations Executive (SOE) was formed during 1942 with the intention of 'setting Europe ablaze' by sabotaging the Nazi war machine's communication and supply network. It was also envisaged that those who were dropped behind enemy lines would liaise with partisans and underground resistance. During the summer of 1942 a Swiss gentleman by the name of Hartmann visited some of the alien Pioneer companies to ascertain who might be suitable for special duties. He moved among members of 87 and 88 Company for several weeks asking questions and assessing motivation for intelligence work. Individual German refugees like Peter Giles (Otto Hess) (see chapter four), and Walter Roome (Walter Ruhm) were sent on SOE missions into Yugoslavia and Germany respectively. In 1944 at the age of forty-two, Walter Roome was dropped into the Rhineland equipped with the papers of a fallen German soldier in order to report back on the effect of allied air raids and other observations of military value. For eight months he lived behind enemy lines until a former colleague from Danzig recognized him and he was immediately pulled out for his own safety.

Precise numbers of Germans and Austrians who trained for SOE are difficult to ascertain, but it is known that approximately twenty-five to thirty men, mainly Austrians, were trained together as a group called 12 Force, a self-designated title. The intention was to parachute these men behind enemy lines back into Southern Austria to link up with anti-Nazis, provide an Allied presence there and if possible capture the strategic aerodrome of Zeltweg. Training took place in Special Training Schools (STS) and the first phase, designed to filter out those who were unsuitable, took place at Special Training School No. 1 at Stodham Park near Liss in Hampshire, a requisitioned country mansion. From there the men were sent to Arisaig House in the western Highlands where the physical pace of training increased and included tough assault courses and the use of weaponry.[1] The men had to be 100 per cent fit to be parachuted into occupied countries. Then came parachute training at Wilmslow near Ringwood, Manchester with the dropping zone at Tatton Park country estate. One of the men, Hermann Faltitschek, was injured during his first jump and broke his spine in three places. He managed to stumble back to billets where he eventually collapsed and was taken to hospital where he received treatment. He chose not to be invalided out of SOE but went with the others to Italy in 1944, assigned different duties because he could no longer parachute. From Wilmslow the men were sent to Brockhall near Weedon in Northamptonshire. Stephen Dale (Heinz Günter Spanglet), a former member of SOE, comments:

> It gradually became clearer what the purpose of our training might be all about. We were by this time about 30 people in total and training got more specialised and more strenuous. Our stamina improved and on one occasion, while still at Brockhall, within the space of about 34 hours or so, we covered 60 miles on foot in battle order, and in between had a small exercise and two or three hours sleep. When we got back to Brockhall most of us felt fit enough to go out to a dance in the nearest village.[2]

Approximately nine months of 1943 were spent at Anderson Manor in Dorset which had been used in 1942 for the training of the Small Scale Raiding Force and commandos. It was here that SOE trainees were sent on regular route-marches and taken by lorry to unfamiliar deserted countryside to find their way back to base. There was still no mention to them of the term SOE, although the nature of their intended operations was becoming apparent from the training. While at Anderson Manor the men anglicised their German and Austrian names and were officially attached to the Royal Fusiliers as a cover for their true identity. One of SOE's members, Walter Freud, a grandson of Sigmund Freud, chose not to change his name because he liked it and believed it would be pointless in the event of capture.

Training at every stage was extensive and demanding. The men learned unarmed combat, weaponry, how to make homemade explosives and open locked doors, how to drive trains and derail them, sabotage, radio technology (the use of suitcase radio sets to send and receive messages), cryptology and how to conduct one's behaviour under interrogation. The final phase of the training in England took place at Hatherop Castle near Fairford in Gloucestershire. In June 1944 the first groups were posted to Italy. They consisted of Otto Karminski, Alan Grant (Noe Czupper), Teddy Lees (Erhard Saar) and Stephen Dale (Heinz Günter Spanglet); and George Bryant (Dr Georg Breuer), Fred Warner (Manfred Werner), Frank Kelley and Jack Rhodes. They were followed a short time later by the remainder of the group from training days. They were stationed in an olive processing factory at Fasano near Monopoli on Italy's Adriatic coast. Intensive training continued with parachute jumps near Bari and mountaineering expeditions in the Abruzzi mountains, east of Rome.

Of those who were eventually dropped behind enemy lines, two were known to have been taken prisoner: Stephen Dale and Peter Priestley (Egon Lindenbaum). Butch Baker-Byrne (Robert Becker) was dropped twice into Germany and Michael O'Hara (Friederich Berliner) was the only one to have been killed. He was captured, tortured and shot. He had also acted as dispatcher for Italian partisans and given the orders to jump. Austrian-born Charles (Karl) Kaiser was group leader of Operation Hamster and on 20 April 1945 was dropped behind enemy lines with Harry Williams (Harry Wunder).[3] Their destination was Rossbacher Alpe in Styria which was formerly a province of Austria. Their brief was to attack communications targets at Bruck-Leoben and Bruck-Graz. Kaiser came to Gleinalpe where he succeeded in contacting a local resistance group and later a deputation of Hungarian Air Force officers coming from Zeltweg airfield. From 8 May Kaiser was operating in Knittelfeld, a Styrian town, and two days later at Zeltweg aerodrome. Together with twenty men he marched into Kittelfeld where he was supported by the local resistance of about two hundred men. Public buildings were seized and the Germans agreed to withdraw. On 9 May he met with the Russians in Leoben and organised Russian protection against SS troops operating in the area. He also tried to arrange the movement of Russian forced-labourers from Kittelfeld to Leoben in exchange for British POWs from Leoben. As a result of going into action, both Kaiser and Williams were commissioned as second lieutenants.

As is apparent from the extracts from unpublished SOE memoirs below, the missions did not run according to plan. It was a risky venture. The men were often dropped from the wrong height or at the wrong location, with the result that they landed miles from their intended zone and sometimes had to survive for days or weeks without their companions. Most of their equipment was dropped after them but often landed in the wrong place. Without equipment the men could not radio their whereabouts to HQ; alone in enemy territory, they had to rely on their training and quick-thinking for survival. With the exception of Michael O'Hara, all survived the war and their mission behind enemy lines.

## ANTON WALTER FREUD

Anton Walter Freud, known to family and friends as Walter, was one of the members of 12 Force who parachuted back into Austria.[4] Born in Vienna on 3 April 1921 into one of Austria's most famous families, his grandfather Sigmund Freud was the founder of psychoanalysis. Walter was born to Sigmund Freud's eldest son Martin, a lawyer and veteran of the First World War, who was decorated no less than four times for bravery having served as a first lieutenant in the Austrian Field Artillery. Walter was not quite seventeen when the Nazis shattered the lives of the 200,000 Austrian Jews, 180,000 of whom were living in and around Vienna. The Freud family was immediately at risk. Sigmund Freud's home on Bergasse was raided just days after the *Anschluss*. Plans began for the family's flight to England. Walter left Vienna for Paris with his parents and sister in April 1938, two weeks before his grandparents. His parents were already experiencing marital problems and emigration provided the excuse for them to separate permanently. Walter came to England with his father and continued his education for a term at Faversham School in Kent. In the autumn of 1939 he began his studies in aeronautical engineering at Loughborough College, where during the summer of 1940 he was arrested while sitting a mathematics examination. He was taken first to a local police station where, despite his protestations of innocence, the policeman told him, 'In war time there are worse criminals than thieves or murderers'. He was taken to the Isle of Man and a few days later boarded the troopship *Dunera* bound for internment camps in Australia.

In the summer of 1941 Walter was released from internment and sailed back to England aboard the SS *Gleniffer*. He enlisted in the Pioneer Corps, training in Ilfracombe and was then posted to 87 Company which was stationed at the Defensible Barracks, Pembroke Dock. Shortly before Christmas 1942 the company moved to the ordnance depot at Long Marston near Stratford-on-Avon where duties were confined largely to unloading incoming supplies and loading outgoing consignments. In January 1943 Walter left the Pioneer Corps for SOE without shedding a tear. He comments: 'Its cap badge showing a pick and shovel was not one that I was very proud of.' Later that month his father wrote to him:

I suppose you have reasons (honourable reasons of course) to keep your whereabouts, unit and occupation a secret and I am glad you find the new surroundings comfortable . . .[5]

After training with SOE, Walter was posted to Italy with 12 Force for the final phase in preparation for his parachute drop. On arrival the impact of the war for ordinary Italians was clearly visible:

There can have been few ordinary Italians whose life was remotely as pleasant as ours. The war had brought them nothing but hunger, destruction and misery – the three riders of the Apocalypse were indeed riding across this normally pleasant and fertile land. The Germans had taken a full measure of revenge for the desertion of their Italian ally. As the Germans slowly retired north, they wrought havoc with Italian installations.[6]

By the end of 1944 Walter was working in Italy alongside German POWs who had been given manual tasks by the Allied Forces. Finally in early spring 1945 Walter's moment had come. Two parties were to be dropped simultaneously into Austria and Walter was to be the radio operator of the smaller one. As he prepared for the mission, reality finally dawned:

> I wondered what sort of reception I would get in Austria. Would the population receive us with open arms, as liberators, or would they lynch us at the first opportunity? Would they consider us as Austrian patriots, trying to save them from the catastrophic results of Hitler's war, or would they treat us as multiple traitors, as Jews and as Austrians who had gone over to the enemy? I had no idea and neither had anyone else.[7]

Walter's companion and boss for the drop into Austria was Hans Schweiger, an Austrian ex-lawyer and older man. Although Hans was not agile, he was reliable and careful. The other group for the drop consisted solely of German-speaking refugees who had anglicised their names. Their leader was George Bryant, another Viennese lawyer and grandson of Dr Joseph Breuer who had cooperated with Walter's grandfather Sigmund Freud on the book *Studien Ueber Hysterie* (1895). The wireless operator for this group was a German refugee Frank Kelley (Otto König). The two other members, both originally from Hamburg, were Fred Warner and Eric Rhodes. The brief for both groups was threefold: first, to make contact with the local population and establish whether they would cooperate with the Allies; second, to carry out acts of sabotage on railways and communications; and third, to establish a British presence in the area because the Russians were advancing towards Austria. If possible, they were to take the strategic air base of Zeltweg in southern Austria. Walter describes the drop in detail:[8]

The green light appeared inside the plane. I could feel the dispatcher touching my shoulder. I quickly stepped out through the open door into the darkness. We were lucky that we could jump at our first attempt. Once my parachute had opened, which it did within a few seconds, I seemed to be hanging in the air for hours. I gently lowered my heavy rucksack on its 25ft line, so that it dangled below me. Unfortunately, its pendular movement was very strong, much more pronounced than during training, and it pulled the bottom strap of the chute away from underneath my behind. As a result, I was uncomfortably supported by my leg straps on my testicles. At long last, I guess after 10 minutes, I landed gently. Although it was almost completely dark, there was a bit of moon and it was obvious to me that I was not at my mountain meadow but in a wide open valley. I could not hear our plane. I couldn't see it, but even if I could, I would not have flashed the 'OK' signal. I had no idea where I was, but it was obvious to me that I was somewhere where I should not be. I believe that I was dropped not from a thousand feet above ground but more likely from seven or eight thousand feet. The reason was not far to see. The highest mountains in that area are about 8,000 ft above sea level and a pilot would be very foolhardy to fly below that level on a dark night. The Mur Valley is only about 1,200 ft above sea level, so I was probably dropped from 7 or 8 times the prescribed height, taking eight minutes at least. During this time I would have drifted for miles.

After landing, I untied myself from my uncomfortable parachute harness and scouted around for the others. I didn't know if they had been dropped or not. I had not flashed the 'OK' signal. I did not dare to shout or to use my torch too obviously as I had no idea who might be in the neighbourhood. I could neither see nor hear anything, except for some barking dogs in the far distance. I didn't even bother to look for the container with the heavy luggage; how can one on a pitch dark night in a completely strange place?

When we were planning the operation, we had arranged a rendezvous for meeting after the drop. It was to be at the south-west corner of the mountain meadow, our selected dropping area, across a little stream. I had had a jocular argument with Schweiger about that location. I told him: 'Look, if we have to cross that stream, we shall get wet feet.' I was no great friend of wet feet in winter. But Schweiger was adamant that this was the best location for our meeting place, for reasons which I have forgotten. So now I looked around for that stream. I could hear some water running in the distance. I quickly hid my parachute in some undergrowth and went off to find that stream; it was not far away. In I went, in accordance with Schweiger's orders. I went in deeper and deeper into the ice-cold water; it was running so fast that it almost knocked me over. When it had reached my belt, I realised at long last that this couldn't be Schweiger's little mountain stream and returned to the bank. Now it was not just my boots that were wet and cold, but all my body up to my belt. It was reasonable to assume that I could do no more that night and hence I went a little way into the wooded slopes of the mountain, unrolled my sleeping bag and crawled inside. I did not dare to take off my wet boots in case I had to make a quick getaway.

Next morning, still cold and wet, I tried to orientate myself. This was not easy; I could be anywhere and there were few distinguishing features in the landscape which could help one to take a bearing. After a time, I understood that the little stream I had been trying to cross had been the Mur river, the biggest one in southern Austria. It is known for its strong currents and I was lucky not to have drowned in it with all the weight I was carrying. I had apparently been dropped not very far from a little village called Oberzeiring, miles from the intended dropping zone. So I set off to walk there, in order to meet the others, if indeed they had been dropped. I didn't know what else to do. I took a compass bearing and started. There were no roads or paths and I made very slow progress up the wooded mountain slopes. There was still quite a bit of snow about. In order to get to our original rendezvous, I had to cross a mountain range. Whenever I thought I was close to the top of that range, there was frustratingly another mountain in front of me. Nearly all the food had been in the big container which was lost and after a few days I was getting hungry. Luckily, I then came across an isolated farm house, my first contact with humanity in Austria. I made sure that it had no telephone wires. I went in and asked whether they had any food for sale. Yes, they said they could sell me, or even give me, a large loaf and some Speck, very fat bacon. In that farmhouse, as in all others which I visited, there was only a young mother with a baby and perhaps one or two toddlers, and the old grandfather. Everybody else had been geared into the German war machine. The men from sixteen to sixty were in the Army, the over-sixties were in the Home Guard, the women worked in the munition factories and the adolescents were doing anti-aircraft duty. My identity was never questioned, nor did I give any explanation. If the inhabitants should be questioned by the police, they could honestly say that they had no idea who I was. I moved on. On my way, I visited a few other farmhouses, always making sure that they were well isolated.

After some further meandering, all steeply uphill, I came across a deserted *Alm-huette*. These are mountain huts [situated] where the cows are driven during the summer months. I thought I could risk staying in that hut for a couple of days. It was difficult to get into, but I managed even without bicycle spokes. When it got dark, I even dared to make a fire and cook myself something. Afterwards, I was violently sick. While I was at that *Alm-huette*, I heard a shot fired; I thought that it might have been fired by my party, but I was too careful to fire back. After the war, when I compared notes with my former colleagues, I found out that a shot was fired by Fred Warner, who was surprised by a German searching party. After one or two nights in that hut, I got my strength back and continued on my trek . . . I continued slowly make my way towards the original dropping zone. After some time, I began to realise that Schweiger, even if he had been dropped, which I did not know, would not be waiting for me any longer. It was obviously pointless for me to continue in that direction and I had to think of something else. I had with me a small radio receiver. With that radio receiver I could hear how the war was proceeding. My bigger receiver-transmitter was lost with the heavy luggage. One day, I heard that the British were at long last breaking through Italy and I thought that the time had now come for me to go to 'my' aerodrome at Zeltweg, to claim it for His Britannic Majesty. I turned around to make my way towards the town of Scheifling, which was the nearest town situated on the main road along the Mur valley. Zeltweg was along that same road, some miles further to the east. By that time, I had had enough of mountains, so I kept to the small roads which led down to the valley. I met few civilians. In my gas cape, I looked not dissimilar to the local woodcutters. I also came across some women evacuees from the bombed towns, who were apparently taking their morning constitutional. I gave them a cheerful 'Heil Hitler' and walked on. Then my life was saved by a grandmother. As I went down the road, I was joined by an elderly local woman. She started to talk to me at once. We came to a little footpath branching off our road and leading across some fields. She asked me for my direction. I said 'Scheifling' and she said that she was going there too and that this little footpath would be a shortcut. So we left the road and proceeded along that path. Not long afterwards we came to the main road along the Mur valley. I looked backwards along it and there, where my original road met the main road, I saw a detachment of SS troops controlling the road junction. Had I not met that old woman who had shown me the shortcut, I would have run straight into them and been shot before I could have said 'OK'. As it was, I was now a hundred yards further on, and even if they had seen me from the distance, they did not bother to take any further action, as I had not crossed their checkpoint. I asked the old woman to take me to the mayor's office in Scheifling, which she did. I thanked her and hoped that all would be well with her grandson.

The mayor was in. He was the biggest Nazi in town and he also kept the biggest shop, a hardware one. I told him that I was the vanguard of the British Army and that I had to get to the aerodrome of Zeltweg in order to earmark it for British, rather than Russian, occupation. Zeltweg is some fifteen miles east of Scheifling and the Russians were rapidly approaching that area. He saw my point at once. He told me that he would certainly take me, but unfortunately none of the cars in his little town had any more petrol, not even for 15 miles. He mentally went over the cars available to him, then his face lit up. The fire engine still had petrol in it! That was good news. The fire engine would do splendidly. The mayor drove and I sat next to him in the front. It was quite a modern engine, with a folding ladder on top and included all the other paraphernalia, including a siren. There was very little traffic about, but whenever he saw anything likely to cause a hold-up or looked like a check-point, he put on the siren and everybody waved us through. Arriving at Zeltweg, we asked our way to the office of the commander. The place was full of soldiers in various uniforms: I noticed in particular many Hungarians in their elaborate head gear. Nobody asked for our passes or any documentation; a fire engine has free access to everywhere.

We stopped outside the commander's office. I went upstairs into the ante-chamber where his secretary sat. I introduced myself in German: 'I am Lieutenant Freud of the British 8th Army, can I see the commander please?' She paled, went into her boss's room and invited me in.

I entered, saluted nonchalantly and repeated 'I am Lieutenant Freud of the British 8th Army; I have come to take over your aerodrome.' The commander, I believe he came from Hamburg, slumped down on his desk and started to cry, 'all our efforts, all our sacrifices, all in vain'. I, being a softy, felt quite sorry for him. It cannot have been fun for him to see a young enemy officer asking him for his aerodrome. I explained to him that I had been especially sent by General Montgomery to ensure that the aerodrome would come under British rule at the end of the war. These were of course all lies. I did not belong to the British 8th Army, nor had I ever spoken to, or even seen, General Montgomery. The commander asked me whether I had a document with me, authorising my demand. I said that I had not, my word as a British officer should suffice. I could see that the man was in a terrible quandary. If he handed over the aerodrome, the still active

SS might take a dim view of his defeatist attitude and execute him. On the other hand, the Russians were near, or even past, the Hungarian/Austrian border, less than 60 miles away and could be arriving any day. The Germans had one great fear and it was the fear of the Russians. They knew what they had done in Russia and to the Russians and were terrified of retribution. To be included in the British zone of occupation would ensure them a safe haven.

After several meetings and negotiations with local Nazi dignitaries it was decided that Freud could have the airfield if agreed by General Rendulic, the commander of the Southern Front based in Linz. Walter was driven by a German major to Linz where the general agreed to the surrender of the airbase. On the return journey they were stopped at a road block and the major was arrested by a group of Austrian units who had mutinied.

They wouldn't let me pass and ordered me to go to the Americans who were rapidly approaching Austria from the west . . . I was driven by an Austrian officer, replacing my German major, to the American front line . . . At the Austrian front line my Austrian officer managed to calm another revolver-waving captain who wanted to shoot me. After this last hurdle was cleared, I made my way very carefully across a badly damaged bridge, hoping that neither side would use me as target practice. On the other side I soon found an American sentry who took me to his headquarters.

Walter was flown to Paris and then posted to Germany for a period of work with the War Crimes Investigation Unit (see chapter eleven). Walter was demobilised as a major in September 1946 and naturalised as a British subject in 1948.

### FRED WARNER

Fred Warner (Manfred Werner, born Hamburg 1919) was dropped in a parallel mission to Walter Freud and Hans Schweiger.[9] Both groups were to be dropped close to each other with the aim of taking Zeltweg airfield near Judenburg in southern Austria and secure it for immediate use by the RAF. Fred Warner's group, consisting of Eric Rhodes, George Bryant and Frank Kelley, was dropped after Freud and Schweiger. When the green light came on, Fred jumped, eventually landing about 20 miles from the intended dropping zone with no sight of his companions. He had been dropped at a much higher altitude than had been previously arranged:

> I was extremely lucky to land in a ploughed field but to my greatest horror, right next to a farmhouse. I managed to get out of the parachute harness and to collapse the 'chute. As I had enough to carry, I quickly hid the 'chute under the thick hedge which surrounded the farmhouse. Still in my jumping suit I gathered my rucksack which I had detached from the harness first of all and made certain that my pistol, an American 4.5 Colt, was in its place, easily accessible, and then made for a small hill nearby which was thickly covered by fir trees. As soon as I was swallowed up by the trees, I got rid of all unnecessary kit: the jumping suit, hat, gloves and the elbow and knee pads. Needless to say, I kept a sharp look-out for my companions – in fact for any kind of movement at all. There was no sign of them. I climbed quickly and quietly to the top of the small hill to try and get a better view of the surrounding countryside and possibly a glimpse of my companions . . . The next few hours I kept on climbing straight up the thickly wooded mountainside, trying to avoid holes in the thick undergrowth and the many fallen trees and branches. Now and then I stopped to listen and to take a drink out of my hip-flask, full of good Scotch whisky. It was pitch dark amongst the trees and when I at last reached the top of the ridge, it was quite a surprise to find a large-sized clearing. The sun was about to rise and my first day in Austria, enemy country, had started. I was getting rather tired and wondered where the rest of my group was. At the far end of the clearing there was a small wooden hut which I found to my great relief was empty. This hut was obviously being used as a temporary shelter by wood-cutters. As there was no one about, I moved in.

[During the night] it was pitch dark inside the hut. I heard men's voices outside but could not make out what language they were talking in. Then someone was trying to open the door of the hut which I had lightly secured by placing a large stone in front of it. I was out of my sleeping bag in no time, gun in hand, I had the good sense to stay on the floor. I waited until the door was nearly open and then called out in German, trying to speak as nonchalantly as possible, and probably not succeeding, 'who is there?' The answer was immediate and to the point – a rally of shots fired from a machine-carbine. I heard the bullets hitting the wooden rear wall of the hut behind my back. Dust and bits of bark were falling all around me. Staying on the ground and not getting up had saved my life. I answered the first rally of shots by firing 2 or 3 shots straight ahead out of the door, now nearly open, and one shot out of each side window of the hut. The shots echoed all round the mountain, breaking the stillness of the night and with each shot fired, a large flame shot out of the short barrel of my Colt. For a moment everyone kept quiet, giving me time to reload my weapon. Whilst doing this I heard a different noise – running feet – and for a moment thought my adversaries were going to rush me. To my great relief, however, they, whoever they were, were running away.

Later when Fred made his way into the nearest town of Niederwölz, he discovered the identity of the men. One was an old farmer, the others from a young compulsory Nazi workforce looking for British parachutists who were known to have dropped in the region. Following the incident, Fred collected his few remaining belongings and ran for about an hour, then walked briskly for a further five or six hours. Thoroughly exhausted, he came across a make-shift wooden hut where he spent the next week:

Luckily for me the shed was half-full of hay. I unrolled my sleeping bag and this time got in without even taking my boots off. I don't know how long I slept but when I woke it was snowing hard. This meant that for the time being I was safe. It kept on snowing for several days and I kept quite warm in my shelter. The only visitors I had were some deer feeding one evening in the clearing. After a few days the weather changed again and from then on the sun was shining brilliantly all the time. I started to investigate my surroundings and found a spot not far from my shelter from where I could watch a road running along a valley far below me. On this road there was plenty of activity, mainly military vehicles interspersed with horse-drawn carts, which I observed with the help of my field-glasses.

Fred's sparse food supply was running out. He packed his belongings and headed towards an isolated house on the outskirts of the village of Weissenbach. Having observed the inhabitants from a distance for a day, he ascertained that any men of military age were away fighting. The occupants were an elderly couple and young woman with two small children. He approached them and they sheltered him for several days. Eventually one of the family's friends arranged for Fred to link up with local partisans. The war was drawing to a close. Local Austrians were concerned about the advancing Russians troops and thus welcomed any officer in British uniform.[10] News came that the intended target of Zeltweg airfield had been taken by the British, with rumours that Fred's companions were there. A local dignitary escorted him to Zeltweg where he was reunited with his SOE colleagues. Conflicting stories circulated about the impending Russian advance but eventually the Russians arrived at the airbase and Fred narrates in detail the ensuing period in his unpublished memoirs. Fred and his companions moved from the airbase to a nearby castle across the river where one of them, George Bryant, had already set up radio contact with their HQ:

Our HQ told us to stay where we were and to assist British troops soon to arrive as best we could. For about a fortnight, no British troops arrived. We kept in wireless contact with our HQ which was about to move up into Austria from Siena (Italy). We tried our utmost to keep out all Russian soldiers who continuously strayed across the river Mur. There was a constant coming and going, civilians needing help or advice – amongst them women who had been raped by the Russians. Others who feared this might happen swam across the Mur as all the bridges were guarded by the Russians. Princess Croy (of the castle) took in everybody, making them as comfortable as circumstances permitted. There was plenty of food as the Croys' estate included many heads of fine cattle, lots of poultry, etc. Eventually orders were received from base, and we transferred charge of the airfield to the Russians.

Fred was then posted to Wolfsberg where he was attached to the Public Safety Section, remaining in Austria until July 1945, where his tasks included general security, investigations, vetting senior police officials and issuing passes for the civilian population. Once he returned to England, he was given orders to join the War Crimes Investigation Unit and posted to Germany (see chapter eleven).

## STEPHEN DALE

Stephen Dale (Heinz Günther Spanglet, born Berlin), survivor of Sachsenhausen concentration camp, came to England in late spring 1939 where he took up odd jobs to support himself. After a year of internment in Australia from 1941 he enlisted into the Pioneer Corps and was posted with 87 Company. In 1943 he transferred to SOE and began training. In June 1944 he was flown to Gibraltar where he joined with three others for their mission. From there they were taken to a primitive holding camp in Algiers before transfer to Fasano near Italy's Adriatic coast. Before the drop, Dale changed his name once again to Stephen Patrick Turner. His group was the first to be dropped. Three days beforehand he developed a swelling on his foot and was sent to hospital. His three companions continued the mission without him and were parachuted into Tramonti in the Dolomites. Dale followed approximately three weeks later with three other SOE members: Peter Priestley, Taggart and his batman. The purpose of their mission was to help partisans in that region by supplying them with arms and explosives. He describes the drop from 10,000ft; he too was separated from his companions:

I was the first to go and my parachute opened beautifully on this my 13th jump. I had never dropped from such a height and it was a lovely experience floating down for a very long time in complete calm, except for the slight air rush after the drone of the four-engine plane had disappeared. At first I could see the chutes of the others above me but then I lost sight of them. I was drifting towards a high, sheer rock face but by spilling air I accelerated my descent and avoided it. I came down on what seemed the only patch of grass in a dried up river bed full of boulders. There were some lights less than a half mile distance which I took to be the lights of the dropping zone. I unharnessed and cautiously approached the lights which were, to my surprise, among some houses and I heard German and Italian voices. It then struck me that I was in the wrong place . . . I made my way up the side of the hill and spent the night there. In the morning I could see Germans spread across the valley. I moved northwards towards the Plöcken Pass. I couldn't move west where I was supposed to be dropped. I knew where I was because I figured it out from my small silk map. I couldn't cross the valley towards Tramonti because of German troops. I moved eastwards. I saw Germans moving south towards me on the hillside. I had no option but to go further up the hill in an easterly direction. I spent another night on the side of the hill. In the morning I could hear voices, so climbed the bank and hid. Two Germans were approaching. I ducked for cover, lost my footing and tumbled. Other Germans started coming towards me, so I put up my hands and I was taken prisoner by SS soldiers . . .

My German and Cossack captors marched me downhill to the level of Illegio. As we were moving along, I with my hands up, one of them saw and removed my watch and then they went through my pockets relieving me of virtually everything I had. Their number grew as we went along and eventually at the edge of the village seven or eight of them stood me against a little mound in a field and in an arc around me, they cocked their rifles, facing me. They were going to shoot me but I felt no fear or panic and there seemed a very strange inevitability about the whole situation, as though it was pre-ordained and which I had to accept. I looked around and I saw a beautiful world, and indeed it was a sunny warm late summer evening in the Dolomites, with just a touch of mist over the mountains, and I felt regret that this had to be the end, but strangely I hoped somebody would find out how I died. However, there was an order shouted in German and I saw an SS officer briskly walking towards the scene and the immediate threat to my life disappeared, but the tension remained.

I was taken to the local HQ at Tolmezzo to be stripped and searched and they started to ask questions. What was I doing in the area? How did I think I would get back to my lines? I was very tired and hungry by this point but there was no use objecting. I spoke German to them because I thought my English may not have been up to it. I explained that my mother was German and I was bilingual, which they accepted.[11]

From Tolmezzo, Dale was taken to a prison in Udine, north-west of Trieste. Twice their convoy was fired upon at road blocks for no apparent reason. On arrival he was given bread and 'coffee', the first nourishment for days. From there he was moved to Coroneo prison in Trieste. Conditions in his cell were appalling with water running down the walls and damp air. After complaints he was moved to the top floor to an airy clean cell. Interrogations continued on a daily basis for up to two hours, but gradually became irregular and less threatening. Dale's main priority was to keep mentally and physically fit and healthy:

I tried to keep fit and alert, which was not easy. Food was scarce. To keep mentally fit I wrote a mini encyclopedia on the whitewashed walls with a pencil stub – anything that I could remember: flowers, rivers, states, countries, capitals, generals, American states, anything. The prison authorities brought in people to look at my work. I resented this. Now and again groups of around twenty Yugoslav partisans would look into my cell. They talked to me and shoved money under my door. I didn't need their money. But I accepted tobacco from them. They were eventually taken to other prisons in Germany or Austria. I used every piece of newspaper I could lay my hands on to stuff between my shirt and skin to keep warm. It was extremely cold in winter and I got chilblains on my hands. People in adjoining cells would disappear and when I asked, 'where is such and such?' I was told that they had been shot. This was not very encouraging news for me . . . I was in a cell in the middle of one of two rows facing each other across a landing with a heavy barred window at one end and a massive steel gate at the other, leading to a spiral staircase. It is not easy to describe the highly depressing effect of a heavy cell door clanging shut behind you, immediately followed by the rattling of a key being turned in the lock. Even though I had heard it often before I arrived at Coroneo, I never got used to it. Isolation and loss of liberty is to some extent probably easy to imagine, but can only be fully felt by experiencing it.[12]

In January 1945 Dale was taken by train to Vienna and onto Kaisersteinbruck camp (Stalag 17a), an enormous camp outside the city with over 50,000 prisoners, mainly Russians but also Yugoslavs, Hungarians and 200 British 'other ranks' escapees. Dale was now in the hands of the German Army rather than the feared SS. It was here that he saw fellow SOE comrade Peter Priestley who had also been captured. Other British soldiers told him of the failed Ardennes German offensive and this served to raise his spirits. Even so, conditions in the camp were grim. The prisoners shared a tiny cell 12ft by 14ft with a single barred window facing barbed wire around the camp. The food was indescribable and brought to the prisoners in a bucket. The grey liquid had a few cabbage leaves floating on the top.

In February 1945 Dale was moved once again, this time with Peter Priestley and one other British prisoner to Oflag 79 near Brunswick which held predominantly British POWs. Little did he know that liberation was still a couple of months away. On 12 April 1945 American tanks rolled into the camp amid much jubilation. It was a great day but one tinged with sadness because President Roosevelt had died:

There was great relief for me. It was six months to the day that I had been a POW and suddenly the tension under which I had lived since 13 October 1944 was no longer there. To be taken prisoner of war is always a depressing experience, but my situation was aggravated by the constant fear of being discovered by the Germans to be a Jew of German origin. The full weight of this pressure upon me with which I had had to live since my capture became only apparent to me at the moment of liberation, and the relief was easily comparable to the removal of the proverbial millstone around one's neck. Also a thought struck me that there cannot have been many individuals who during one war spent time as prisoners behind British and German barbed wire. Our liberators were, as victors, quite naturally on top of an emotional wave and generously showered us with food, cigarettes, chocolates, chewing gum and anything in the clothing line that they did not absolutely need.[13]

Since Oflag 79 had been a Luftwaffe barracks, the prisoners were stationed next to an airfield. A few days after liberation, Dale and Priestley were airlifted out of Austria to Brussels and a couple of days later flown back to England. It was an emotional time for Dale who wrote: 'On arrival I felt like the present Pope who makes a habit of kissing the ground when getting off a plane.[14] Although I did not kiss it, I certainly bent down and touched the tarmac with deep affection – it was a poignant moment to be back in England, and although I had no home of my own to go to, I knew that I had come home.'

That was not the end of Dale's military service. He had not yet been demobbed and in November 1945 he returned to Germany, posted to a port operating company of the Royal Engineers (RE) in Hamburg. He knew the port so well and, of course, spoke fluent German. He then moved with the Royal Engineers to Gottingen engaged in denazification work at the *Reichsbahn Zentral Amt*, the Central German Railway Stores Administration. His particular task was to trawl through thousands of questionnaires and cross-examine employees of the German railways. Anyone suspected of being a Nazi was handed over to Field Security. During his time there he brought in two high-ranking Nazis – one a brigadier in the SS, the other in administration in the Nazi Party before 1933. His reactions when returning to Germany:

I walked through Berlin and Hamburg, the places I knew best. There was a tremendous amount of destruction and disorganisation. I was pretty well unaffected, with no sentimental attachment. I was happy to leave Germany in 1939, but did not wish all the bombing and misfortunes on the German people. But, it was inevitable. It was acceptable in the pursuit of the end of the war. It was senseless destruction but we wanted the war to end. I walked through the ruins of Berlin, with its heaps of rubble, the women were clearing up – this I didn't enjoy seeing, but accepted it as necessary. I harboured no feelings of vindictive pleasure.[15]

### MICHAEL O'HARA

Michael O'Hara (Friederich Berliner) was the only member of 12 Force who never returned from his mission. He was remembered by a colleague, Captain Hillman MC, MM in an article for the journal *The Royal Pioneer*:

Towards the end of 1944, O'Hara climbed aboard the Halifax which was to take him on his last journey in life. A few hours after the huge plane had taken off into the dark night, an elderly lady sat in her warm room behind blacked-out windows in a city in southern Austria when a faint knock sent her startled to the door, through which stepped 2nd Lieutenant Berliner, alias O'Hara. This lady, a widow, was one of the few people left unintimidated by Nazi slogans and the constant threat of arrests by the Gestapo. O'Hara immediately set to work and in a matter of hours he tapped out his first message to headquarters on the shores of the Adriatic. There followed weeks of excitement, passing police pickets by producing false documents, evading searches by Gestapo officials with police dogs and meetings with men of the Austrian Resistance Movement in cellars, attics and outlying farms.

In the meantime, O'Hara's activities had not remained unnoticed, and one night early in 1945, O'Hara escaped over rooftops, through darkened streets with bullets of his pursuers whizzing past his ears. The Gestapo had been tipped off by one of their agents who had succeeded in penetrating O'Hara's organization and had surrounded his hideout at midnight. Undaunted by this setback O'Hara clutched his W/T set, the only piece of belongings he was able to grab in the dark whilst men were hammering at the door, and made off into the country where he knew he would be able to link up with a detachment of Yugoslav partisans. But then it became evident that fate had decided against him, and after a few days of being not only hunted by German troops but also threatened with death by a number of distrusting Yugoslavs who saw in him a traitor, he fell into the hands of the enemy and was immediately denounced by one of his fellow prisoners as a British agent . . . That night O'Hara, on whom documents were found in the name of Chirgwin, spent the night in Graz prison, badly bruised after having been subject to the most fiendish tortures by Gestapo Kommissar Herz. Sharing his bed was an Austrian merchant, who survived the mass killings which were to end O'Hara's life, to tell the story.

Further days of beatings and questioning and more beating followed. Every time Michael O'Hara returned to his cell, his wounds were washed and attended to as good as conditions permitted by his five cell mates who were, with one exception, to die with him. And so the bell tolled for my friend Michael O'Hara. One evening in April 1945 when the Russian Armies were racing up to meet their Allies in Austria, steps clattered in the corridor of the huge prison. Doors were flung open and prisoners, Austrians, Yugoslavs, Czechs, French and Belgians, were kicked by SS guards out of their cells into the corridors where they were manacled to each other looking like frightened animals . . . No sooner had O'Hara cringed in agony when his name was called out, and resigned to his fate, he stepped out in the corridor shouting his farewell, 'Goodbye my friends'. In a steady drizzle, the lorries drove through dark empty streets to the SS Rifle Range at Wetzelsdorf. As the deadly shots fell, Michael Berliner, alias O'Hara, must have fallen as a soldier without remorse or self-pity.[16]

**1.** Kitchener Camp, near Sandwich in Kent. Max Strietzel is playing the violin in the background. *(Courtesy of Michael Streat)*

**2.** No. 88 Company, Pioneer Corps, Kitchener Camp, early 1940. *(Courtesy of William Howard)*

**3. Left:** Rudi Herz, one of the refugee-architects who oversaw the rebuilding of Kitchener Camp. (*Courtesy of Sonia and Dennis Dell*)

**4. Centre:** Pioneer soldiers, Ilfracombe, autumn 1940. (*Courtesy of Michael Streat*)

**5. Bottom:** Soldiers of 249 Company, Ilfracombe, 1940. (*Courtesy of Ros Rosney*)

**6. Top:** Pioneer Corps Orchestra at Seaton Barracks, Plymouth, 17 March 1941. (*Courtesy of Fritz Lustig*)

**7. Centre:** The entertainment section of the Pioneer Corps, Plymouth, March 1941. *Back row, left to right:* Privates Frank Taylor (Engl), Cecil Aronowitz, G. Guttmann, Fritz Lustig (partly hidden behind Guttmann), Jimmy Wedge, S. Mark, Jack Norman, Herbert Kruh (behind Norman), Fred Leeding, H. Karg-Bebenberg, H. Hirschfeld, Hans Geiger (behind Hirschfeld), H. Adler, H. Moses (behind Alder), P. Wiesner, W. Kornfeld. *Front row:* Rudolf Jess, Corporal Nickolai Poliakoff (Coco the Clown), Tamara Poliakov, Helen Poliakov, Lt Phinees May, ballerina Hanne Musch (Mrs P. Wiesner) Pte H. Gurschner. (*Courtesy of Fritz Lustig*)

**8. Right:** Private Carl Jaffe and Hanne Musch in *White Cargo*, Garrison Theatre, Ilfracombe, February 1941. (*Courtesy of Fritz Lustig*)

**9. Above:** Pioneer Corps soldiers, Ilfracombe, autumn 1940. (*Courtesy of Michael Streat*)

**10. Left:** The grave of Private Emil Mesner, East Ham Jewish Cemetery, Marlow Road, London. (*Courtesy of Herbert Mesner*)

**11. Below:** A section of 249 Company, Pioneer Corps, 1942. (*Courtesy of Herbert Landsberg*)

**12. Above:** 69 Company, Pioneer Corps on parade, Darlington, June 1943. (*Courtesy of Myrna Carlebach*)

**13. Below left:** Richard Lehniger (on the right with beret), served in the Small Scale Raiding Force, with his Bavarian cousin, Leo Felix. (*Courtesy of Irene Walters*)

**14. Below right:** Ken Adam, RAF fighter pilot, climbing into a Typhoon. (*Courtesy of Sir Ken Adam*)

**15.** John Waxman of 3 Troop, No. 10 Inter-Allied Commando, who was attached to the Parachute Regiment for D-Day. Pictured here with his brother Werner Waxman of the RAF. (*Courtesy of John Waxman*)

**16. Above left:** Colin Anson of 3 Troop. (*Courtesy of Colin Anson*)

**17. Above right:** Ernest Goodman, Coldstream Guards. (*Courtesy of Professor Ernest Goodman*)

**18.** Members of 3 Troop, No. 10 Inter-Allied Commando at Eastbourne. (*Courtesy of Colin Anson*)

**19. Above:** The 5th Battalion of the Coldstream Guards enters Arras. Ernest Goodman is second in line, his friend Archie Newman is the fourth man. (*Courtesy of Professor Ernest Goodman*)

**20. Below left:** Wolfgang Likwornik pictured here in the uniform of the Black Watch. He transferred to the Gordon Highlanders for action overseas. (*Courtesy of Peter Lee*)

**21. Below right:** Geoffrey Stuart of A Squadron, 8th Kings Royal Irish Hussars. (*Courtesy of Geoffrey Stuart*)

**22.** C Squadron, 8th Kings Royal Irish Hussars landing near Arromanches on D-Day+3 . . . (*Courtesy of Willy Field*)

**23.** . . . unloading tanks from the Tank Landing Craft onto the beaches of Normandy. (*Courtesy of Willy Field*)

**24.** The devastation of Caen. (*Courtesy of Geoffrey Stuart*)

**25. Left:** Willy Field in Pioneer Corps uniform, later transferred to the 8th Kings Royal Irish Hussars. (*Courtesy of Willy Field*)

**26. Centre:** Geoffrey Stuart (second from left) with his tank crew, Normandy, June 1944. (*Courtesy of Geoffrey Stuart*)

**27. Bottom:** Ken Ward (seated in middle) with Eric Marsland (gunner) and Charles Adam (driver) in action on their Sherman Firefly tank, Normandy, 1944. (*Courtesy of Ken Ward*)

**28.** A tank crew of 8th Kings Royal Irish Hussars with captured Nazi flag, en route to Hamburg, April 1945. (*Courtesy of Dennis Goodman*)

**29.** William Ashley Howard, Royal Navy (middle). (*Courtesy of William Howard*)

**30. Right:** Sidney Graham, Royal Navy, Sicily, summer 1944. (*Courtesy of Sidney Graham*)

**31. Far right:** Leo Horn, the Wiltshire Regiment. (*Courtesy of Leo Horn*)

**32. Left:** Alice Anson (née Gross), Women's Auxiliary Air Force (WAAF). (*Courtesy of Alice Anson*)

**33. Below left:** Paul Hamilton who parachuted into Normandy on 5 June 1944, the eve of D-Day, as a 12th Battalion Parachute Regiment Pathfinder, ahead of the main airborne landings. (*Courtesy of Nigel Hamilton*)

**34.** The staff of No. 2 Distribution Centre of Combined Services Detailed Interrogation Centre (CSDIC), in front of Latimer House, early 1944. Most are German refugees who served in the British Forces. Bill Sales, Neumann, Vigart, Huppert, Hollaender, Kraft, Peter Ganz, Garry Casey, Graham, Sabersky, Neuhaus, Bentham, Heilbronn, Strauss, Freddy Wellmann, Rudi Oppenheimer, Bobby Manners, Richard Stern, Walter Beevers, Mann, Tonie Marshall, Maxi Langley, Well, Allan Henley, Claus Mayer, Father Shipton, Harry Jakobs, Robert Aufhäuser, Franken, Peter Bendix, Felix Fraser, Robert Neave, Sterne, Frank Stevens, Berchstecher, Mark, Sirot, Rees Nichols, Jellicoe, Hubert Bailey, Erskin, Falk, Charles Lipton, Scot(ty), Bratu, Bruce Eldon, West, Marefield, Spiller, Segell, Werner Stark, David Feist, Tugendhat, Bamberger (Bambi), Lindsay, Hart, Brent, Horton, Eric Schaffer, Leon Kendon, Wulwick, David Stearn, Wolfgang Meyer, George Pulay, Johnny Rapp, Teddy Schächter, Freddy Katz, Douglas (Konny), Eva Metzger, Johnny King, Francis Seton, Franklin, Männlein, Ellis, Fred Bentley, Peter Baines, Jimmy Leader, Walter Leatham, Oscar Hamm, Blake, Freddy Benson, Johnny Gay, Peter Tükheim, Deeds, Warner, Herbert Lehmann, Fritz Lustig, Innocence Grafe, Franz Huelsen, Peter Kaufmann, Hubert Simon, Francis Hellman, Godfrey Scheele, Fleiss(i), Ruth Schein, Ena Fothergill, Mary Gomes, Anne Bell, Joann Fisk, Susan Cohn (Lustig), Robin Eltringham, Doreen Wilkinson, Eve Henry (Bamberger), Muriel Richardson, Jane Hopkins, Lucy Haley, Joan Stansfield, Ilse Hirsch, Inge Jaeger (Beevers), Gerda Engel, Dora Garret. *(Courtesy of Fritz Lustig)*

**35.** Some of the members of 12 Force, Special Operations Executive. *Back row, left to right:* Eric Rhodes, Frank Kelley, Paul Mayer. *Front row:* Hermann Faltikschek, -?-, George Bryant. *(Courtesy of Eric Sanders)*

**36.** Walter Freud of Special Operations Executive, who was demobbed as a major. *(Courtesy of David Freud)*

**37.** Susan Lustig (née Susanne Cohn), ATS. *(Courtesy of Susan Lustig)*

**38.** Captain Howard Alexander who captured the Nazi war criminal Rudolf Hoess. *(Courtesy of Howard Alexander)*

**39.** George Rosney in search of his parents at Theresienstadt concentration camp, near Prague, May 1945. He discovered that having survived nearly two years there, they were transported to Auschwitz in 1944 where they perished. *(Courtesy of Ros Rosney)*

**40.** The Victory Parade, Berlin, July 1945. *(Courtesy of Willy Field)*

ERIC SANDERS

Eric Sanders (Ignaz Schwarz, born Vienna 1919) arrived in England in October 1938. Having carried out work on a voluntary basis for the German-Jewish Refugee Aid Committee at Woburn House in London, he then worked as a dairy boy on a farm. In February 1940 he volunteered for the Army and was assigned to 88 Company of the Pioneer Corps, stationed overseas in France with the BEF. Once back in England after the evacuation of Dunkirk, his company was given various labour jobs around the country. He was on detachment in Carmarthen in Wales when approached by Hartmann to join a special unit.

> There I stood in rubber boots in a ditch next to Corporal Urmacher. We were both shovelling mud out of that trench with a degree of despair when a man came running down the slight hill and shouted for me to go back to the office. I was being transferred.[17]

In 1943 Eric, then as Ignaz Schwarz, was transferred to Special Training School (STS) and trained for SOE. In September 1944 he was sent to Italy, first to Fasano near Monopoli and then Siena. He was assigned to Theo Neumann as his radio operator for their intended mission, due to his proficiency with radio in being one of the fastest in sending, receiving and coding messages.

> Theo wasn't actually Jewish, but was a Social Democrat from Vienna. Once in England he was connected to the exiled Austrian Social Democrats who still maintained contacts with anti-Nazis in Austria. It was thought that Theo's links could prove useful for SOE operations in trying to link up with underground resistance in Austria once we were dropped back into the country. In Italy, a group of us were stationed apart from the main group in a fisherman's cottage on the coast. Our detachment consisted of Hermann Faltitschek, Theo Neumann, Michael O'Hara, John Miller (Hans Wirlandner) and myself. We

also had Austrian and German POWs in the house. O'Hara was the first to go into action.

I was stationed with Theo Neumann and Hans Hladnik, both of whom would frequently disappear for a day. During their 'disappearance' they successfully smuggled themselves into a German POW camp, mixed with the prisoners as if POWs, not an undangerous situation. They were successful in finding two men who were reliable anti-Nazis who could be dropped ahead of us. They became a kind of reception committee. I was responsible for training the first of the anti-Nazi men in radio, coding, decoding and fieldcraft. The first was eventually dropped and succeeded in sending back messages to HQ but by this time the German front was collapsing and the army was no longer interested in his messages.

I waited a whole year to go into action. I really wanted to do something positive against Hitler and the Nazis. They had thrown me out of Austria, and I had been badly treated at school. Now that I was in SOE, I was tough, strong and fearless, but not brave. But the war collapsed before Theo Neumann and I could be dropped at our intended zone at Styria in southern Austria. Whilst we waited, we lived a wonderful life with nothing much to do. I went into Siena every day. We lived in a villa with plenty of wine and good food and enough money. It was privileged in every way, but we did not go into action and that was the most frustrating period of my whole army career.

By then it was 1945, so SOE was disbanded. The men of 12 Force were assigned to other military service, often relating to the denazification process in Germany and Austria or the hunt for Nazi war criminals.

Chapter 6

# THE ROYAL AIR FORCE

A major unfulfilled ambition for the vast majority of Germans and Austrians in the British Forces was to join the Royal Air Force (RAF). Many aspired to become pilots. Disillusioned with life in the Pioneer Corps, they sent off repeated applications with little success. The few who succeeded in getting into the RAF were generally assigned to mechanical and support jobs. Their German background was not only a barrier to becoming pilots but also receiving a commission. However, there were exceptions. Of German-Jewish origin, Oliver Owen Bernard, who was a member of the Communist Party of Great Britain from 1941 to 1943, trained as a pilot with the RAF from 1943 to 1944.[1] It is not clear whether he saw action as a pilot. George W. Berger, of Austrian descent, piloted Mosquitoes on photo reconnaissance missions for Coastal Command. He also flew Sunderlands on Arctic convoy patrols and was awarded the Distinguished Flying Cross (DFC), later becoming an instructor on Mosquitoes.[2] In stark contrast to the trials and tribulations endured by many refugees classified as enemy aliens, Fred Tuckman (Fred Tuchmann) left Germany on 15 March 1939 but was naturalised as a British citizen on 31 July due to his mother being British-born. Consequently, when war broke out he was among the few ex-Germans with British nationality serving in the British Forces. He became a wireless mechanic. After the war he became a successful businessman and served for ten years as a respected British Euro MP, in recognition of which he was awarded an OBE by the British government and the *Bundesverdienstkreuz* by the German government. Berlin-born Ken Adam (Klaus Hugo Adam) became one of the few, and possibly the only, German fighter pilot in the RAF during the

Second World War. The following profiles offer an intimate insight into those who served with the RAF.

## KEN ADAM

Ken Adam (Klaus Hugo Adam) was born in Berlin in 1921 into an assimilated upper-middle class German-Jewish family.[3] His father owned much property and the famous Berlin sports store S. ADAM, which was frequented by well-known athletes and sportsmen and women. During his childhood, Ken was unaware of his Jewishness until 1933 when Hitler came to power. It changed everything for this prosperous family, and Ken began to feel different from some of his friends. His father was arrested by the Gestapo but was fortunately released after forty-eight hours. It was a warning for the family.

Ken's mother and older brother Peter were the motivating force in getting the family out of Germany. In 1934 Ken and his younger brother Dieter (Denis Adam) emigrated to Scotland where they attended a small public school in Edinburgh. They were not happy at the school and when their parents came to London a few months later, they joined them. Ken's mother rented a house in Hampstead and turned it into a successful boarding house, enabling Ken and Dieter to be educated at St Paul's School. Their father died in 1936 at only fifty-six years old. The education of the boys was left to their mother who became the strong element in the family. After leaving St Paul's in 1937 Ken enrolled for evening classes at London University's Bartlett School of Architecture. During the day he was articled to a firm of architects and civil engineers, C.W. Glovers & Partners, in Gower Street. There he switched to war work and designed air-raid shelters and illustrated books on air-raid precautions. For this work he was exempted from internment in 1940. During that year he volunteered for the British Forces and was sent to Ilfracombe to join the Pioneer Corps immediately with the rank of corporal.[4] He spent about nine months there training the other refugee Pioneers, but his real ambition was to become a pilot in the RAF:

I wanted to fly. At that time you could not get into fighting units of the British Army. I was firing letter after letter to join the RAF and was always turned down. And then very much to my surprise in April 1941, I was accepted and was transferred to Scarborough for elementary training. There may have been other reasons for my transfer to the RAF. My commanding officer was initially Lord Reading who was then replaced by Colonel Coles and I became friendly with one of Coles' daughters. Once I was placed under open arrest because, whereas I should have been drilling a squad somewhere, I was walking down the promenade at Ilfracombe with Deidre Coles. Her father wasn't there unfortunately and when he came back two days later, I was confronted by him. He was a very bright man. He said, 'You have to conform with military discipline and I have no personal objection to you taking out my daughter, who I understand is very fond of you, but you must not flaunt that relationship openly.' I fired off another application and was shortly accepted by the RAF. All other people did not succeed at that time.

Ken served with the RAF from 1941 for the duration of the war, changing his name from Klaus Hugo Adam to Keith Howard Adam.[5] He became Ken Adam after the war. He began his initial training at Scarborough: drill, physical fitness, square-bashing, Morse code and navigation. From there he was sent to 11 Elementary Flying Training School in Scotland where he experienced his first flight in a Tiger Moth, trained by a well-respected Battle of Britain pilot. In June 1942 he went to Moncton, Canada for the next phase of his training. After a short time he requested a transfer to the United States and was sent to Lakeland, Florida for his main flying instruction. From there he was posted to Cochrane, flying monoplanes. Finally, having spent a year in the USA, he was sent to 55 OTU in Annan Scotland for further instruction in flying and aerial combat. On 1 October 1943 he was posted to 609 (West Riding) Squadron, a top-scoring single-seater fighter squadron and flew operations over Europe in Typhoons. On 11 May 1944 he was part of the formation of Typhoon squadrons and American bombers that attacked the Bruneval radar station near

Le Havre on the French coast. It was not a straightforward assignment because the station had reinforced concrete bunkers:

> Our plan was to fly into inland France, go into echelon starboard, and then dive down and attack towards the sea on our way back to England. Well the first thing I noticed, because I was one of the last men in, was that planes were going down in flames before we'd even got over the French coast. I heard it over the radio and thought, 'My God!' And then the next thing I found, when we were attacking, was that the German anti-aircraft guns were just aiming at the first plane because if they didn't hit it, they hit the one behind. So I slid out to one side and came in at an angle, which probably saved my life. We'd never had serious losses before. But suddenly, in one show, the first really important one, we lost three aircraft. To lose three people was traumatic for all of us. In fact, when we landed back in England there was general depression. There was one pilot who baled out – Junior was his name – and since I was the last one to attack I saw him hit the water. I sent out a Mayday to scramble Air Sea Rescue and I circled him until my petrol became too low and I had to leave. But they never found him. We were probably the most effective close-support weapon the army had, and our losses were horrendous, really horrendous. As a vague estimate, from the beginning of 1944 to November 1944 we lost nearly twice the establishment of the squadron. Not all were killed: some became prisoners, but still a terrifying loss. Because, although we were incredibly effective, we were also unbelievably vulnerable . . . Flying at 400 mph at ground level and trying to avoid trees and high-tension cables and pylons and church steeples. We often came back with tree branches stuck in our radiators![6]

During August 1944 the RAF carried out intensive bombing of German troops in the Falaise area of France. Ken describes the impact on him when he visited the area:

> What affected me most and I will remember for the rest of my life, was the aftermath of the battle for the Falaise Gap. After it was all

over, 609 Squadron was given a day off and we decided to drive into the Falaise area to get a first hand view from the ground of the results of the battle and our rocket attacks. Unfortunately our truck was trapped in an armoured column moving at a snails' pace, since the road or what was left of it was choked with wreckage, swollen corpses of men of the SS divisions, dead cattle and horses. The stench of death was everywhere. We tried to breathe through our handkerchiefs which we had knotted over our mouths and noses, to little avail. The sickly sweet smell of death stuck to our uniforms and bodies for days to come. This was my first contact, on the ground, with the dead and what had been the enemy. Attacking a target from the air, one felt strangely removed from the realities and horrors on the ground. This was our first decisive defeat of the German Army, in which 609 Squadron and other Typhoon squadrons of 84 Group played such a vital role, but my feelings of elation at this victory were muted by the carnage of dead bodies and even more so the grotesque spectacle of countless dead horses with their limbs rigidly sticking up in the air. It was an experience I will never forget.[7]

Ken flew countless sorties over France and survived a number of incidents of enemy fire, including an attack on 11 November 1944 on the Gestapo headquarters at Dunkirk. That same month he received a commission and attained the rank of flying officer. At the end of the war, when his squadron returned to England, Ken was posted to Wunstorf, near Hanover in Germany on an extended commission as acting flight lieutenant in charge of 10,000 Luftwaffe POWs who were formed into labour units for the reconstruction of airfields.

After the war his charisma and talents were directed into the film industry when he became the production designer for some of the best-loved films in cinematography over six decades, including seven James Bond films and The Madness of King George which won him his second Oscar. Ken received an OBE in December 1995 for his services to the film industry. In 2003 he received a Knighthood from the Queen for his services to the film industry and British-German relations. As he himself admits: 'I was what they call a natural pilot, a born pilot. I proved that.'

CLAUS MOSER

Claus Moser was born in Berlin in 1922 into a well-off banking family. The Nazi rise to power obviously affected the family such that in 1936, Claus left Germany with his parents and brother for a new life in England. They took a house in Putney and Claus was educated at Frensham Heights School in Surrey until 1940. In May 1940 he was interned at Lingfield and then Huyton along with his father and brother. By this time he had already been accepted for study at the London School of Economics (LSE). The Director of the LSE wrote to him at Huyton to say that he had heard that Claus had been interned and looked forward to his release. At the end of the letter he commented, 'you may be interested to know that the housing estate where you are interned belongs to my wife'. Claus was released after a few months and from 1940 until 1943 studied at the LSE, graduating with a First Class Honours in Statistics. In the summer of 1943 he decided to enlist. Recruitment was much harder than anticipated because of his German background:

I was longing to get into the war and do my bit in fighting Hitler. One of my professors at LSE was Harold Laski, so I went to see him. He said, 'you're a statistician. The nation needs you. Try the civil service.' I tried the civil service but this was barred to me because of my German background. So I went back to Laski and he said to me, 'if you really want to go into the war, you must join the RAF. I will speak to Air Marshal Sir John Slessor.' The answer came back – because of my nationality, I could not be accepted for the flying side of the RAF. I visited Laski again. On this occasion he said to me, 'we have tried the civil service, we have tried the RAF. What we really need are Bevan boys.[8] If you really want to help this country, go down the mines.' I replied, 'I haven't got the guts to do that.' I then walked into the RAF recruitment office in Euston Road where they desperately needed recruits. I was asked about my education and background and explained that I had a first class degree in statistics from LSE. The reply came, 'That's wonderful. I've got just the job for you – flight mechanic.'[9]

Claus was delighted at having been accepted. He had little understanding then that he had signed up to the lowest grade within the RAF. In mid-1943 he was sent to Cardington in Bedfordshire for training, one of many new recruits who were kitted out with their new uniforms that day.

Cardington was a significant time for me because it was my first warning of a major problem that lay ahead for me: until then I had had a rather protected life. We had lived a very privileged life in Berlin – at least until Hitler – moving in similarly privileged circles. School in England was also a bit exclusive. I never had much opportunity to mix with typically working class people so I was quite uneasy at this first encounter with the wider section of the population at Cardington. The first day we had to get into our uniforms and put on our kit. There I sat on my bed, amongst dozens of others, trying to work out how to put on my kit and all the straps. I appeared to have one strap missing and I got into a panic. No other chap would help me. I had to face the corporal and got a terrific telling off for losing one of my straps. After two days I was posted to Skegness for physical training which included long runs on the beach in freezing temperatures. I felt terribly inferior to all the other much fitter chaps. I had a miserable time for many weeks.

The time came for Claus to decide which part of the RAF he would work in. He sought a commission, but once again his German background was a barrier and a commission was out of the question. He became an instrument repairer class I, repairing and checking the cockpit instruments in a plane before it left on a sortie. He was sent to No. 12 School of Technical Training at Melksham in Wiltshire for specialist trade training which he enjoyed, although he was hopeless with technical tasks:

This period strengthened something I didn't get over until much later – for perhaps the first time in my life I was very unpopular. I had not experienced that before. I got very upset and tried to work it out. It had nothing to do with my background; no one knew about that. I spoke good English from being educated at a fine school here. There was no problem with anti-semitism or religion. It was about being cleverer than the rest and always having an answer for everything which did not make for popularity. Gradually I improved that.

Claus changed his name to Michael (Mike) Moser which he used for the duration of his RAF career. Then began a series of postings, the first of which was to Manston near Margate in Kent with a Mosquito squadron. It was here that damaged bomber aircraft from sorties and raids over Germany crash-landed. Throughout the day Claus became used to announcements over the radio that aircraft were coming back with a number of dead bodies and survivors on board. The buzz of planes constantly coming and crash-landing created an atmosphere of excitement and elation. Claus continued his work as instrument repairer. From Manston he was posted to two bomber bases in Yorkshire, Pocklington and Driffield:

Here my job was much more significant. There were lots more instruments to repair in these aircraft. I was often called out in the middle of the night because planes were to leave on bombing raids. I would run across the runway at midnight to check that all the instruments and oxygen supplies were working in the aircraft that had been allocated to me. It turned out to be a very responsible job. By this time I was a leading aircraftsman. The responsibility of our work was highlighted one night when an electrician in my team failed to check that the bomb release mechanism on an aircraft was working. The bomber returned from its mission over Germany having failed to drop any bombs. It could have cost the crew their lives. The electrician was court-martialled for that error.

I felt that I was now at the front of the war. I still tried several attempts to get a commission and each time my background was a barrier. I felt I could have done much more. In terms of being a refugee and Jewish – this was not a problem. Being a German was a total barrier, even though I was stateless and not yet British. It was a great disappointment to me.

By the end of 1944 or early 1945 Claus had been posted to Bomber Command Headquarters at High Wycombe where he became part of a research team. During the early months of 1945 he was charged with assessing how much damage the RAF had done in the bombing raids over Germany. As different parts of Germany were coming under Allied control he went on trips to these areas to assess the damage. For example, a trip would be planned for Cologne or München-Gladbach to interrogate surviving heads of businesses and factories to ascertain whether the official RAF reports of damage were in fact accurate. Claus acted as interpreter, the only point at which his German background accorded him any importance in the RAF. The European headquarters of this operation was in Versailles and sorties into Germany were planned from there. A team of three were sent to assess bomb damage: Claus, his boss (a RAF group captain) and his driver. Claus and the group captain were responsible for all the interrogations. One day this work was to have devastating consequences for Claus:

My career was short-lived because in May 1945 the three of us set out from near Cologne in the staff car to visit some factories. On that occasion the group captain insisted on driving. I don't remember the precise details of the crash, but he drove us into an American Army lorry. The group captain died outright and I didn't see the driver again. I was sitting in the back of the staff-car at the time of the accident and was thrown through the dividing window. I survived only because an ambulance was passing at that very moment. My jugular vein had been cut, usually a fatal occurrence, but the ambulance medics saved my life. I was unconscious for four days in an American field hospital. After that, I was sent to an RAF recuperation centre in Belgium for a couple of months. I was seriously ill, my jaw was broken and I had cuts over my face. I was flown back to England and sent to the famous East Grinstead Hospital led by the greatest plastic surgeon of our time, Sir Archibald McIndoe. He was treating severely injured pilots, amongst others, all of whom were dreadfully injured, often with burnt hands and burnt parts of the face. On the first day, Sir Archibald came to see me and said, 'We start operating tomorrow. But there is one rule – you must watch some of my operations to see what an art it is and to realise that most patients here are in a terribly worse state than you.' So, I found myself in a largely RAF community with aircrew and soldiers, often particularly good-looking, now disfigured by their appalling injuries. During the nine months that I was there, I really learned about human survival. I gained an understanding of the human spirit and what people can do to help each other to survive, however physically damaged. Sometimes Sir Archibald would speak to us and say that such and such a patient had committed suicide the previous night. He would explain what it was that a man in such awful conditions could not take: least of all he could take sympathy, especially from a girlfriend. It was easier to cope with statements like, 'you look terrible, ghastly' than 'it will be alright. I'll stick by you.' Sympathy was not really a help.

As part of recovery for all of us, the so-called 'Guinea Pigs', regular trips to the theatre and nightclubs in London were arranged with girls to dance with. I recall one occasion when we were invited to the Palace to be received by the King and Queen. The late Queen Elizabeth, the Queen Mother, once asked me to talk to her about the war. She mentioned that it was her role to be involved in every part of society, to meet people with all sorts of troubles, and that few occasions moved her more than meeting those dreadfully burnt airmen and soldiers from East Grinstead. 'Their spirit was wonderfully moving,' she said.

After a number of operations at East Grinstead, Claus was posted to Bomber Command Education Service at High Wycombe, promoted to the rank of sergeant. There he taught RAF personnel about politics and economics until his demobilisation in 1946. He reflects on his wartime career:

It was not a distinguished career but I felt that I did my bit to defeat Hitler. I learned a lot about human beings. My service in the RAF enabled me to learn how to relate to a wide range of people which helped me for my later public service activities. I would not have missed it for the world. It helped to shape me as a person.

In peacetime Claus was active in public service, with academic posts at the LSE and Wadham College, Oxford; in charge of government statistics for many years; in banking at Rothschild's; and in the world of the arts – above all at the Royal Opera House and the British Museum. In retirement, studying and playing the piano became a central activity.

## KEN AMBROSE

Ken Ambrose (Kurt Abrahamsohn, born in Stettin) joined the RAF on 5 July 1943, passed the required intelligence and aptitude tests and was sent for initial two-week training at Babbacombe near Torquay in south Devon. He comments: 'I decided that I wanted to fly against Germany. Above all I would have a clear conscience and know that I had done what I could for the war which concerned my people more than any other.' He was allocated to 26 EFTS at RAF Theale near Reading and received twelve flying lessons with an instructor. Just before being posted overseas to South Africa for his main training, he changed his name from Kurt Abrahamsohn to Kenneth Ambrose.[10] At the beginning of 1944 he was sent to Durban and then to a flying training school at Potchefstroom, an hour's train ride from Johannesburg. But he was not destined to become a pilot:

I flew just over a hundred hours in a Tiger Moth, mostly solo. I was then posted to another airfield to fly twin engines to become a bomber pilot, but I had a job to get the two engines to synchronise. My spatial awareness was not good and after ten hours, often misjudging the height for landing, I was not allowed to fly again. I was out. During the winter of 1944/45 I found myself on the way back to England, to Eastchurch on the Isle of Sheppey for failed aircrew, awaiting reallocation.

At Easter 1945 Ken was assigned as 'Interpreter German Technical', in the rank of sergeant, posted to a small group of officers in the British Bombing Research Mission (BBRM), who were going to Germany to assess RAF bomb damage:

Our headquarters were in a little chateau outside Paris. The war was nearly over, but not quite. We were instructed that if we went anywhere near the Rhine, we had to wear tin hats because the Germans were still shooting from the other side. We were billeted on the outskirts of Cologne which had been bombed to pieces. Our work was interesting. We visited the local *Bürgermeister* or directors of hospitals, anywhere where we could gather information on our bombing raids. The officers interrogated them and I acted as interpreter. We visited bombed sites to see what had happened in human terms, damage to buildings, etc.[11]

As the Allies advanced into Germany, the unit moved to Hanover and was stationed just outside the city at Bad Nenndorf. The unit was renamed British Bombing Survey Unit. In Bad Nenndorf Ken worked as a translator in the unit and travelled occasionally back to London. Most of his time soon became taken up with finding and helping Jewish survivors at the displaced persons' camp in Deggendorf, southern Bavaria. In a letter dated 16 September 1945 he expressed his feelings on returning to a defeated Germany:

We are, it is true, in a state of 'no war', but if you saw what I see around me every day and then read the *Economist* as well, you would hardly call it peace. It is for the peoples of Europe, but especially the Germans, a state of very grim war-existence without the shooting, and there is not safe ground anywhere in sight on which to build a new life.[12]

In December 1945 Ken was posted back to headquarters in London where he translated documents seized from the German authorities, sometimes of a highly technical and scientific nature. He was also engaged in translating documentation relating to V2 rockets. He worked there until his demobilisation in 1947.

## WERNER WAXMAN

Werner Waxman (Werner Wachsmann) served as flight mechanic in the RAF. Born on 4 August 1925 in Oppeln near Breslau in Upper Silesia, he was not the only member of his family to enlist in the British Forces. His elder brother Wolfgang served in 3 Troop of No. 10 Inter-Allied Commando. Their father, Paul Wachsmann, had served in the German Army in the First World War and had been awarded the Iron Cross Second Class. Werner has vivid memories of the Nazi regime:

> Frightening images are clear in my mind even today of Hitler Youth aged between 8 and 12 with swastika armbands, Nazi uniforms, each with a leather cross strap and dagger, riding around on scooters. But the tragedy for both myself and my brother growing up in Nazi Germany was realised at school. Whenever there was a disturbance in class, we and another Jewish lad always received the blame. Later on it was particularly frightening to witness senior Nazis smashing up Jewish shops and daubing graffiti on Jewish businesses.

It was proving impossible for the Wachsmann family to obtain an *ausweis* (exit permit) to leave Germany. Well aware of how serious the situation was becoming for Jews, in 1934 their mother Emily tried to smuggle Werner and Wolfgang over the border into Switzerland. This failed and they were turned back. In 1935 their mother secured a visa for them to emigrate to England because she herself had a British passport, having been born in Glasgow. British nationality enabled her to emigrate with her two sons that August. Their father Paul was unable to leave with them.[13] Werner arrived in England without a word of English. The family lived in a house in South Woodford, Essex, bought for them by Emily's father. Life was harsh, the family was poor and they lived mainly on potato or garlic bread soup. In

1939 Werner left school at the age of fourteen to work in a factory near Walthamstow, building an electrical plant.

In 1941, at the age of sixteen, Werner received a letter from a government department which requested that he work as a Bevan boy in the mines. He refused. Just before his eighteenth birthday in mid-1943 he went to the RAF recruitment centre in Euston Square, London, where his voluntary enlistment was turned down because of his German nationality. He then received a final notice from the government requesting him to report for mining work. He took the notice to Euston Square and begged to see someone higher in the RAF recruitment centre:

> I was asked why I wanted to enlist. I replied that working in the mines would not give me the chance to fight the Nazis who had cause so much suffering to my family and millions of others. Fighting the Germans would give me the chance to thank Britain for refuge. I am prepared to die for that fight. I then received my call-up papers to join the RAF. I changed my name to Werner Waxman, known to my colleagues as Jimmy. From 4 October 1943, I was trained at Skegness and from there sent for aero engine-flight mechanic training at a station near Cardiff [St Athan]. Once fully trained (superior), I was posted with a Liberator squadron. Liberators were 4-engine bombers and the United States had sent over masses of equipment before they joined the war in 1942. It was my task to service the four engines on the Liberator aircraft. For this work I was based at St Eval in Cornwall. Then the whole squadron was transferred to Elgin, Morayshire in Scotland. Whilst in Scotland, we were engaged in 12-hour North Sea patrols on anti-submarine missions. In the belly of the aircraft we had lots of depth charges. I eventually received the rank of leading aircraftsman (LAC). We were so short of air gunners that after my 12-hour shift filling aircraft with fuel and servicing engines, I was asked to be a mid-upper gunner on the North Sea patrols. I did not know how to work a gun, so I was taken to a hangar for training. I had 10–15 minutes instruction and that was it. I must have carried out any number of sorties.

After Scotland I was transferred abroad to Bombay with 85 Squadron, involved with Mosquito aircraft this time. We were sent to Bombay for kitting out and acclimatisation. From there we travelled to Madras by train where we prepared for squadron assignments. The whole squadron was sent to the city of Batavia in the Dutch East Indies. In Batavia, I was in charge of the motor pool – responsible for overseeing and organising the movement and servicing of vehicles. From there we went to Kuala Lumpur. It was by now the summer of 1945 – shortly after the Japanese had surrendered on 10 August. I was sent to Kuala Lumpur to join 84 Squadron. I remember driving in a 3 tonne truck through the Johore Causeway that joins Singapore to Malaysia. There, I was returned to my original flight mechanic engine work. After VJ-Day, the whole squadron was moved to Seletar air force base in Singapore.[14]

Werner spent much of his wartime career on the vital task of servicing many different kinds of aircraft and engines, from Rolls-Royce Merlin engines to Beaufighters and heavy bombers. He refuelled the aircraft after each sortie and repaired their engines when required. Werner remained in Malaysia until he was shipped back to England in 1947. He was demobilised in Kirkham on 23 July 1947.

## ALEX KLEIN

Alex Klein served under his original name. Born in Vienna in October 1924, his family fled to Cologne after *Kristallnacht* in an attempt to reach the Belgian border. Alex decided, against his parent's wishes, to try to reach the German/Belgian border on his own. He left Cologne, aged fourteen, with a rucksack on his back, but was stopped and interrogated by Nazi officers en route. They laughed at such a small boy trying to reach the border alone and turned him back. It was his youth which, in the end, saved his life. He continued his journey, avoiding the Belgian border control, making his way through woods and lanes until he reached the main road to Verviers, always avoiding the border guards. The 45km journey on foot took him 8 hours and he finally stumbled into a café in Verviers. He found refuge in a hostel in Brussels until May 1939 when he came to England with the Kindertransport. His parents eventually escaped Germany into Belgium and to England. Alex found work in a sweat shop until his enlistment in the British Forces. In June 1943 he volunteered for the RAF and chose to be trained as a wireless operator:[15]

> When I mentioned my plans to my mother, she was aghast for me to take this step as I was only just over 18 years of age and I had no need to expose myself to go to war in the armed forces. But my mind was made up. I wanted to do something myself for the country that gave me refuge, in the fight against the Germans to enable us to win the war. My aim was to be a pilot but I should have realised that I was too young and did not have the English education needed for this task, and having only had four years in a Jewish grammar school in Vienna before the Nazis closed it down.

On 9 June 1943 Alex was sent to RAF Padgate for basic training and from there to Stanley Park, Blackpool for initial training as a wireless operator. Apart from the day-to-day training, he lived the life of a civilian in Blackpool until his transfer to RAF Compton Bassett, Wiltshire, on 7 October 1943 to complete his training in wireless telegraphy. He passed his tests, being able to read and transmit Morse code at twenty-five words a minute. On 17 February 1944 he was transferred to RAF Chigwell in Essex, a camp where different units were being formed ready for the invasion of France. Alex was assigned to 72 Wing, which was formed into a radar/wireless unit and then became part of the 2nd Tactical Air Force. Its task was to assist and guide the aircraft involved in bombing raids to pinpoint targets. On 13 September 1944 his unit proceeded to Cardington to await embarkation which followed four days later.

> We went across to France via Southampton. From there we made our way to Mons, Belgium which had just been liberated and we were received with great enthusiasm. People invited us into their

homes to entertain us and could not do more to help us. We then proceeded to a location in the Ardennes, only a couple of miles from the frontline. This was where we carried out our first work in conjunction with aircraft involved in bombing raids. The method was for two radar stations to follow the flights to their targets and when they flew too close to their targets we gave signals to the aircraft in conjunction with the radar about when to release the bombs. When the Germans counter-attacked us in the Battle of the Ardennes, we were very lucky to be able to retreat before they overran our position. We went back to Mons and in early 1945 moved into Holland where we carried on the work as before with pinpoint bombing of German targets.

In April 1945 Alex was transferred to another unit in Germany doing the same work. He was there until the end of the war, and after a period of leave in England, stayed in Germany until May 1946. Afterwards he was posted to a unit in Rennes, France where he undertook administrative duties until his posting to Paris in February 1947. On 21 September 1947 he was discharged from the RAF and made his way back to England.

I was pleased that it was all over and that I had not come to any harm. I enjoyed my years in the RAF. I experienced no anti-semitism and was able to meet boys from many parts of England, Wales and Scotland, something which I would not have been able to do at home. It taught me a discipline and I did my share of duty to a country which I have learned to love.

Alex was naturalised as a British citizen in 1947.


## SIDNEY GOLDBERG

Although Sidney Goldberg was born and raised in Leipzig, Germany, he held a Polish passport because his father was a Polish national.[16] As a Jew living in Nazi Germany, his life was at risk, so he emigrated to England. He wanted to avoid conscription into the Polish Army because he could not speak a word of Polish. When he enlisted in the British Forces in 1941 he was technically a 'friendly alien' and this may have determined his career in the RAF. He volunteered as a radio operator and trained at a wireless school in Blackpool. He was posted to an operational bomber station at Wyton near Huntingdon on various duties, which included teaching German to air crew. In about June 1942 he was transferred to a fighter base at Swansea in South Wales as part of 'the pick and shovel gang'. In July/August 1942 he was assigned to the RAF 'Y' service, secret intelligence and German radio telephony communications, based at Newbold Revel. His duties thereafter consisted of intercepting communications between German aircraft and their bases and vice versa. The messages were thinly coded, but usually transmitted in plain language. Sidney's knowledge of colloquial German was vital to the post. In November 1942 he embarked for North Africa, landing on 8 December at Bône (now Annaba) in Algeria. There he was involved in setting up a mobile unit at Ain Draham over the border in the Kroumerie Mountains of Tunisia for the interception of German aircraft communications. At that time wireless operators in his unit were intercepting Enigma for a while. He recalls:

Tunisia was a stop-gap operation effectively, to stop Rommel coming up from the Western Desert and escaping towards the west. We had with us a small element of Americans and a large contingent of French colonial troops who had been left behind by the change in circumstances. To get the best reception possible we had to be as far forward and as high as possible. We had moments of anxiety when Rommel attacked the Americans at the Kasserine Pass in February 1943 and we were left wondering what would happen to us. We were armed with rifles and ammunition. We were equipped to fight if we had to. Montgomery came up from the Western Desert and fought his way towards Tunis. The battle for Tunis was for me the highlight of my RAF career. We worked extremely hard and there were battles going on all around us. The German Air Force was already in decline. When Tunis fell in May

1943, we moved in and set up again there, but we were effectively preparing for the invasion of Sicily. I was then sent with a detachment to cover the invasion of Sicily. We stayed there only for a short time because our work was taken over by personnel who had come up from the Middle East. We returned to Algiers where we were stuck in a transit camp for 3–4 months. I regard the summer of 1943 as *the* turning point in the war with the invasion of Sicily and Italy. The Luftwaffe, having lost a very large part of its transport fleet, suffered a steep decline in the effectiveness of its day-fighter force and a disastrous decline in its morale.

In January 1944 Sidney returned to England and was stationed at Morecambe where regrouping and preparations began for what later transpired to be the invasion of Normandy. In May he was moved to Chichester and was attached to Combined Operations. On 15 May he arrived at HMS *Vectis*, a shore establishment, at Cowes on the Isle of Wight where he boarded one of three fighter direction tenders cruising up and down the Solent for three weeks. At midday on 5 June he was transferred to the headquarters ship for the Canadian landing on Juno Beach and boarded HMS *Hilary* for Operation Neptune, the assault phase of the invasion of Normandy:

We set sail the evening or late afternoon of 5 June and arrived off the Normandy coast in the early hours of D-Day. I now know that I was the only representative of my branch aboard any of the headquarter ships on D-Day. My main task was to give advice to Naval commanders who had no experience of RAF intelligence. I was there for three weeks. On 1 July I returned to Southampton for a period of leave. On 8 August 1944 I landed in Normandy for a second time with my unit, 383 Wireless Unit, covering the advance of the Canadian 1st Army. We made our way towards Belgium on the northern flank and moved to Lille in France from Radinghem, crossing to Ghent in Belgium, listening for Luftwaffe traffic. We covered shifts for eight hours at a time over 24 hours. We were on course to finally enter Germany, crossing the border near Lingen where we set up camp. Our unit included German or Continental

Jews, ex-refugees who had knowledge of German and English Jews who could speak Yiddish; in all about thirty.

Once back on German soil, Sidney was assigned to air disarmament duties, controlling large units of the German Air Force. Life was more comfortable because they were billeted in buildings rather than tents.

We were in charge of German Luftwaffe POWs. They were kept in their own camps under their own officers minus their rank and insignia. We controlled them and intercepted their telephone wires and listened to their conversations. We discovered from the conversations that they were communicating with other Luftwaffe bases. Our task was also to demilitarise the German Armed Forces. We confiscated their equipment and ammunition. They were then formed into labour groups (*Dienstgruppen*) to carry out work for the British Forces. The war was over. We didn't know what the future held for us, but we knew now that we were set for better things.[17]

*Chapter 7*

# THE ROYAL NAVY

For centuries the Royal Navy has formed an impenetrable defence to protect Britain's coastal borders from invasion. Its long history and traditions encompassed all that it meant to be British and as such it was virtually impossible for non-British subjects to join its ranks. That changed during the Second World War when the Admiralty admitted a small of number of Germans to carry out specialist intelligence tasks. The number of enemy aliens who served in the Royal Navy was a tiny percentage of the 10,000 who volunteered for the British Forces. Precise numbers are difficult to ascertain, with figures varying from twenty to forty. Norman Bentwich in his book *I Understand the Risks* cites around eighty who enlisted in the Royal Navy from 1944. From the profiles below, it is known that some successfully joined earlier than 1944. Although their numbers were relatively small, their role became fundamental in intercepting German military signals as well as the translation of coded German naval orders. Accuracy was of the utmost importance as was speed of translation. The Admiralty was aware that it was difficult for British people who spoke German to understand rapid German codes during the heat of battle, proving even more difficult with provincial accents and intonations. Those who successfully entered the Royal Navy received their basic training at a former Butlins holiday camp at Skegness, requisitioned by the government and renamed HMS *Royal Arthur*. From there they were transferred to Chatham and allocated to various ships or naval bases. In spite of their contribution to Naval intelligence operations, the highest rank that they could attain as enemy aliens was petty officer.

Harry George Stevens (Heinz Georg Steiner) joined the Navy in 1944 and was assigned as an electrical officer to a minesweeper. Petty Officer Vernon, who had worked on radio receivers at Kitchener Camp, was posted to the destroyer HMS *Westminster* and later transferred to HMS *Volunteer* for D-Day action. Afterwards he was engaged in the fight against E-boats with the French destroyer *Le Combatant*, and awarded the Croix de Guerre. Petty Officer Russell, original name Landsberg, was killed in action serving on HMS *Quorn* during the Normandy invasion. From 1944 to 1945 R. Karo was posted to HMS *Cottesmore*, which was involved in thwarting E-boats in the English Channel. Operations with HMS *Cottesmore* also included the Antwerp run, the bombardment of the Normandy coast after D-Day and the assault of Walcheren in November 1944. At the end of the war Karo was assigned to the translation of German documents for the Admiralty.

### WILLIAM ASHLEY HOWARD

William Howard (Horst Adolf Herzberg, b. Berlin 1919) had been under surveillance by the Gestapo and was forced to flee Nazi Germany for England in October 1938. Shortly after the outbreak of war he volunteered for the British Forces. The choice was limited at the time and so he joined the non-combatant Pioneer Corps, training at Kitchener Camp from February to April 1940 with 88 Company. He recalls:

> The training consisted of hours and hours of square bashing. Our sergeant major, a bullnecked Irishman with a ferocious temper, told us that never in his life had he had such a tough assignment in turning us into soldiers. In April 1940 we joined the BEF in France. Work included loading and unloading freight in the docks of Le Havre. In mid-May the Germans swept through Belgium into France. We were briefly armed and told to fight side by side with our British comrades. Three weeks after Dunkirk we were evacuated from St Malo with German gunfire audible in the background. There was great rejoicing when we arrived hale and hearty at

Alexandra Palace and then proceeded to Westward Ho! During the height of the blitz my company was active in the East End of London clearing bomb damage. We were billeted at a school in Mile End Road. Every night the continuous drone of enemy bombers overhead followed by exploding bombs was not conducive to a good night's sleep. But we survived.

In early 1941, 88 Company was stationed in South Wales on camp construction work. It was here that William first heard rumours that the ban on enemy aliens joining fighting units had been lifted. He made a number of attempts to join a special task force unit or an armoured regiment, but ultimately the Royal Navy beckoned. He had transferred to 220 Company of the Pioneer Corps and was stationed in Gloucester when in the autumn of 1943 he responded to a notice requesting volunteers for the Royal Navy, who had to be fluent in English and German. He volunteered with forty-six others from his company, but only two were accepted, and he was one of them. At the end of 1943 he received his call-up papers from the Admiralty and began training in Wimbledon. This included translation exercises and familiarisation of Naval code which was regularly updated by Naval Intelligence. He then received full training at HMS *Royal Arthur*, Skegness and anglicised his name from Horst Adolf Herzberg to William Ashley Howard.

His first assignment was to HMS *Tanatside*, a Hunt class destroyer operating in the English Channel on anti E-boat patrols. He was employed in the interception of enemy radio transmissions at sea, mostly coded information which he was required to translate and pass immediately to the bridge. The VHF radio receiver had a range of approximately 20 miles, within combat range of the enemy, hence the importance of his work in detecting their location quickly. His work was top secret and so he was given the rank of special writer with the codename Headache. This codename seemed particularly appropriate because during his two months aboard HMS *Tanatside* he cannot recall intercepting a single message. He had many a headache wondering what he was doing aboard ship.

His work gained concrete results when he was posted to HMS *Bellona*, which was attached to the Home Fleet at Scapa, engaged in various operations in the Channel and off the coast of north-west France. She also patrolled the Norwegian coast to help prevent German ships coming out of Norway. At this time William was engaged in listening for enemy surface activity within combat range. In April 1944 HMS *Bellona* was allocated to Operation Neptune for the Normandy invasion as a reserve bombing ship in the Western Task Force. The crew waited for the final instructions for D-Day. At the beginning of May 1944 William was instructed to report to Lieutenant Hazelton of Naval Intelligence at Portsmouth. He was then assigned to light cruiser HMS *Bellona* with the Home Fleet. He was directed below deck and deposited his gear. A Royal Marine bugler boy appeared and announced, 'Cap'n wants to see ye, at the double'. William eventually came face to face with Captain Norris, a tall upstanding man who generated authority and respect. He remembers the conversation that day:

'Leading Writer William Howard, Naval Intelligence, reporting for duty, Sir.'

'What do your duties consist of?' he enquired haughtily.

'Intercepting enemy R/T in combat zones, Sir,' I replied.

'So you are fluent in German?'

'Aye aye, Sir.'

'Where did you learn the language?'

'At school, Sir.'

'Which school was that?' he asked.

'Hindenburg Oberrealschule, Sir.'

'Where was that?'

'In Germany, Sir,' I replied.

'But you are British.'

'No, Sir.'

'I do hope the Admiralty knows what it is doing. Dismissed!'

It was an unpropitious beginning. I was somewhat dismayed, but I had to prove my worth. Once every four to five weeks the Admiralty sent me a security envelope marked *Top Secret* containing the latest enemy naval code. This proved to be incredibly accurate, as I myself discovered; a masterpiece produced by the Enigma team at Bletchley Park. At times when I managed to intercept these coded interchanges it brought heights of excitement. I had my moments which helped towards the destruction of the enemy ships off the coast of Norway on the Russian convoy routes.

The events surrounding D-Day remain vivid in William's mind. In his unpublished memoirs he writes:

Some of my shipmates and I were strolling in the streets of Bangor Lock near Belfast when naval patrol Jeeps hollered instructions for all ratings and officers to report back to their units. We knew then that the big day was imminent. We sailed out along the west coast of England on course for Portsmouth. Our Captain, C. Norris, confirmed over the intercom that Operation Overlord was on. He wished us God-speed. The mood on my mess deck seemed carefree. There were signs of enforced *bonhomie*, but this masked an underlying fear and anxiety. My own feelings were fatalistic. I was there. There was no turning back.

Some time during the afternoon of 4 June the captain's voice boomed over the intercom, 'Do you hear there. I have just received a signal from Admiralty that D-Day will have to be put back for at least 24 hours due to prevailing weather conditions.' We waited. Then on 6 June the captain's voice announced that D-Day has come. 'We will be fighting alongside US 4th Division – the US Task Force. May God bless us all.' This turned out to be Omaha Beach where US forces suffered 94% fatalities.

It was getting dark. I stood on the upper deck looking up. The sky was virtually invisible. My view was blocked by hundreds of Allied aircraft moving overhead with a continuous drone. The sight was awesome and at that moment I began to feel confident that victory was in our grasp. At about 2 a.m. we were ordered to our battle stations. Minesweepers were ahead of us – the first to go in. I sat facing my VHF radio set. There was complete silence along the radio waves. At about 4 a.m. the silence was broken by ferocious gun fire. The battlewagons with a range of approx 20 miles sent salvo after salvo towards the enemy defences along the French coastline. The gun fire continued for a considerable length of time. Once the battlewagons stopped the cruisers took over. The whole ship shook with every salvo. Nerves of steel were called for.

I picked up the first American commands on my set as dawn was breaking. The language was plain and strong, with no attempt to send it to us in coded form as laid down by British procedure. I was amazed. Thereafter naval gun fire continued intermittently. Later that morning I managed to leave the plotting office to go to the upper deck and see for myself. There was a hive of activity. I saw huge command ships, the USS *Augusta*, destroyers, channel steamers, white hospital ships and the landing craft. Well over a thousand RAF and US bombers were dropping their loads on enemy coastal defences. After all is said and done, the most onerous gut-wrenching task befell the boys of the infantry. The assault troops faced the full brunt of heavy German gun fire on Omaha Beach. I could see the landing craft bobbing up and down in heavy seas. These men were the real heroes. History was unfolding in front of our eyes.

Our trial came four days later when the Luftwaffe made a determined effort to create a re-run of Pearl Harbor. Whilst damage to shipping in our section was considerable, and we lost many ships, remarkably HMS *Bellona* came through unscathed. We were expecting a direct hit at any time. It felt claustrophobic in the plotting office with bombs dropping all around us. Whilst we were manning our positions Commander Reginald Firth, wearing a heavy duffle coat and binoculars around his neck, opened the hatch and exclaimed loudly, 'Don't worry chaps, I'm here.' It was a confidence which belied belief and yet it took the tension out of a terrifying time.

After a week along the Normandy coast, HMS *Bellona* joined the 10th Cruiser Squadron, Home Fleet for the remainder of the war. In July 1944 she escorted carriers for an air strike on the German battleship *Tirpitz* located off Altenfjord, Norway. She was engaged in numerous successful attacks on enemy ships close to the south-west coast of Norway. William's translation work led to the sinking of a number of enemy ships:

It was on 6 August 1944 that HMS *Bellona* and four destroyers wiped out a German convoy off the Brest peninsula. The radar had picked up that German ships were in the vicinity. The information was passed to me. They were within striking distance. Suddenly I picked up excited German voices over the radio. When translated, I realised that they had given their precise location. I contacted the bridge and passed on the relevant information. Shortly afterwards I heard a hell of a racket and we blew them out of the water. No one on my ship really believed that my work was important until then. After that, I had established my credentials and I received a number of privileges.

During the autumn of 1944 William was approached by the naval commander to teach German to the crew so that when they went ashore they could converse with the local population. He earned 2s 6d a lesson and was thereby able to supplement his basic naval pay. He was asked whether he would teach the officers, to which he readily agreed. He earned their respect and was given no restrictions on going ashore. Towards the end of 1944 and into 1945 HMS *Bellona* was part of the escort of convoys to Russia, destination Kola Bay, frequently having to evade enemy U-boats. Due to his outstanding service in the Navy William was recommended for a commission by his captain, but because of his place of birth it was refused by the Admiralty. William was demobilised with the rank of petty officer at the end of 1945 and received British Nationality on 1 August 1946.

## JULIUS CARLEBACH

Julius Carlebach was one of the few German refugees who refused to change his name on enlistment into the British Forces.[1] He held firmly to the belief that he was born a Carlebach and would return to Germany as such. He was born into a prominent rabbinic family in Hamburg. His grandfather was rabbi of Lübeck and his father, a well-loved orator, was the Chief Rabbi of Hamburg. His maternal grandfather was Julius Preuss, one of the most famous medical historians in Germany. Julius' father declined two offers to bring him out of Germany stating that he would stay with his community. Before his arrest he sheltered many people who were on the run from the Nazis and was under constant Nazi surveillance. He, his wife and four youngest children were deported to Riga in November 1941 where, in appalling conditions, he ministered to the needs of his community in the concentration camp and offered an education to the Jewish children there. Only one son survived the concentration camp.

Julius came to England on the Kindertransport with one of his sisters Judith, lodging for a time with an Orthodox rabbinic family. His memories of those first few years in England were unhappy ones. He worked for a while for a Jewish furrier and then a scrap metal firm. After a period of internment on the Isle of Man, he volunteered for the British Forces and was sent to the Pioneer Corps, first with 248 Company and then 69 Company.[2] When he heard of vacancies in the Royal Navy he applied and was surprised to be accepted because he did not have a British-born father, but the need for German-speakers proved a higher priority. It was a privileged existence as he himself explains:

Whatever there is going, the Royal Navy gets the first pick. I remember for example every ship carries a canteen where you buy things. And on the small ship everybody does their own cooking because you don't have cooks in the kitchen. So I went to the canteen for the first time and asked for a bar of chocolate and the Petty Officer behind the counter said, 'How many?' So I said, 'Eighteen'. So he put out eighteen bars of chocolate!

Julius served on HMS *Blencathra* under Lieutenant-Commander Dickens, the great-grandson of the famous author Charles Dickens. He was assigned the task of regularly updating the intelligence ledgers which were kept for the Navy under lock and key. During the D-Day landings his ship made twenty-five crossings to ferry Americans to Normandy. He also took part in the battle of Antwerp and was on board the first destroyer to enter the port of Rotterdam since the German occupation of the Low Countries. At the end of the war he interviewed Germans in Hamburg, the town of his birth.

## SIDNEY GRAHAM

Sidney Graham was born Szaja Gumpricht to Polish parents but raised and educated in Danzig, West Prussia, now Gdansk, Poland. When he came to England with the Kindertransport in February 1939 he was a German-speaking refugee with Polish nationality who could not speak a word of Polish. This influenced his decision not to join the Polish Army in Britain during the war. He lived with a family in South Tottenham, London until his school was evacuated to Holland in Lincolnshire. After about a year he returned to London during the height of the blitz. The Jewish Refugee Committee found work for him as a market gardener on a farm in Scotland. From there he made several attempts to join the Royal Navy, but was encouraged to join the Polish Forces. However, Sidney did not give up hope of joining the Royal Navy and finally in August 1943 received a letter to attend a medical examination. That was the start of his Navy service.

After training, Sidney was sent to Ayr in Scotland and given the choice of a post as steward or telegraphist. He chose the latter and was sent to HMS *Scotia*, another former Butlins holiday camp shore establishment. There he received specialist instruction for about six months in general coding, Morse code, radios and transmitters. From there he was sent for two weeks to an unnamed stately house in Wimbledon in south London, a deceptively ordinary house with no guards on the gates. Here he was trained in listening into German Morse transmissions, something which was to become his main role in the Royal Navy. He was then sent to Chatham in Kent to await a posting.[3] He recalls:

I was sent back to Scotland, to Greenock, to board the P&O cruise liner *Orontes* which was packed with Army, Navy and Air Force personnel. I was heading for HMS *St Angelo*, the naval base in Malta, the headquarters of the Mediterranean Fleet. We were part of a large convoy which zigzagged its way west towards the Azores and then turned south towards the Bay of Biscay and Gibraltar. I was dropped in Malta with other personnel and the rest of the convoy continued *en route*. After two days in Malta I was sent to a naval base in Augusta, Sicily where I stayed for six months listening to German Morse transmissions which came from German commands on land and at sea. It was an extremely busy time because the German transmissions were continuous at that time. I never knew what the coded messages were. My job was to listen for them and pass the information to the Admiralty. Decades later I discovered that these messages were being sent to Bletchley Park for decoding.

As the land forces moved through Italy and beyond Rome, Admiral Cunningham of the Mediterranean Fleet moved the HQ to the Palace of Caserta which then became the army, navy and air force headquarters. I was moved from Sicily to Caserta where we had a large communications office. I again listened into German Morse transmissions until April 1945. Then one day the warrant officer called me into his office. I did not know that the war was effectively over. He said to me, 'They tell me that you are going to Naples tomorrow to join a party of men.' I was issued with a gun in case it was needed. I went to Naples where the Admiralty was gathering a group of men with transmitters and everything required to set up a wireless office. We were then put on a flight of three Dakotas with all our gear to Trento, the nearest landing strip to Bolzano. We landed and took all the gear in a small convoy of lorries along Lake Garda and into Bolzano in the lower Dolomites. Here we were a group from the Royal Navy in the middle of a mountainous range in Italy with no sea in sight. It was bizarre and yet our brief was critical. We were to set up a wireless office and then go to the German communications centre just outside Bolzano and prevent the retreating Germans from destroying all the information stored there. This included strategically important maps of all their minefields along the Italian coast. We succeeded and sent back the relevant information to our HQ so that the Admiralty could send out the minesweepers. When we arrived at Bolzano the US troops had not yet arrived. Huge crowds of people cheered us and threw flowers. We were the first of the Allies to reach them. There was a lot of lawlessness in the town, so ironically the German soldiers at the communications centre guarded us and our equipment from looting. The 101st Mountain Division of the US forces arrived two days later. An officer drew up in a Jeep pointing a gun and saying, 'Who the hell are you?' I replied, 'we're the Royal Navy. What took you so long?' He was certainly not expecting to find the Navy in the lower Dolomites. The US troops were extremely friendly and for ten weeks we were fed by the US troops. And what food! We had tins of chicken not corned beef, breakfast like we had never seen during the war with plenty of eggs and bacon.

After ten weeks Sidney was sent back to Naples. The war was over and so was his specialist work. He was then sent to Malta and from there to a Naval base in Alexandria, Egypt. He remained there for a year as an ordinary wireless operator. At the end of 1946 he was demobilised with the rank of leading telegraphist. Then began the painful task of tracing his relatives. Sidney's only surviving sister who was then living in Palestine informed him that all the rest of their family had perished in the Holocaust. They were last seen in Lublin and were thought to have been murdered in Treblinka.

*Chapter 8*

# INFANTRY

It is a surprising and little known fact that German-speaking refugees were among the ranks of Britain's most elite infantry regiments. They trained in the Black Watch, the Coldstream Guards, the Gordon Highlanders, and the Argyll and Sutherland Highlanders, to name a few. Because of their knowledge of several European languages, they were often sent ahead of their regiment on reconnaissance patrols behind enemy lines and carried out interrogation of German POWs. The infantry regiments were involved in some of the fiercest fighting in Normandy after D-Day and during the Rhine crossings. They spearheaded major advances, often at night, into enemy territory and usually at a slow pace. Conditions were tough, as portrayed in the official War Diaries. Sleep was in short supply, casualties and fatalities were extremely high, with some regiments losing a substantial number of their commanding and commissioned officers. These crack regiments, with a long and proud tradition of their own, were called upon to lead the main offensive, including the major campaigns into Belgium, Holland and Germany. On occasions after an advance or capture of a village or town, hundreds of POWs would be taken in a short space of time. All had to be interrogated and this required a knowledge of fluent German. This is where the German-speaking enemy aliens were so valuable. The following profiles provide some insight into the dangerous circumstances under which they served, but also the importance of having them in the infantry. They continued to mask their German and Austrian origins from the prisoners who they were interrogating. If they themselves were captured, as with any enemy aliens in the forces, they risked being treated as traitors. Under the circumstances, their sacrifice is all the more exceptional.

ERNEST GOODMAN

Ernest Goodman (Ernst Guttmann) was born on 26 February 1925 in Breslau (now Wroclaw, Poland) in the province of Silesia to Herbert and Rose Guttmann. Hitler's rise to prominence changed his life:

My family felt persecuted in increasing measure as decree followed decree until they were separated, expropriated and marked for 'the Final Solution' unless they could escape . . . I remember, as time went on, the boycott of Jewish stores, Brown Shirts in the streets yelling anti-Jewish slogans, the occasional disappearance of Jews in concentration camps, Hitler Youth lads calling us names in the street on the way to and from school, and an attack on me by a young thug in the street. I saw banners affixed to buildings and masses of swastikas. The banners read, 'The Jews are our Misfortune' and 'Whoever buys from Jews is a Traitor'. Did they mean me, I wondered? Clearly I had become an object of hatred and wondered why, but nobody seemed to have an answer to my question. Parents were unable to keep the truth from their children because the ugly truth surrounded them at all times.[1]

On 21 August 1939 Ernest left for England as part of the Kindertransport, biding farewell to his mother at Breslau station:

I struggled to get my suitcase on the rack above the seat and got off the train again. My mother said we would soon be reunited, not knowing that war would break out within a few days, to be good meanwhile and to enjoy farm work. Several times she asked me whether I had my tickets and passport and the bag with the sandwiches she had made. She fought back tears as she told me to go back into the train to join several other children, all boys, I believe, in the compartment. For a brief moment she disappeared behind a post on the platform where I saw her sobbing while she tried to hide. As the train began to move I left the compartment where children were pushing each other to wave to their parents. I stood at the door and looked out until I could no longer see my mother waving with her handkerchief as she got smaller and smaller and finally disappeared.[2]

Ernest lodged with his aunt and uncle in London before going to a YMCA training centre at Egginton near Derby. From there he was sent to work on various farms around the country for the next couple of years. His experience reflects that of many refugees who found their treatment and conditions on the farms extremely harsh. Meanwhile his mother had succeeded in leaving Germany for Bolivia in South America. At the end of 1942 Ernest and his friend Adolf Neuberger (who later changed his name to Archie Newman) volunteered unsuccessfully for the RAF and were advised to try the Army. In the summer of 1943 they were both called to Northampton where they swore allegiance to King George VI and received the King's Shilling. At the end of 1943 they received orders to report for training at Maryhill Barracks in Glasgow, dubbed 'Merry Hell' by soldiers. Ernest comments:

I enjoyed learning about weapons, taking them apart and reassembling them, to shoot accurately and drill with precision. The psychologist, whom we had to see, and who administered aptitude tests, thought I had a much more mechanical aptitude than I admitted and wondered whether one day I might perhaps wish to join the Tank Corps. But meanwhile, he suggested the infantry where cannon fodder was required urgently. Archie and I chose the Northamptonshire Regiment that had distinguished itself in battle and was the regiment near the county where I last resided. We also hoped that we would train at Talavera Barracks in Northampton, quite near the agricultural hostel at Newport Pagnell that we had left to join the army. And that is exactly what happened. Both of us were posted to Talavera Barracks for a ten-week infantry training period. . . . Two days before our training company's big formal passing out parade prior to specialised training, those of us who were at least 5ft 9in tall, and first-class shots or marksmen, and who thought they would like to try for one of the elite regiments of the Brigade of Guards, were asked to report to the gym. There were about twenty of us, all volunteers, addressed by non-commissioned Brigade of Guards officers who looked at each of us, inspected our records and asked whether we thought we were up to it. A few days later we climbed on a truck and went to Pirbright, the Guards' training camp. It was at this point that I changed my name from Ernst Guttmann to Ernest Goodman.

Pirbright was tough and the six weeks there were the toughest the British Army had to offer. Strict discipline, tough physical training and mental stamina – training, testing and re-testing were the order of the day. The daily 'fast drill' added to the toning of one's concentration. Extra drill for minor disciplinary infractions and competence in the knowledge of weapons and their use all were designed to produce disciplined, tough and alert fighters with initiative and imagination. My friend Archie and I were now proud members of His Majesty's Coldstream Guards. I felt in excellent health and condition, fitter than ever before, and before very long managed the toughest assault course in the British Army with little difficulty. When 'volunteers' were drafted for a street fighting course in Battersea (London), to be billeted in Chelsea Barracks, I was one of those chosen. For two weeks we worked with a platoon of commandos: learned to fall down stairs, to jump out of windows, climb the outside walls of buildings, enter buildings through the roof and to clear the enemy out of houses. We received lectures and demonstrations from NCOs who had been on the St Nazaire raid and from other heroes of many a raid on enemy-held installations and territories. The bombs fell around Chelsea Barracks, but we slept through everything . . . I felt free, independent and thoroughly in love with London and all that it afforded, but was also ready to report for further training and other duties having to do with the invasion of the European continent by the Allied Liberation Armies. I was nineteen, had now left the training battalion and 5th Battalion was being formed. We were to be part of the infantry of the Guards Armoured Division (XXX Corps under the command of General Sir Brian Horrocks). The shield with the ever-open eye was sewn onto our battledress tunics along with the number 5. The Coldstream Guards' flash was ready on our shoulders.[3]

Around D-Day, Ernest carried out highly confidential and sensitive duties near Newhaven, southern England, work which has not yet been declassified.[4] Then came Normandy when he joined his battalion near Caen and they made their way slowly towards Falaise to close the gap and trap the German 7th Army. The Canadians were also there, as were Poles and Americans. One third of the German 7th Army managed to escape leaving behind their equipment and thousands of dead soldiers. Dead horses lay in the streets ready to be carved up for meat by a hungry population. The smell of decay and the sight of the many dead and dying left a lasting impression on a very young soldier. Then came the days of battle, the staunchly defended hedgerows, the mortars, the 88mm guns, digging, moving forward, dodging shells, occasionally clearing the battlefield of the dead and wounded, waiting for artillery to pound the enemy and frequently being attacked by 3in mortars, the massacre of Falaise where 10,000 Germans were killed and 50,000 prisoners taken, the dust, the stench of death. Then there were the mopping-up operations such as Arras where Ernest's battalion was the first British infantry patrol to enter. He and his German-refugee friend Archie Newman were involved with their comrades in street-to-street fighting:

Then came the crossing of the Seine and Somme, followed by the liberation of Brussels and gigantic victory celebrations. North of Brussels there were canals to be captured, possibly with bridges intact. I have vivid memories of the Albert and Escaut canals because we were short of fuel, ammunition and food. Eventually supplies arrived but unfortunately, not for the first or the last time, German assets and fanaticism were underestimated. It was early September and we were to prepare the spearhead operation for the assault on the Rhine and the 'Fatherland'. General Kurt Student's

First Parachute Army was given the task of defending the borders of Germany along a 60-mile line. The fighting was ferocious but that well-equipped defensive line had to be cracked and the fanatical fighters removed one by one. Here we also came up against the Hermann Goering Training Battalion [Hermann Goering Division], hardened and hard-bitten young Nazis. We quickly lost four officers and twenty-two men in the places which remain quite vividly in my memory.

Eventually I sustained a gunshot wound. I had one more narrow escape while making my way out of the front line to a forward field dressing station. We had advanced beyond the German lines and I had to get through the hardened Nazi positions to reach my division or some unit – any unit – of the British Army. As the sun rose on that chilly morning I crawled on my stomach through wet ground for a good part of a mile, whilst listening to German soldiers perhaps only twenty to thirty feet to my right. I was wet and dirty in my blood soaked battle jacket and my socks were drenched inside my boots. From time to time I stopped and stayed perfectly flat on the ground and listened, as I had been taught in all my field craft exercises, hoping not to be spotted, especially as I was not armed. The Germans were in no mood to take prisoners in those last ditch defensive battles and I would have been killed on the spot had I been seen. I was in pain and also needed to relieve myself urgently but obviously could not. Eventually, while lying on the ground listening to the loud pounding of my heart, I no longer heard Germans in the vicinity, stood up slowly and on stiff legs walked, muddy and wet, until approximately an hour later I saw our division's tanks in a wooded area with ever-open eye insignia on their fenders and soon the van with a red cross on the roof and both sides of the vehicle. Having identified myself to the satisfaction of the sentries on duty, a medical officer removed some lead from my arm, surgically cleaned the wound, packed it with sulfa powder, dressed it and then had several of us who had arrived at that dressing station in the past twenty-four hours or so, sent by road to a hospital in Brussels. That hospital was overflowing with wounded Allied and German soldiers. Together with many others I spent the night on a stretcher in the hospital corridor, and next morning a small reconnaissance plane flew several of us to an airfield in Normandy, near the invasion beaches. After three weeks in a tent hospital on the beaches, where I had to swallow many large sulfa tablets for gangrene, I was flown to an American base at Swindon [Membury, Wiltshire] and from there to Bromsgrove near Birmingham to spend another six months in one of the largest military hospitals. Here after a couple of operations and a skin graft, I contracted rheumatic fever and was very close to death for several days.

One night, one of the nurses asked me whether I was at peace and did I want to see a priest who happened to be visiting another ward? I was in great pain and there was no adequate treatment for that malady at the time except opium. I told her that I was ready to die, not unhappy at all, and looked forward to the release from pain. I felt her hand over my clenched fist until the sun rose. She was to have gone off duty at 7:00 the previous night. The night she stayed at my bedside was a strange and wondrous one. It was the fourth night in succession that my temperature rose to 104 degrees Fahrenheit and I felt as though I was soaring through space, slowly dropping through the darkest night, on and on seemingly for hours until there appeared the brightest, whitest light imaginable. I am still unable to describe the brightness of that light. And through all the pain and discomfort of swollen joints, my head throbbing, my mouth and throat dry, all my bones feeling that they were cracking in many places, I smiled as a feeling of well-being came over me and as though her hand had saved me from soaring out of life's orbit. When I was fully awake, the pain was less agonizing and I knew that I had passed the crisis point of my illness. I soon gained strength thanks to that nurse and to the generous employees of a nearby factory. I had no family to visit me and the nurses informed the many regular visitors to sick and injured soldiers from nearby mills and factories that I was alone, very sick, near death and would very much appreciate their visits. From then on the word got around all the factories in and around Birmingham that a very sick and lonely soldier needed them. As a result, people saved some of their meagre rations for me. Just before leaving Bromsgrove, I heard that my old friend Archie Newman had been badly wounded and was paralysed. I was depressed about his condition. Happily he survived, though partly paralysed until his death in 2004.[5]

After Bromsgrove, Ernest was sent to Trentham Park convalescent depot in north Staffordshire where much exercise and sport was the order of the day in preparation for returning to his unit.

We were to be toughened up. Before returning to our units we had to appear before a board of physicians before leaving to be physically re-graded. I was down-graded to a C2, just one grade above discharge because of the wound that scarred my left arm and the rheumatic fever that might, in time, affect my heart. I received a ticket to Pirbright and there was assigned to all kinds of different duties. Later I was asked to join the Regimental Police that kept order and patrolled the camp near a public road for hours to ensure that no theft was committed. It was at Pirbright Camp that I heard of the Allied victory and later I was one of those picked to line the street for the great victory parade in London. During that historic parade, I stood in The Mall, the wide, tree-lined street leading to Buckingham Palace, cap badge and boots polished to high gloss. The great wartime leaders, soldiers and statesmen among them, the British Royal family and the heads of state of many of the Allied countries and of those just liberated, Winston Churchill, his War Cabinet, General Eisenhower, Field Marshal Montgomery and many of the Allied generals and admirals. At that moment particularly, I thought back to the Kindertransport, getting off the ferry in Harwich at the end of August 1939 and all that had happened since that day. That the evil Nazi regime had been destroyed and that I had played a small part in that process was gratifying to me.[6]

Demobilisation was still a long way off. Ernest requested that his company commander transfer him to Westminster Garrison, Wellington Barracks, London. He consented and there Ernest carried out all the garrison's duties, mainly guarding the Bank of England and the palaces. One day he noticed an advertisement calling for German-speakers in service to give German conversation lessons to those soldiers who were to be posted to Germany. This he did, teaching a group of about forty service personnel.[7] During the spring of 1946 he returned briefly to Germany when he escorted some prisoners back to Germany, some of whom were to stand trial for war crimes. He was reunited with his mother in 1950 after the birth of a son. In 1953 he emigrated to the United States with his family where he completed his education and became a professor of political science, later accepting a number of visiting professorships in Germany.

### GUY BISHOP

It was purely by chance that Guy Bishop (Günter Gustav Brüg, born in Gera) was included in one of the last Kindertransports to leave Germany. He arrived in Britain on 5 July 1939 and comments: 'My unexpected inclusion on the Kindertransport was the beginning of a chain of good fortune based almost entirely on extraordinary co-incidences. I had not even been on any waiting list when an aunt, who worked with various Jewish organisations in Berlin, phoned to say that a girl scheduled to leave on the next transport had scarlet fever and that I could take her place if I could be ready in five days.'

Guy landed at Harwich and was sent to a refugee camp at Barham House, Claydon in Suffolk. His new life was generously sponsored by a businessman, Mr Sanderson, who paid all his expenses and boarding school education. During the blitz Guy was evacuated to Bath where a family by the name of Bishop became his surrogate family. He took their surname when he anglicised his name in the army a few years later. He volunteered for military service as soon as he was eligible and in April 1944 joined the army a few days after his eighteenth birthday. He was sent for infantry training and was then transferred to the prestigious Black Watch:[8]

I saw active service from December 1944 on the Continent in the Intelligence Section of the 7th Battalion, The Black Watch, Royal

Highland Regiment, 51st Highland Division. I saw active fighting until armistice. I vividly remember crossing the Rhine in 1944. I was given a special fluorescent scarf to wear for the crossing, now donated to the Imperial War Museum in London. Several hours before the main assault by the 51st Highland Division, I was sent across the Rhine to gather intelligence and to help prepare the landing area and to mark any minefields. I was part of a team of army specialists that included Royal Engineers with mine detectors; heavily armed bodyguards; Royal Corps of Signals operators and Pioneers to mark the perimeters of minefields with broad white tape which I carried on my back on a drum like those used for garden hoses.

As darkness fell, we were floated across the Rhine in an amphibious landing craft, with engines turned off to avoid detection. As soon as we reached the heavily defended opposite riverbank, I jumped off the landing craft and crouched next to the vehicle. When the other soldiers lined up to jump off, they were silhouetted against the Rhine and immediately came under machine gun fire. All the men were killed instantly. After some hours, the Allied artillery barrage blanketed the landing area. After being pinned down for hours by German machine gun fire, I was now trying to survive our relentless softening-up of the German defences. Marooned as I was, I could not explore the landing area to discover the minefields which were a serious hazard. When our troops finally landed, my lonely vigil was over and I returned safely to my unit and started to interrogate German prisoners. A little later, I began to write the sad letters to the next-of-kin of the special task force [of] which only I had survived.[9]

After the armistice, Guy acted as interpreter at several surrender negotiations at brigade and division level. He was then transferred to the Intelligence Corps and was involved with the denazification procedures of the Military Government in the British Zone of Germany until demobilisation in February 1948. He reached the rank of warrant officer, CSM and was reputed to be the youngest to do so.[10]

Guy lost most of his family in the Holocaust. His father Ernest died on 7 December 1938, just five days after being released from

Buchenwald concentration camp. His mother was deported to Lublin on 10 May 1942 and declared dead in 1945. His sister Hannelore survived Auschwitz and Belsen and then emigrated to the United States.

## WOLFGANG LIKWORNIK

Born into an assimilated Viennese Jewish family in 1924, Wolfgang Likwornik escaped Austria sometime after the *Anschluss* to join his aunt and uncle in France. From there he came to Britain in May 1939 and found work as an apprentice printer in Glasgow. In the summer of 1940 he was interned. In December 1943 he enlisted in the British Forces and was sent to Maryhill, near Glasgow for infantry training. His army records show that he may have been under military age when he volunteered because the words 'age limit to be waived as a special case' appear on one of the official forms. On 27 January 1944 Wolfgang was posted to the Black Watch and just a few weeks later transferred to the Gordon Highlanders. His private diary shows that he landed in Normandy on 15 June 1944 and proceeded to join the 1st Battalion of the Gordon Highlanders at their 'resting camp' at Bayeux where they had retired until the next orders for battle.[11] They remained in Bayeux or Ranville for nearly two weeks.

On 1 July Wolfgang moved with the 1st Battalion to Longueville, laying anti-tank minefields between two villages. On 9 July the battalion was sent from there to carry out a raid on a factory compound at Colombelles, 3 miles north-east of Caen, taking three POWs nearby. The following day the Germans heavily bombarded them at Longueville base with artillery and mortar fire. The Gordon Highlanders prepared for a night attack on Colombelles with the 5th and 7th Black Watch. At 1 a.m. on 11 July, they began their assault and finally secured the factory premises and destroyed chimneys being used as observation and sniper posts by the Germans. Coming under heavy mortar attack, they proceeded to clear buildings in Colombelles. They experienced difficulties in clearing the towpath for military vehicles to pass along and had to withdraw to Longueville. Part of the 1st Battalion was then engaged in clearing the south-west corner of Colombelles of enemy presence, during which time some of their officers were wounded. The Germans counter-attacked with the fearsome Tiger tanks and a general withdrawal was ordered under a smoke screen, but they still suffered losses, so the whole battalion was moved back to Ranville.

On 15 July the River Orne was crossed and the Gordons withdrew into reserve near Douvres-la-Delivrande. On 18 July they came under German air attack and were ordered to begin the advance towards Caen. On 22 July two platoons were sent out to dig night positions near the Lisieux road. On 25 July the battalion moved back to Ranville for a period of rest. By 6 August the 1st Battalion had moved to Grentheville preparing to take offensive action to drive the Germans east over the Seine. At this point they were under the command of II Canadian Corps. The battalion moved in trucks and then on foot towards Garcelles Secqueville which they attacked and took after 90 minutes. Casualties were light and 90 POWs were taken. On 10 August Polish forces handed over St Sylvian to the control of the Gordon Highlanders. On 15 August they advanced to Glatigny and dug in for the night. They were attacked by German aircraft, losing three men and suffering twenty casualties. On 16 August Wolfgang's private diary confirms entries in the regimental diary that the battalion moved to Percy-en-Auge. Before they settled for the night, they were ordered into vehicles in pitch darkness to advance towards St Maclou, beyond the River Dives. German forces were taken by surprise and surrendered or fled. Bridges had been blown up and the enemy was entrenched on the other side. The following day the Gordons crossed the Dives at Bretteville where a bridgehead had been established and they headed for the high ground at Ste Marie-aux-Anglais, attacking at 11 a.m. and meeting stiff resistance. On 18 August the Gordon Highlanders sent patrols to the River Vie, ahead of the rest of the men. They came under heavy fire as they tried to cross open countryside opposite Grandchamp. They began to erect a bridge across the Vie, under constant gunfire. The following day at 8 a.m. amid thick fog, the 1st Battalion crossed the river and was engaged in fighting in the apple orchards at the foot of the ridge codenamed Ben Lomond. They suffered losses continuously, especially among the officers. By 22 August the Gordon Highlanders entered Lisieux. Progress was slow because of German resistance. The War Diaries record that the 1st Battalion was now very weak on numbers, but began to clear houses and occupy the Lisieux-Paris road. They had a tough time until reinforcements arrived from a brigade of the 7th Armoured Division (tanks). They dug in at Barneville-sur-Seine a week later, under mortar fire. On 30 August they advanced to Forêt de Mauny and took twenty-one prisoners in the nearby woods. The 5th and 7th Battalions took about 100 POWs at Bardouville, a place recorded in Wolfgang's diary. It is likely that he was sent to these battalions for prisoner interrogation.

On 2 September 1st Battalion covered 70 miles in nine hours. They arrived at Veules-les-Roses at 2.15 p.m. where they held a memorial service, followed by a dance in the village hall. The next target for them was the heavily fortified coastal port of Le Havre. The RAF had already been sent in to soften the target (see Ken Adam's profile in chapter six). On 10/11 September 1st Battalion moved at 3.55 a.m., clearing Fontaine-la-Mallet by 7 a.m, taking 80 POWs. A further 100 prisoners surrendered to other battalions of the Gordons. They prepared to settle for the night but were ordered to advance towards the coast of northern Le Havre. A further 200 POWs were taken, and they met no resistance. Prisoners by this time had amounted to a total of around 600. On 11 September they entered Le Havre. Then followed a two-week period of rest and training when they moved back to Villainville.

At the end of September the 1st, 5th and 7th Battalions crossed into Belgium and received a hearty welcome in Antwerp. They entered Holland on 1 October and held the frontline until relief arrived on the 3rd. There followed two weeks of relative quiet, with patrols being sent out and the occasional shelling from enemy positions. Then they were sent to a divisional leave camp in Eindhoven for twenty-four hours to enjoy the first bath for months and replenish with clean clothing. 1st Battalion carried out a number of raids in the region and took prisoners, with Wolfgang interrogating them; as confirmed in the diary of Lieutenant-Colonel Martin Lindsay.[12] A much larger offensive was impending – to clear the area south of the Maas in anticipation of the crossing. All three battalions (1st, 5th and 7th) were engaged in the battles of the Maas. On 22 October, 1st Battalion rounded up twenty-four German paratroopers at Schijndel. On 23 October, the anniversary of the second battle of El Alamein, the men were given a special ration of rum. On 24 October, 1st Battalion was on the move again to St Michielsgestel, advancing to the Boxtel area the following day. From there patrols were sent out, but no enemy found. During the night the battalion formed up to attack towards Oisterwijk and two days later suffered severe casualties and fatalities, and entered the town on 27 October. Over the following days, they proceeded to Loon op Zand and Sprang. When they moved into 's-Hertogenbosch on 31 October, they began training in assault boats on the Wilhelmina canal. At Nieuwkuik, the battalion sent out rigorous patrols to ensure that there were no Germans south of the Maas. On 6 November they were relieved by troops of the 7th Armoured Division and the Gordons withdrew to Vught. 1st Battalion moved to Heese where they continued assault training in boats and carried out reconnaissance missions. On 14 November they began their attack on the canal, losing twelve men and sustaining twenty-two casualties. Two days later they reached Roggel and advanced with tank support. They crossed the Zig canal on 17 November, supported by the Black Watch. Wolfgang interrogated twenty prisoners who had been captured.[13]

On 25 November, 1st Battalion was driven to Nijmegen and crossed the River Waal bridge to relieve American troops of the 101st Airborne Division who had landed there. They remained in the city until 4 December and enjoyed a period of leave east of 's-Hertogenbosch. From 16 December the Ardennes Offensive was launched when German troops tried to take lost ground and head for Antwerp and Brussels. A month-long battle ensued. On 21 December the Gordons crossed the Maas east of Maastricht, and were at the threshold of the Ardennes. Reconnaissance missions were sent out southwards, with a period of training. Orders came on 7 January and the War Diaries note that the companies 'began to construct sledges of corrugated iron to carry their blankets and greatcoats, as this was to be a cross-country business and all tracks were snow-bound'. They advanced along the slopes of the Ourthe valley, heavily congested with battle traffic, heading for Verdenne. As they crossed the valley, they came under heavy attack. On 10 January they took Ligniéres and linked up with the 6th Airborne Division. Two nights later the temperature was recorded as -35°C. On 13 January the 1st Gordons lost twenty men as they advanced across country towards Nisramont. The Germans were in retreat by this time. Patrols were sent to the River Ourthe and eight prisoners taken.

The Gordons were about to experience their fiercest fighting since Normandy in Operation Veritable, which they prepared for with special training over several days. The purpose was to drive the Germans back over the Rhine. The 1st Battalion moved to Linden on 7 February and received a thorough briefing. That night, RAF bombers carried out a heavy air attack and the following morning the artillery began their bombardment. That same day, 1st Battalion crossed the Maas at Mook, vehicles were kept to a minimum because they were entrenched in mud. On 11 February they had to clear the trenches along the river of Germans. The following day they attacked south of Gennep on the German border, supported by tanks and made a charge, killing thirty Germans. Headquarters was then set up at Heyen. The battalion paid a heavy price for the Gennep-Heyen operations which left four men dead, thirty wounded, and only seventeen effective officers in their ranks. The next objective was Goch where once again they suffered heavy losses with 1st Battalion losing three officers, seven wounded officers and one missing, twenty-one other ranks killed, fifty-nine wounded and forty-eight missing. The total casualties suffered by the 1st Battalion in the battle for the Rhineland alone amounted to 20 officers and 183 other ranks.

During early March, training began for the last major assault – the crossing of the Rhine into Germany. Full military power was assembling with the Gordon Highlanders: air cover, artillery and airborne troops. On 25 March, 1st Battalion with the Black Watch completed the capture of Rees. The 1st Battalion followed the 5th Black Watch in crossing the Rhine in Buffaloes. The next target was Isselburg before the final advance to Emsburen. Villages were cleared en route, often with stiff final resistance from the Germans. On

17 April the 1st Battalion moved into an area east of Wildeshausen where patrols brought in many POWs and deserters. On 20 April Delmenhorst surrendered without a fight. Wolfgang Likwornik served through the whole campaign with the 1st Battalion of the Gordon Highlanders from June 1944 until the end of April 1945. It is known that he was sent behind enemy lines and towards the end of the war also interrogated POWs.

At the end of the war Wolfgang was posted to the British Army of the Rhine (BAOR), and returned to the city of his birth for the first time in six years. He was engaged in translation work for the British High Commissioner in Vienna. During his lifetime Wolfgang barely spoke about his wartime experiences except to hint that he had worked behind enemy lines. He told his son that he was impressed with the courage of his officers who led from the front, armed only with a pistol.[14] In May 1945, in a rare gesture of recognition of his bravery, he was awarded a Certificate of Gallantry from the commanding officer of his battalion. He was demobbed as a corporal in August 1948 and changed his name to Wilfred Lee in the following year.

Peter Lee, Wolfgang's only child, lost three grandparents in the Holocaust. His paternal grandfather Pinkas Likwornik was imprisoned in Gurs camp in France and on 9 March 1943 was transported to the death camp at Majdanek and gassed. His paternal grandmother survived the war in France, came to England for a short time and returned to Vienna in 1949. His maternal grandfather Max Ostermann perished in Auschwitz and his maternal grandmother died in Theresienstadt at the age of forty-three from diabetes through lack of medication and food. After Wolfgang's death in 1974 Peter came across the stainless steel typesetter's ruler which his father had used when he was an apprentice printer:

He had inscribed on it – Wolfgang Likwornik, so this was before he changed his name to Wilfred Lee. When my father died in 1974 my wife and I cleared out the house and so acquired the ruler. A few months ago, I came across the ruler again and when I turned it over to look at the inscription, I found that my father had used a file to obliterate his name and this must have happened after I left home. If he had done this when he changed his name, I could understand it but to do it so late in life, I find quite shocking. This was his last denial of his past, his roots and his culture. When I look at that ruler, I see my childhood – and I stand in the blackness cast by the shadow of the Holocaust.[15]

## RONALD WALTERS

Ronald Walters (Rudolf Walter, born in Breslau) left Germany with the Kindertransport in June 1939. He was one of about 200 young people at the Zionist Youth Training Centre at Whittingehame House, the estate of Lord Balfour, in Scotland. In June 1940 he was interned at Lingfield racecourse for approximately six months before returning to Whittingehame to work on the land and train for a life in Palestine. In 1941 he was sent to Glasgow for war work as a toolmaker. In 1943 he volunteered for the army and on enlistment anglicised his name to Ronald Walters. He received his basic infantry training at Maryhill Barracks, Glasgow and was then posted to the Argyll and Sutherland Highlanders which were stationed at Perth. Having completed his training in Perth, he was then sent on a special course to become a signaller, operating wireless sets and telephone lines. On 6 November 1944 he was sent overseas with the 2nd Battalion Argyll and Sutherland Highlanders and saw fierce frontline fighting in Germany. His regiment suffered heavy casualties. They crossed the Rhine:

Before we crossed, gliders were sent ahead of us. We were stationed on the west bank. The sky was black with gliders – it was very impressive and memorable. We crossed to the east bank. This was after Arnhem. We entered Germany from Holland and were amongst the first to break into Germany. We experienced heavy fighting on the ground. Then we crossed the Elbe, during which time my battalion was shelled. On 29 April 1945, I was wounded at Lauenburg, a laceration of the skull and blinded for a period. I later regained my sight. I was flown back to England and received treatment at the military wing of Friern Barnet hospital in north London. After recuperation in Lancashire, I was invited for an interview in London because translators were needed. I was posted to Presteign, a POW camp in Wales, and promoted to the rank of staff sergeant, assigned to the categorisation of prisoners.

Ronald was demobilised on 2 August 1947. He married a fellow refugee, Ilse Rosenbaum (born in Vienna) who had served with the ATS in Ilfracombe, North Devon.

## LEO HORN

Leo Horn (Leo Schwarz) was born in Berlin in January 1924 to Chaim Baruch Schwarz and Jochweta Schwarz. On 28 October 1938 his father was arrested and taken to Zbonczyn, a border town between Germany and Poland where thousands of Jews were sent to a 'no-mans-land'. Four of his brothers had already emigrated to Palestine between 1932 and 1937, leaving Leo (the youngest) and his sister in Berlin with their mother. Leo's parents ultimately perished in Auschwitz, ironically the town of his father's birth. On 17 January 1939 Leo left Berlin for England with the Kindertransport and on arrival he was among thirteen boys taken by Rabbi Weintrobe to be with families in Swansea, South Wales. His sister joined him in England soon after. Later he joined a *Habonim* Zionist youth group in their hostel in West Hampstead, London. In 1942, while living in the hostel, he first learnt about the terrible fate of Europe's Jews. He had received a number of Red Cross letters from his parents who were in Auschwitz. This knowledge led to his decision to enlist in the British Forces in 1943: 'my parents were in grave danger and I wanted to fight'.[16] Before joining up he worked for a time for Higgs Electric Motors carrying out essential war work. He was eventually granted permission to leave this 'reserved occupation' to enlist in the Army. At the end of 1943 he joined up and trained for three months with the Royal West Kents at Maidstone in Kent, after which he was assigned to the Wiltshire Regiment and changed his name from Leo Schwartz to Leo Horn. One of his closest friends from those training days died in action, something which a veteran finds hard to forget. Leo recalls: 'Whilst training in Maidstone a non-Jewish friend invited me to his home for a meal because I had no family in England. We became really close friends and he was eventually posted with me. He was killed in action in Germany and I survived. It was a difficult task for me to go and visit his parents later.'

Leo landed in France after D-Day with 5th Battalion the Wiltshire Regiment (129th Infantry Brigade). They made their way in a convoy of lorries through France towards Holland. He recalls that period:

Our regiment was stationed in Nijmegen in Holland. It was known that I could speak German and so I was sent out on many of the patrols when we were looking for the location of German troops and mines. We had to mark out the mines so the rest of the regiment could avoid them. In the winter of 1944/45 when the Germans broke temporarily through the American lines, our whole brigade was attached to the Canadians. We were positioned behind the American lines. It was freezing cold. We were placed on a hill and told to dig in and stay in our foxhole. The earth was so frozen that we couldn't dig in. It was impossible. We were waiting for the Germans. It was a very scary time, but the Germans never came because the Americans had hit them hard. We fought two particularly hard battles, once when we tried to break through to Arnhem to help those trapped. We were fighting day and night. The route to Arnhem was along narrow roads with woods on either side. The Germans were well entrenched and we had great difficulty getting through. In the end we couldn't break through to Arnhem in time. We experienced ferocious fighting and heavy casualties.

When we entered Germany we encountered a second round of heavy fighting and resistance. I was wounded when we entered Goch just before the Rhine crossings. We were shelled by artillery and I was wounded in the leg. Five or six of us were grouped together at the time. Others were wounded far worse than me. I managed to stumble to a house which was a temporary first aid centre. I waited on a stretcher to be transferred to hospital. Eventually I was taken by Jeep onto an amphibious vehicle through Holland. At that time the country was partly under water when the dykes were released. I was taken to a Canadian hospital in Belgium where we experienced a pecking order for operations: first the British, then the Canadians, then the Germans. The shrapnel was successfully removed from my leg and after recuperation I was sent back to my regiment. I rejoined the Wiltshire Regiment which had just crossed the Rhine. My boss called me into his office and offered me an apology. He had not known that I was wounded in action and in hospital. No one had told him. He thought that I had deserted. I replied, 'You really thought a thing like that of me?'

The war was nearly over. The Wiltshire Regiment encountered light resistance and fighting near Hanover. Losses were mainly due to their own mistakes with friendly fire. At the end of the war, Leo was required to report to the Interpreters Pool in Brussels.

I was sent to Brussels on an interpreters' course and issued with a motor bike after one day's instruction on how to use it. I was posted to Iserlohn in Westphalia, the Headquarters of the Second British Army. DDOS, the office of the Ordnance Corps, was in Iserlohn. I became the interpreter to the colonel in charge of all the supplies. We could take over anything: factories and equipment. We were interested in a large pipe factory which we requisitioned. Engineers arrived from England to dismantle it and transport it back to England for the technology. With the war over, I received an order to see the major in his office one day. He said, 'I've got a special job for you. It's hush hush. Go and requisition as many skis as you can for the British Army.' I was given lorries and Jeeps with drivers. Skis were made in factories in Bavaria, then in the American zone. I drove into Wuppertal in the British zone where there was a sports shop and asked the German owner to accompany me to Bavaria in the American zone to requisition skis. Our group went to the first factory and impounded whatever skis they had. We went to the next factory, and the next. Nothing. They had been forewarned.

Eventually we went to the burgomeister and explained that the British Army wanted skis and they would be given a special form signed by DDOS and myself promising payment for them. We returned to the factories and sure enough there were plenty of skis for us. What did the British Army want with so many skis? Churchill had intended to invade Russia because the Russians were going into Austria and the Balkan States. He gave the order for the British Army to receive skiing instructions in anticipation of invasion. I was given ski training in France and we were issued with the best quality skis and boots.

Leo was demobilised in December 1948 with the rank of sergeant. After the war he discovered the shocking truth that fifteen members of his father's family and four of his mother's had perished in the death camps. He has no regrets about his role in the British Forces: 'I felt good that I had joined a fighting unit, particularly when I knew what had happened to my parents and family in the Holocaust.'

## Chapter 9

# AIRBORNE FORCES

The paratroops and airborne forces had their fair share of German-speaking refugees in their ranks. On 5 June 1944, just hours before D-Day, the sky was littered with parachutists who would prepare the area for the invading forces. They were heading for the Caen canal to take a strategic bridge, necessary for the Allied advance. Their chances of survival were minimal. Fatalities and casualties were extremely high and many of the first waves of parachutists died before they made it to the ground, killed by German snipers. Others were wounded on landing. Frederick Gordon (Gaensler), who had served in the alien Pioneer Corps and Royal Scots Fusiliers, transferred to the Parachute Regiment and was among the first group of 60 men to be dropped into Normandy on D-Day. Another refugee who parachuted into Normandy then was Viennese-born Paul Hamilton (Paul Herschan):

On a quiet English summer evening we drove through the aerodrome gates [amid the] cheers of the RAF. The human bombs were in high spirits. We drew our parachutes which had been previously fitted and went out to our aircraft which was lined up with many others at the side of the runway. The mechanics were giving it a last minute overhaul. The aircrew arrived and shared our last cup of tea and a cigarette . . . We scrambled forward in the fuselage to take our take-off positions as the four 1,600-hp engines roared to life . . . Owing to the fact that we all had enormous kitbags and lots of other bulky equipment we couldn't sit down. So we just stood there chewing gum and letting the minutes creep by. It was freezing cold but there were beads of perspiration on all the blackened faces. Then at last we got 'twenty minutes to go'. We hooked up, opened the jump door in the floor and all the lights went out. Next we got, 'Action stations!' It was shortly after this that we felt the aircraft rocking violently as flak burst near. One of the engines coughed, spluttered and stopped. We went into a steep dive. 'Red on' and then the 'go'. We followed each other out as fast as possible. I was number 17 and the man in front of me hesitated at the edge so I pushed and jumped on top of him. I had stepped into the slipstream and for an instant I was being knocked about by it. Then the good old brolly opened and I was oscillating gently down.[1]

Having successfully invaded Normandy and over several months slowly pushed their way through France, the Allies faced a daunting strategic task: how to cross the Rhine into Germany. This would not be easy with die-hard German forces entrenched along the river and surrounding areas. Field Marshal Montgomery came up with a strategy – Operation Market Garden, an airborne force to be dropped into enemy territory near Arnhem in Holland in anticipation of the Rhine crossing. On 17 September 1944 the operation began with Luftwaffe bases being hit and German posts near the drop zones heavily attacked. The 21st Independent Parachute Company was the first unit to parachute into the area as pathfinders to prepare for Market Garden. Among them were German and Austrian refugees, many of whom had started out in the Pioneer Corps. Their brief was to drop flares and offer radio guidance for the colossal incoming forces of the 6th Airborne Division. They carried out local reconnaissance missions and interrogated German POWs. The German-speaking contingent was a vital part of that operation. But the campaign was a military disaster for the Allies because they had not anticipated the stiff resistance from die-hard Nazis. The 9th and 10th SS Panzer Divisions regrouped and created a formidable defence against any advance. The ensuing battle of Arnhem led to casualties on a massive scale. British Forces tried to break through to Arnhem to provide relief but were hampered by German troops. They arrived too late and found utter devastation and carnage.

John Hubert Stanleigh (Hans Schwarz, born in 1919) was one of those who served with 21st Independent Parachute Company at Arnhem. Having spent about six weeks in Oranienburg concentration camp north of Berlin, he came to Britain after *Kristallnacht*, enlisted in the Pioneer Corps and then transferred to the paratroopers. Before Arnhem he was involved in preparing the dropping zone ahead of the men and equipment that would be parachuted into the area. He comments: 'We dug in at Oosterbeek and there we witnessed the shooting down of Lancaster bombers by the Germans. We were to defend the town against enemy attack. I was engaged in the cross-examination of POWs.'[2]

Edward Norton (born in Mannheim) was attached to the 6th Airborne Division. His task was to go ahead of the division with the land-borne unit of 6th Airborne and pick up the latest enemy order of battle information. He crossed the Rhine and joined with the airborne gliders:

It was a shocking sight, with all the smashed up gliders. We encountered heavy mortar fire. I walked around the dropping zone and found an abandoned German officer's rucksack. In it, there were details of the whereabouts of petrol, oil and lubricant supplies, and food depots. Within two hours of my discovery, the RAF was able to bomb these sites. We moved on. I acquired a car and it was my job to get information on what was happening to German troops. We were advancing so fast that I was sent out with another man to gather information on German movements. We had to watch out for the 'werewolves' – underground Nazi resistance groups. We were also engaged in collecting weapons from the local people so they couldn't be used against Allied forces.[3]

A number of German and Austrian refugees made the ultimate sacrifice at the Battle of Arnhem, including Privates Walter Landon and Timothy Bleach (Adolf Bleichröder) who was fatally wounded by a German patrol while trying to evacuate British soldiers across the Rhine. Timothy Bleach is buried in the Oosterbeek military cemetery in Holland.[4] Also Walter Lewy-Lingen, the son of a

German high court judge, who served in the 21st Independent Parachute Company. He was killed in the area on 20 September 1944. Lieutenant Rudolph Falck of the 6th Airborne Division was killed on 26 September 1944. They had all started out in the alien Pioneer Corps.

Numerous others from the paratroops and airborne forces were wounded, and not all at Arnhem. They included glider pilots Sergeant Louis Hagen who received the Military Medal and Sergeant Simeon. Also among the wounded were Sergeant Harold Bruce (Schilling); Bobby Shaw (Robert Schlesinger); Eric Stevens (Schubert); Private Descarr (Dossmar); Sergeant Martin Maxwell (Max Meisels); and Lieutenant H. Pollack (Pollak) who was wounded in Italy, then served with the 21st Independent Company before transferring to the SAS. He was also awarded the Military Medal.[5] Private Mane Spiegelglass was awarded the Distinguished Conduct Medal (DCM).[6] Sergeant Martin Lewis (Lewin), who had arrived in Britain with the Kinderstransport and served in the Pioneer Corps, was involved in the invasion of Italy and wounded behind enemy lines. He recovered and was dropped with his company at Arnhem. The bravery and courage of the men of the airborne forces is attested in the following profiles which provide some insight into the perilous situations under which they served.

PAUL HAMILTON

Born into a large prosperous Jewish family in Vienna, Paul Hamilton (Paul Herschan) came to England in 1939 on the Kinderstransport, sponsored by a prominent English psychiatrist Dr Hugh Crichton-Miller. He lodged with the Crichton-Miller family and was educated at Taunton School in Somerset. In 1942 he volunteered for the British Forces and joined the alien Pioneer Corps in Glasgow. He chose his *nom de guerre* when he saw a bus destined for Hamilton.[7] He volunteered for the RAF as a rear gunner, was accepted but advised that it would be a long wait. After a few months he was transferred to the Green Howards in Wakefield and afterwards posted to the Parachute Regiment, joining the newly formed 12th Battalion.

He then retrained as airborne infantry, and underwent parachute training at Ringway near Manchester. He served most of his army career in the 12th Battalion the Parachute Regiment and the 6th Airborne Division.[8] He spent nearly two years from 1942 until 1944 acquiring military experience with army commandos in Scotland and an attachment to the American 101st Airborne Division, and trained to be a sniper. On 5 June 1944 Headquarters Company 12 Para jumped as pathfinders with the primary role of taking the landing zone for the 5th Brigade of the 6th Airborne Division in readiness for D-Day. They were instructed to take a bridge on the Caen canal and hold the flank in the event of a German attack on the British beach landings. Just before the transport planes took off, the battalion chaplain [a Christian] gathered together the Jewish soldiers to reassure them that he had memorised the Jewish prayer for the dead, the *Kaddish*. The risks were high and those who were about to be parachuted into Normandy were well aware of them. Paul was parachuted into France as a pathfinder and wrote about his experiences that fateful day:[9]

I realised that I was being fired on: streams of red and green tracer were going past me. I suddenly observed that I was only about 50 feet off the ground right over a big wood. I prepared for a tree landing and went through just between the trees and had a hard landing on uneven ground. I quickly recovered my kitbag from a tree, slit it open with the dagger. I then cocked the rifle and fixed the bayonet and put on my pack. I instantly realised that we were in the wrong place – next door to a German anti-aircraft battery. So I left the wood on the other side but didn't see or hear any of the others. I was not to see them again. Then I noticed a movement in the hedge. I challenged it, no answer; so I charged. Yes, there was a German standing against a tree. I was faster than he. He died without a sound – a fat man. I continued on my way and found an officer and a few men from my battalion. They were quite lost and I was pleased to lead the way with a sergeant who was a personal friend of mine. My ankle was giving me hell but somehow I kept going. The sergeant and I spotted a post with two Germans in it with an anti-aircraft machine gun. We stalked them and eliminated them, taking each one. There was no noise.

We had covered about 1½ miles fairly well but now we were spotted and came under heavy machine gun fire. We took cover and got into a defensive position. They soon forgot about us as they had to fire at the gliders which were now coming in. The others then continued. I knew that I couldn't make the rendez-vous owing to my sprained ankle. I would do the rest of the journey the next night.

As dawn was breaking 100 Lancasters came over and bombed a 4-gun battery nearby. They used blockbusters and they flattened it out in seven minutes. . . . As soon as it was light I surveyed the position and found that I was in the centre of a German company position. There were three platoons, one on each side. It was a sniper's paradise. So I got to work up and down a hedge. Each time one of them exposed himself I fired. Then I always shifted my position at once – it was very important in my precarious position. They were fooled and started firing wildly in all directions and it made me feel good.

That evening at 9 p.m. I saw a sight I shall never forget. About 400 gliders coming over, wave after wave protected by a big fighter screen. At a given point they were released and went in to land while the glider tugs swung round and turned for home. By this time I had collected a little party (glider pilots). We had a short council of war. . . . We advanced cautiously along hedges and through ditches avoiding trip wires which were all over the place attached to anti-personnel mines. I was keeping on compass course which would get us to the Canal de Caen just to the right of our battalion position next door to the Orne bridges. Everything was OK for about a mile. Up till then we had had plenty of cover. Now we had to cross about 300 yards of open country. We opened out still further and doubled 50 yards at a time and then went down to observe. I was up in front and spotted a slit trench about a hundred yards ahead. We crawled forward within 50 yards and then I went forward while the others gave me cover. I had luck and got within ten yards of it until I got the German challenge, '*Halt! Wer da?*'

I rushed forward and dealt with the single Nazi corporal who was in it. But not before he could yell out 'Kamerad'. This done the others [British] advanced up to me. Then some more Nazis came up from the reserve position. We prepared to put a bayonet charge in, for they don't like that at all. But our friend who was a bad soldier threw a bomb and it slipped out of his shaky hand. I didn't know that it landed behind me or I should have had time to pick it up and throw it on. One of the splinters hit me in the leg. I knew that we didn't have a chance, so I told the others to clear out: they did. I couldn't get up so I rolled into the best cover I could find and started shooting. The Nazis threw more grenades and I was hit again and again. Still I wasn't going to throw my life away without a fight. I managed to pull myself together and threw my own grenades back at them but I don't think they hit anything. However it kept them at a respectable distance. Then I continued firing until my rifle got blown in half. Now I was defenceless so I rolled right into the ditch. Then I got the special morphine syringe which we all carry in the paratroops' outfit and injected it. This was a godsend and within five minutes all pain was gone. I surveyed the situation; both trouser legs had been blown off just above the knee, blood everywhere, on my face, left arm and both legs. So I got my field and shell dressings out, also the spare pair of socks. With these I covered the worst wounds. However I hadn't the strength to do up the safety pins or apply a tourniquet. It was clear to me that I was losing too much blood. I said to myself – *well this is it. You have had it.* The funny thing is that it didn't worry me. A pity to miss one's life. Yes, but still I had achieved a little. My people were avenged. I finished off my water, said a prayer and fell asleep.

I woke up as two Nazis dragged me out of the ditch. 'Himmel, he is still alive. These English!' Too true I thought, never say die! When they lifted me to their pillbox, I passed out.

Paul regained consciousness to hear German soldiers complaining. Their morale was low and they had little enthusiasm for further resistance. They were being bombarded on all sides by mortar from advancing British forces. A short time passed with the sound of Bren and tommy guns as Lord Lovat's British commandos continued their assault on the German post and dragged Paul out. He was taken to a stable where he was given basic medical attention, then loaded onto a Jeep, headed for the coast. He writes:

> The seaborne forces were moving up to the front. Their morale was high and when they saw our red berets, they shouted, 'Good show the paratroops, not arf!' Up the suicide squad.' It made us feel a lot better. They pressed their own precious cigarettes on us with a smile and then staggered onward under their load. Such men cannot fail; more than ever I am convinced that the Tommy is the best soldier on earth.
>
> We spent the night in an evacuation hospital near the beach. The Germans bombed and shelled the place all night. In the morning we were loaded on a DUKW and drove down the beach. What a scene of destruction. Smashed landing craft and vehicles and bodies too. Bulldozers were clearing the place and the Pioneers were busily unloading supplies. The DUKW drove straight into the water. There were ships as far as the eye could see. The navy were firing salvo after salvo at inland targets.

Paul was taken back to England on a damaged naval vessel, three surgeons on board performing emergency operations. That was not the end of his army career. He was determined to return to action and achieve combat fitness again. Eventually Paul rejoined his battalion, promoted to sergeant. On his return he was shocked to find that only sixty men out of the original 600 who jumped were still in the battalion. The re-formed 12 Para then took part in Operation Varsity, the airborne landings for the Rhine crossing. Paul was part of the advance through Germany, including the final dash for the Baltic at Wismar on the coast of Mecklenburg Bay, half-way between Lübeck and Rostock. As a sergeant in the Intelligence Section of the battalion, he commanded a heavily armed Jeep in the spearhead and undertook almost continuous skirmishes with German units. During their rapid advance, Paul was required to translate on a number of occasions.

After the German surrender, Paul was sent with 12 Para to India in readiness for Operation Zipper, the recapture of Malaya and Singapore. The Japanese surrendered a few days before they were due to instigate the operation and so they then spent three months restoring order and guarding Japanese war criminals in Singapore. The battalion was then sent to Indonesia where they were caught up in sporadic fighting with the nationalist independence movement, the remnant of the Japanese puppet government. Thereafter Paul was transferred to the Royal Army Education Corps and spent six months in Ceylon, now Sri Lanka. His last military duties were as a staff sergeant, acting warrant officer, restoring order on the troop ship back to England in late 1947 when there was a semi-mutiny by disgruntled conscripted servicemen.

Paul was immensely proud that he fought for Britain during the war. He had fully expected to die on D-Day and saw his life thereafter as a bonus. He regarded himself as wholly British and formally took British citizenship in 1947. After the war he became a respected architect, whose work included Paddington Maintenance Depot (which won the Concrete Award in 1969), the Alton and Barchester housing estates, the Birmingham Central signal-box, Bletchley signal-box, the early refurbishments at London's Liverpool Street station, and Helen House Children's Hospice.

Two of Paul's relatives also served in the British Forces during the war. His cousin Paul Fried joined a Czech squadron in the RAF as a fighter pilot. Another cousin, Dan Muller, served in the Pioneer Corps and was later captured at the fall of Crete. He spent four years in a German POW camp in Silesia chained to the ankle of another Jewish soldier. The senior British NCOs in the camp reputedly went on hunger strike until the conditions of the Jewish POWs were improved.

## ANTON LUCAS

Anton Lucas (Anton Ignaz Löwenthal) was born in September 1919 in his mother's tiny home village of Popovice in Bohemia, from where his parents returned with him to Vienna. While his Jewishness had never been the subject of discussion, the Nuremberg Laws presented an unexpected problem. He was the product of a mixed marriage and his birth had not been registered with any Jewish community. He was therefore designated a *Mischling I Grades* (1st degree half-caste) and as such could be drafted into the German Army, a rule which applied until 1941. In a diary entry on 4 August 1938, his sister Elsa wrote: 'The military are making things difficult for Toni. They don't want to certify that he is Jewish.' On 9 September 1938, after unbelievable difficulties and hours of queuing at the British Consulate, Anton finally obtained his exit visa. He left home two days later. That day Elsa wrote:

> Anton left an hour ago. . . . He was given a new suit and hat. . . . I acted happy and as if everything was fine and promised myself not to cry . . . then came the worst moment. I had wanted to say good-bye with a smile on my face so as not to make things harder for him. But he had already gone in to see Mee [a term of endearment for Camilla, his youngest sister] and I could hear her throwing up and my bravery just evaporated. And then he came up to me with tears in his eyes, trying awkwardly to smile. As fast as I could, I said to myself 'things will be better for him in London', but as he stood before me with that hat which was much too new, I was filled with only the one thought: now you won't see him for a long, long time. He kissed me without saying a word. We didn't say a single word. I quickly turned away and disappeared into the bedroom where Mee was still howling.

Anton arrived in London on 13 September 1938 and lodged with his father's brother, Arthur, a sculptor from Berlin. Within weeks of arriving in London, Anton, until recently a student at the Kunstgewerbeschule (school of arts and crafts), started work on a portfolio of designs which he then sold to textile manufacturers and design companies. Initially he was successful, but by late summer 1939 the textile industry was cutting back. War was imminent and Anton's most lucrative work with Courtaulds dried up. His precarious financial position and that of his uncle's declining income exploded into a row with his aunt and Anton moved out. Then began the most desolate period of his life. On 18 June 1940 he wrote to Elsa who had by this time escaped Vienna for England:

All Austrians and Germans in Class C are going to be interned. However, I am no longer filled with the horror as I used to be at that thought. Since I don't have any work anyway, I'm just pleased that I shall no longer have to struggle with the day-to-day problems of living. I did go and try to get registered with the Pioneer Corps this morning, but the doors have already been closed.

Just over three weeks later he was interned on the Isle of Man. From there he volunteered for the British Forces and was drafted into the Pioneer Corps, serving with 229 Company.[10] On 25 November 1940 he wrote to Elsa from Didcot near Reading in Berkshire:

On Sunday we had breakfast on an RAF airfield. And lunch. Both meals were the best I had had for 4–6 weeks. . . . We're here to work on a depot. What sort I don't know but it's supposed to be a very large one. Our company has been housed in tin huts, which look like small aeroplane hangars. There are about 16 men in each one. Our beds are iron frames with mattresses which, after a month of sleeping on straw sacks on the ground, seems almost like luxury. But the luxury is forgotten the minute one steps out of the hut. The mud is often ankle deep and at 6.30 in the morning it's a real problem getting back from the wash-room without being covered in dirt all over again. The food here is good because the company has got its own continental cooks . . .

In October 1942 he wrote: '229 Company marched all the twenty-six miles from Bulford to Marlborough . . . our billets here are such a contrast to our old ones as heaven to hell. Of course I have settled down now after the first shock. We are in double bunks, 8 men to one old disused stable. But the food is excellent on the old continental standard again.' This time he wrote in English and it marked the permanent change away from German.

In October 1943 Anton volunteered for the Royal Armoured Corps and on 10 February 1944 was posted to the Airborne Armoured Reconnaissance Regiment (AARR).[11] He landed on 5/6 June 1944 with 6th AARR in a Horsa glider in support of D-Day operations and was in France until September 1944. From 25 December 1944 until 25 February 1945 he took part in 6th AARR holding operations in the Ardennes during the Battle of the Bulge. He returned to England for a short period and then departed once again for action overseas, this time as part of the 6th AARR land fighting element for Operation Varsity, the final push across the Rhine. On 4 April his squadron was ambushed by a battery of twelve 88mm guns. Heavy fighting ensued and the whole squadron was lost through casualties. Anton was wounded and taken prisoner, during which time he was careful to mask his original Austrian identity. He was taken to a German field hospital but treatment of his leg wound was interrupted by a British counter-attack in which he was rescued, but then recaptured by German forces. Gangrene eventually set in and amputation became the only life-saving intervention.

On 16 April 1945 Anton was returned to England for hospitalisation, after which he was able to recuperate and await his prosthesis at Dresden House, the retirement home in Hove where his sisters had come to live in 1939. His sense of humour was still intact but there was a streak of cynicism in his letters of that period, betraying life's bitter experiences. He looked far older than his actual age of twenty-six. In December 1945, after several months of healing and waiting, Anton was fitted with an artificial leg. He remained in England and eventually married a Romanian lady whose entire immediate family was killed when the Romanian refugee ship the *Struma* was sunk by a Russian submarine in the Black Sea in 1942. Anton was discharged from the army in February 1946.

### GIDEON BEHRENDT

Gideon Behrendt (Günter Behrendt) enlisted in the Pioneer Corps before volunteering for the Parachute Regiment in 1943. He was drafted into a 'German' platoon (consisting of men of German origin), changing his name from Günter Behrendt to Gene O'Brian.[12] In his privately published memoirs *The Long Road Home*, he writes:

The discipline was stricter now, the physical demands more strenuous than in our previous unit. While we were used to marching 15 or 20 miles a day, now we started off with a 'comfortable' day march of 45 to 50 miles. At first, the commandos and paratroopers trained in the same camp; later we split up for specific training and studies . . . As time passed we came closer to fulfilling our initial purpose – the start of the Second Front. The African campaign had already tilted the military situation in the Allies' favour. Sicily had been taken and now fighting was taking place in Italy, with daily advances toward the north. Every day we were preparing ourselves for the assault on Northern Europe. . . . Although we never knew for sure when it would happen, the day we had been training for came nearer; the day we would jump into occupied Europe to fight and terminate Hitler's reign. The day of revenge? Oddly enough, the urge for revenge had by then already been replaced by sober and professional considerations just as no good boxer would enter a ring blinded by hatred, but keeping to the rules. By the end of May 1944 we were moved to a closed camp. All leave was cancelled. No one was allowed to leave or enter this huge camp. So we knew: this was it. We had roll-calls several times a day, opportunity to see several movies in as many large tents, but most of the time was occupied playing cards. Many chaplains came to conduct services, amongst them a rabbi who called us for prayers. Most of us went because it was a parade and an order, but then we slipped away like sand between the fingers. We knew that no prayer would help us do what we had to do, no angel from above and no rabbi from down here. Our rabbi must have done his homework overnight because he admitted that his approach the day before had not been a success with us since it seemed that praying was not our favourite pastime. Therefore he had loaded his Jeep with 'goodies' such as chocolate, sweets and cigarettes. He also brought a booklet for each of us called *A Book of Jewish Thoughts*.

About a week or so before D-Day a very special guest came to wish us luck. It was no other than Winston Churchill in person. We received him enthusiastically. He did not stay very long nor make long speeches but I remember him saying that we did not have to read about history 'since you are about to make history!' He ended by stating that 'Had I been younger, I would surely have been amongst you'. Winston received a roaring applause.

Late one night, which happened to be 5 June 1944, we had our last briefing, dressed very carefully, checked and re-checked every item and drove to the landing strip to board our planes. We were ready for the great, historic occasion. I don't think any of us had thoughts about history or heroism on his mind, only pure efficiency. Any mistake could mean personal disaster and harm to the next man. The next man looked as blackened as myself and I could recognise my comrades more by their voices, movements and the form of their bodies than by their looks. Here the long training together paid off. Our night flight did not take overly long, only long enough for a quick eye-shut to remember every part of the training and in particular the last briefing before battle. The rumbling and droning of the engines made talk impossible and who wanted to talk anyway! At certain times in the past I tried to imagine what it would be like on this particular fateful flight. Where would my thoughts be? With my brother Heinz? With my relatives over there? However now that I was up in the air my thoughts were blank. D-Day was about to dawn, my hour of reckoning had come.

The green light was on! I jumped out of the sky amidst thousands, like tiny insects amidst enormous swarms of locusts, not to devour but to liberate Europe from its evil curse, from the occupation of Nazi Germany, to meet the Germans who thought themselves to be the master-race. We landed just before dawn. The operation went according to plan with not much more than the expected opposition. Other units were less lucky and suffered many more casualties especially on the first day. Our strenuous training had paid off and every man knew his job. Now speed was of vital importance. Before sunrise we had already formed into units, ready for action. Our supplies and the lighter equipment was dropped directly by containers called 'cigars' and gliders brought the heavier stuff like field guns, Jeeps, more ammunition and all the other requirements. Our main objective was to cut off enemy reinforcements and supplies on their way to the beach heads, thereby reducing German pressure on our invading land forces who had started the invasion that very morning and were battling to build up their positions from the beach heads. We believed that we would soon be returned to England after completing the task. We soon merged with our land forces but fighting continued. We remained in our positions and even advanced eastwards. As soon as our HQ was established, I went out on routine reconnaissance patrols; most patrols were at night. Patrol work was a full-time job, always followed by a debriefing . . . I was so busy doing my job, the first days under heavy fire, that I did not know what day it was, even less about the general situation.

The heavy fighting continued and the advance was mainly done by armoured units and motorized artillery, with fierce resistance left aside in pockets to be mopped up in due course. I saw many burned and shot-out tanks. Allied as well as German iron monsters, standing only a short distance apart. None of them seemed to have given an inch of ground to the enemy before they fired and destroyed each other . . . The first month or so in France, I slept in the oddest of places, never twice in the same spot, foxhole or ditch, never more than a few hours, sometimes just a fraction of an hour; but I did drink a lot of cider instead of water and at times enjoyed the taste of creamy home-made butter in several farmhouses.[13]

Eventually, Gideon's unit returned to England to replenish its ranks and stock up on supplies and equipment. Gideon was ordered to stay in France and transferred to an armoured division for special reconnaissance duties, attached to the 3rd Battalion the Scots Guards. He began his new duties by commanding a Humber scout-car, an armoured vehicle with a crew of four men: a driver, a gunner, a radio operator and Gideon himself. The car was equipped with canon on the turret and a machine gun next to the driver. They moved eastwards towards Belgium, in constant contact with battalion headquarters. Gideon was called upon to interrogate POWs. German forces were in retreat and Gideon and his team finally entered Belgium in September 1944, heading for the Dutch border. In March he crossed the River Weser under the command of Field Marshal Montgomery, amid heavy air and artillery bombardments. Just before crossing the river, he was promoted to corporal. He writes poignantly about the meaning of the end of the war for him:

> And then the guns went silent. It was all over. Germany's unconditional surrender was signed at the beginning of May. The signing of the surrender is a historical date today, but at that time it seemed entirely unimportant. There may have been jubilant festivities in London, New York and other places, but for me there was no jubilation because by that time I had already seen photos and heard about the atrocities committed at the concentration camps, Bergen-Belsen and others. Our division had passed close by Bergen-Belsen on our way to Lüneburg and I had not known about the existence of such a place. The extent of the horrors the Nazis and their henchmen had perpetrated in other places of Europe, particularly in the East, only came to light at the end of the war. I was as shocked as the rest of the world, but the hurt went deeper into my soul.
>
> Hitler was said to be dead. The Nazis had surrendered. The German people seemed to have accepted their defeat. Large parts of Germany lay in ruins and ashes. I had achieved what I set out to do: I had helped towards the downfall of Hitler and his thugs. I had been one amongst the millions of simple people who fought for justice and freedom.[14]

# Chapter 10

# WOMEN IN THE FORCES

While little has been written about the contribution of German and Austrian refugees to the British Forces during the war, even less has been recorded about the women. Gathering their testimonies has not been an easy task. Those who are still alive are now in their late eighties and early nineties and have not been forthcoming in sharing their experiences; often because they feel that their contribution is not significant. There was no female equivalent to Kitchener Camp. Many of the refugee women who came from Germany and Austria arrived on domestic permits or with the Kindertransport. Some came with their families or already had relatives living in Britain. Those employed as domestics, often in large houses, found that they were poorly treated and suffered exceptionally long working hours with back-breaking physical work. It is estimated that just under 1,000 German and Austrian women volunteered for the forces, most of whom were drafted into the Auxiliary Territorial Service (ATS). Among the continental recruits were highly trained professional women, doctors and professors, who had held high-level positions in Germany before they fled.

Once they had completed their basic training, their duties were usually limited to domestic work, cooking and serving in the officers' mess. Around 100 continental ATS girls spent nearly four years in Ilfracombe, the North Devon town which had seen the training of over 3,000 refugee men for the Pioneer Corps.[1] Their duties in the ATS consisted mainly of cooking and domestic duties for the Royal Army Pay Corps which was stationed there. Dorothea Hirschfeld's story is typical is this respect. The twin sister of Willy Field (see chapter two), she came to England on a domestic permit in June 1939.

During the war she enlisted in the ATS and after training was sent to the army transit camp at Huyton near Liverpool where her duties were initially limited to cooking and serving in the officers' mess. When news came that her brother might be on the ship returning to Liverpool from Australia, where he had spent a year in internment, Dorothea took a chance and went down to the dockside to greet him. She was not disappointed. They had an emotional reunion. After a period of around nine months at Huyton, Dorothea was transferred to a military hospital at Kimnel Hall near Abergelly in North Wales. From Kimnel Hall, she moved to Catterick Camp in Yorkshire and worked as a physical training instructor. In her spare time, she worked in the officers' mess for the Royal Corps of Signals based there.

The profiles in this chapter demonstrate that while the female 'enemy aliens' did their bit for the war, much more use could have been made of their knowledge of German. Their contribution was a modest one, with just a few engaged in exceptional top-secret duties. Their stories would add to an honourable archive if the surviving women could record their contribution for posterity.

ALICE ANSON

Alice Anson (née Alice Gross) volunteered for the forces and was posted with the Women's Auxiliary Air Force (WAAF). She was born in Vienna in September 1924 to Edith and Otto Gross. Her father, director of a bank in Vienna in the 1920s, had served in the Austro-Hungarian Army in the First World War and been decorated for bravery. Her grandfather owned a factory in the city and had a wide circle of friends abroad. Alice left Vienna in October 1938 to stay with some of her grandfather's friends in England. In February 1939 both parents escaped Austria via Czechoslovakia and came to England. Living first in Coulsdon in Surrey, Alice was treated as a member of the host family. She helped with the children and carried out household duties. Nine months later war had broken out and she was billeted with a family in Cricklewood, north London. Eventually she was apprenticed as a dressmaker to Debenham & Freebody in Wigmore Street for nearly four years. Soon after the outbreak of war, the company changed from dressmaking to essential war work, making army uniforms. Alice recalls: 'I made straps for the belts in the army battledress trousers for a year and a half'. She then took up a job with a dressmaker in South Kensington before moving to The White House in Bond Street, a high-class dress and lingerie shop, as a dressmaker.

Alice volunteered for the forces and in March 1943 her call-up papers finally arrived. She was accepted for the WAAF, a rare posting for an Austrian national.

I was sent to Innsworth, Gloucestershire where I was kitted out with my uniform. I learnt marching and drill. After four weeks everyone received their posting. I wanted to be a driver but there were no vacancies so I was assigned as a clerk. I was eventually sent to Madeley in Herefordshire, a training camp for aircrew signals with over 800 men and 100 women. We were billeted in Nissen huts on a WAAF site. I worked in head office, routing people. So for example, if someone failed their exams I completed the paperwork for them to return to unit (RTU). I also organised all the travel warrants. After about eight months I asked to be re-mustered for training as a photographer. I was posted to No. 1 School of Photography at Farnborough, Hants for twelve weeks of training with exams every week. At the end of the training I was graded LACW – leading aircraft woman, a better result than I had dared hoped for. From Farnborough I was posted to RAF Croydon, where we were billeted in private houses. We spent all our nights sleeping in the Morrison shelter because of the bombing raids, and constantly wore steel helmets due to the start of the V1 bombardment, one of the first of which landed in Croydon. From there I was posted to RAF Gatwick. The headquarters building was known as the beehive because it looked like a beehive, now a listed building outside Gatwick airport area. My duties consisted of helping the dentist because there was no photographic section on the base.

From Gatwick, I was posted to HQ Bomber Command at High Wycombe which had an underground photographic section. We were responsible for processing the 5in wide film strips which came in from the bomber target cameras. Once developed and printed, the photographs were taken next door to the photographic interpreters. Sometimes they came back to us for enlargement depending on what the interpreters had seen on the image. On one particular occasion, a photo was sent back to us and a section of it marked about the size of a postage stamp. We were asked to enlarge just that area. We had to photograph it using glass plates in those days and enlarge it to 20in x 16in. This was then sent back to the interpreters and that was how we found where the V1 flying bombs were launched in northern France.

From High Wycombe I was sent to Sturgate, Lincs, again attached to Bomber Command and carrying out printing and developing work. It was here that F24 cameras were attached to the aircraft and their films came back to us for developing.

Alice volunteered for active service overseas and in March 1946 landed at Heliopolis in Egypt. From there she went to RAF Ismailia to carry out photographic duties and then a work station, 107 Maintenance Unit (MU). Later she was posted to RAF Deversoir with three other photographers, working in an office of the warrant officer alongside German POWs who were happy to be doing congenial work and were well looked after. There she was engaged in taking photographs for the military authorities of important events, such as parades, or the funeral of an ATS woman killed by an insurgent bomb.

Alice was demobilised at Christmas 1946 and returned to London. In 1951 she married fellow-refugee Colin Anson, formerly of the commandos. After the war she worked as a society photographer covering social events for *The Tatler*. During her time with the magazine, she took official photographs at the silver wedding anniversary of the then Duke and Duchess of Norfolk, and at a tea given by Mrs Atlee at 10 Downing Street, among other events.

## BRIGITTE EISNER

Brigitte Eisner (née Brigitte Loeser) was recruited by MI6 to work at a top secret propaganda station at Milton Bryan, a tiny Bedfordshire

village just a few miles from the cipher school at Bletchley Park.[2] Born
in Berlin in 1923 to Alfred, a gynaecologist, and Susanne, a fine
violinist, the Nazi rise to power affected the family. Dr Loeser was barred
from practicing in a non-Jewish hospital in Germany and for a time
worked in a Jewish hospital and also attended private patients. In 1934
he and his wife Susanne visited London and found a boarding school,
Hayes Court in Kent, for their elder daughter Renate. With work for
Jewish doctors increasingly impossible in Germany, Dr Loeser emigrated
to England in 1935. He re-studied medicine because the British Medical
Association would not recognise the qualifications of German-refugee
doctors. Having passed his examinations after only nine months, he
arranged for the rest of the family to leave Germany. Brigitte recalls:

> We boarded a ship at Hamburg on its maiden voyage to New York,
> but we disembarked at Southampton where we were met by my
> father. Once in London, we lived in a small service flat in Mayfair
> which had only two rooms and I attended Hayes Boarding School
> in Kent. With the risk of invasion of the Kent coast, I was
> transferred to Kingsley School in Hampstead which later that same
> year was evacuated to Tintagel on the north Cornish coast. During
> 1940, three other refugee girls and I were told to leave the area
> which had become 'restricted' or face internment. We were enemy
> aliens and not permitted to remain in the area. Our head mistress
> appeared before a tribunal to plead our case to remain in Tintagel,
> but this was not granted. We returned to London to sit our final
> exams at Henrietta Barnett School in North London.[3]

In 1941 Brigitte applied to the Royal College of Music and was
accepted. In 1943 she received her call-up papers, but managed to
postpone enlistment in order to finish her studies. In early 1944 she
received a letter asking her to attend an interview at Bush House in
central London, at the same premises as the BBC:

> When I arrived there, I remember lots of barbed wire everywhere.
> I was taken into a room where I waited for several minutes before a
> tall thin man came in. He began to talk to me in fluent German.

I replied in English. We talked a lot and then he asked whether I could do any typing. I replied that I hadn't done any typing for 2-3 years because I was a cellist. He asked me to show him some typing and I refused because I needed to practise first. That was it – I thought that I haven't got the job. Whatever he was going to offer me, was not to be. Then four days later I received a letter with a train ticket. Destination: Bletchley Station. I was instructed to take enough clothes for a fortnight. I travelled by train to Bletchley, where a car was waiting to collect me on my arrival. Another man also alighted at the station and got into the same car. We were driven for around forty-five minutes to a secret location. I did not know where I was going. We arrived at gates and a huge barbed wire fence with guard dogs. I remember that the dogs were barking at us. The man got out, showed a pass and we were allowed to enter the compound.

Brigitte had arrived at Milton Bryan, a complex of red brick buildings surrounded by a 12ft wire steel mesh fence, patrolled by Alsatian dogs and security guards. It was here that MI6 had established a clandestine radio station named Deutsche Kurzwellensender Atlantik transmitting German radio broadcasts. It housed the latest technological equipment and included a direct telephone line to the BBC and Air Ministry. This complex later expanded its work to include another radio station Atlantiksender. Most of the personnel working there were of German nationality, either refugees or prisoners of war. Among them were the anti-Nazi figure Max Braun; the porcelain manufacturer Philip Rosenthal; Dr Otto John, a German resistance leader; Fritz Heine, secretary to the Social Democrat Party in Germany until 1933; and General Werner von Fritsch. The POWs were ex-Luftwaffe, Germany Army and U-Boat personnel. German-speaking refugee women were also drafted into the operations there. The station had a link to the POW camps at Wilton Park and Latimer which were under the auspices of the Political Intelligence Department (PID). When necessary the head of operations at Milton Bryan, Sefton Delmer, requested POWs to be transferred from the Wilton Park and Latimer camps to work at his radio station. It was of paramount importance to ensure the station's credibility, to use reliable and varied information which was obtained in a number of ways:

The primary source was the interrogation of prisoners-of-war who provided up-to-the-minute details of military intelligence, gossip, troop movements and other items that could be used for subversive purposes. Two members of the Milton Bryan staff were employed in reading all the letters written by U-boat POWs as well as the births, marriage and death notices published in German newspapers. With these, they started what became an enormous reference file from which the *Atlantiksender* was able to offer congratulations to a U-boat commander on the birth of a baby or its sympathy to a torpedo mate on the death of his father. Reconnaissance photographs of German cities were taken by Mosquitoes after bombing raids. The developed prints were taken by dispatch-rider to Milton Bryan where photo-interpreters examined them. After comparison with a library of guide-books and large-scale city plans, the *Atlantiksender* was able to announce the names of the streets and the actual numbers of the houses in them that had been destroyed just hours after the event.[4]

The station also used misinformation to feed propaganda to the Nazi war machine. The success of Milton Bryan depended on close cooperation and collaboration between many different military departments and secret headquarters. Brigitte Eisner recalls her first day and the work there:

I was taken to an office at the entrance where lots of questions were asked for identification purposes. I was then driven through the gates where I saw lots of prefabricated buildings. At the end, there was a two-storey brick building. We entered, walked along the corridors to a door where I was instructed to go in and wait. It was an office like any other office. After a few minutes in came a huge man with an open shirt, hairy chest and shorts secured with a tie, big black beard and a twinkling face. The man was Sefton Delmer, the head of the whole outfit. He was British-born but had grown up in Berlin and therefore spoke German with a Berlin accent. I was told about the work on site. I understood later that this was nothing to do with Bletchley Park, although Sefton Delmer was in touch with them from time to time. The work was explained to me: 'We broadcast to Germans for 24 hours a day. We pretend to be a German station, located near the English Channel. We do not say where in our broadcasts. The broadcasts are all in proper German, not refugee-German, so that our work cannot be traced back to refugees who have left Germany. You will be working alongside German POWs.'

I was totally taken aback by the fact that I would be working alongside German POWs. This seemed preposterous, but I stayed. We were told not to make friends with the POWs, but of course many of us did. There were lots of other German refugee girls working at this site. We were billeted in two private houses in the nearby village of Milton Bryan and transported to the main site everyday by bus.

The broadcasting consisted of up-to-date news. There were good maps of Germany posted around the building. When certain towns were bombed by the Allies, it was mentioned by the broadcasting station. Exact street names were given to provide it with authenticity. Most Germans began to listen to this radio station which, unknown to them, was transmitting from Milton Bryan in England. They believed the information which they were hearing to be authentic and from a bone fide German station.

During my time at Milton Bryan, I worked first as a typist. We typed from a machine to give instructions to the German Army via our news broadcasters. Two editors were in the adjacent room. They wrote the script for the news readers and we typed up the script and collated material. It was all highly confidential of course and we were never allowed to ask questions. We had four old fashioned ticker machines in our room (tele-printers) and the information was printed out from these. We worked on the ground floor of the building. The first floor was out-of-bounds to us and was used for other intelligence activities. We worked in shifts, some of us filed material, some of us typed. The place was simply known as 'M.B.'

(Milton Bryan). We wore civilian clothes, working for a fortnight at a time with two days off when we were permitted to go home. For me, that meant returning to London. The irony of it all became clear when I returned home on leave. I was not allowed to talk about my work, even to my parents. I discovered that every night they were listening to this radio station transmitting from Milton Bryan and thinking it was a bone fide German station!

Then I had a fall and broke my arm. I was unable to type and so I was assigned as an assistant at Milton Bryan to a German non-Jewish lady who had married an Englishman. There was so much material coming in that she needed assistance. I learned something of the filing system, but also much more about the work because I had open access to all the files. Editors would often ring through and ask me, 'have you anything on such and such . . .' I had a pretty clear idea of the confidential material.

Brigitte worked at Milton Bryan until 1945. Once the British Forces had broken through the zone from where the station was supposed to be broadcasting, they had to cease the programmes. Brigitte returned to London and was assigned work in the newsroom at Bush House until her official release papers came through in December 1945. After the war, she became a professional musician. She concludes:

At the start of the war, I was an enemy alien. Ironically at the end of the war, I received a letter from Anthony Eden thanking me for my war work. Being at Milton Bryan was one of the most interesting and exciting times of my life.

### SUSAN LUSTIG

Susan Lustig (née Susanne Cohn, born in Breslau 1921) emigrated to England on a domestic permit in July 1939. She obtained work in north London, but on the day war broke out her employer dismissed her as she did not want a 'German' living in her house. Friends of Susan's parents, an émigré dental surgeon, employed her as a domestic and trained her as a chair assistant in his practice. In 1943 she was called up for war work and chose to join the ATS, in preference to working in a factory. Her first posting was to Fenham Barracks in Newcastle upon Tyne to train in a continental platoon. After initial training, she was detailed as a dental orderly. She recalls the early days in Fenham Barracks:

> We did our basic training and slept in a huge barracks on hard wooden beds, twenty-six of us to a room. We were told we had to polish the floor underneath the beds which I thought was quite unnecessary. When I refused, I was put on a charge which meant that I was sent to see a senior officer who decided what punishment I deserved. I had to wash the dishes in the sergeants' mess for a week. I was also put on a charge for not standing at ease when we were waiting on the parade ground for a visit by the Princess Royal [Princess Mary]. I wasn't very good at obeying rules. Even so, I loved the army. When I started as a dental orderly (I was working for three dentists), I discovered that I was expected to administer the gas anaesthetic which was something I had never done before. The first time that I did it, the patient turned blue because he was allergic to the gas. Fortunately the poor man recovered quickly. Later it was decided that there was no 'establishment' for female dental orderlies, so I had to become a medical orderly and was sent to a military hospital in York for four weeks training.[5]

Having completed that, she was posted to Nottingham for three months, where her main job was delousing ATS girls. While on leave in London, she met another ex-refugee ATS girl whom she knew from Breslau. Her acquaintance was a sergeant and attached to the Intelligence Corps, and she put Susan's name forward to transfer to her unit. In December 1943 Susan was invited for an interview at the War Office for selection and tests. About four weeks later she was posted to a POW camp at Latimer House, formerly a stately home, at Chalfont and Latimer in Buckinghamshire. Upon arrival she was promoted to the rank of sergeant:

The camp at Chalfont and Latimer was top secret because POWs from all three services who were considered to have important information were held there for interrogation. It was all very exciting. I had a railway ticket to Chalfont and Latimer Station and was told that I would be met there. A very smart naval officer was waiting to meet me in a Jeep, whose driver said to me, 'I bet you a packet of cigarettes that you'll be a sergeant by tonight.' I didn't believe him, but it turned out that he was correct because everyone there had at least the rank of sergeant.

I was allocated to a typing pool, but as my typing was rather poor, I was soon transferred to another department where I had to check the documents of the POWs in the camp. One day I came across the papers of my former English teacher from Breslau who was a POW. I knew that he wasn't a Nazi, so I put in a good word for him and he was transferred quite quickly. In March 1944, I was moved to the sister-camp at Wilton Park near Beaconsfield where I was engaged in similar work. It was here that I met my future husband Fritz Lustig, who came from Berlin and was a sergeant major in the Intelligence Corps.

Susan left the army immediately at the end of the war because married women were given preference for demobilisation. She had attained the rank of staff quartermaster sergeant, equivalent to sergeant major in the army. Her first civilian job was with the Preparatory Commission of the United Nations in London, where she worked as supervisor in the duplicating section.

### ANNA HARVEY

Anna Harvey (née Anna Simoni) joined the WAAF at Innsworth, Gloucestershire in 1943. She trained initially at Wilmslow and was then posted to No. 5 School of Technical Training at RAF Locking near Weston-super-Mare in Somerset where she trained as a flight mechanic (air frames). From there, she was posted to Flying Training Command at South Cerney near Cirencester, and later to Southrop in the Cotswolds and Moreton Valence near Gloucester. She worked on twin-engine Oxfords. Whilse stationed at South Cerney, she worked in a hangar and was distressed by the practice of pouring aviation spirit on the floor to whiten it:

It was a waste of a commodity urgently needed for more important purposes and for which British seamen risked their lives. One day I took the matter so much to heart that I sat on my toolbox and cried. The corporal noticed, put his arm around me and asked me what was the matter. I explained that every day the newspapers reported ships being sunk and men burnt whilst bringing us the petrol we needed. The war in the Atlantic was horrendous, and at South Cerney, the stuff was poured all over the hangar floors. He told me that nothing could be done about the aviation spirit because 'orders are orders' and that if I was unhappy I should apply for a transfer to a satellite station which was just opened to women. That happened and I was transferred to South Cerney satellite station at Southrop in Gloucestershire where I was much happier. Instead of giving the aircraft a 'main service', I was now giving them an 'inter-flight service'. We also had privileges not previously granted to us, such as the use of bicycles for work and leisure. And we were permitted to wear civilian clothes when off duty. I was one of the few WAAFs who succeeded in 'taking to the air' occasionally. During my time as a flight mechanic I had the opportunity to take over the controls from time-to-time, under the supervision of an instructor. Our pupil pilots learned circuits and bumps, going round and round and take-offs and landings. Our instructor pilots, against the rules, allowed the flight mechanics to take over from the pupils when they thought it was safe to do so, which was fantastic.[6]

During the winter of 1944/45, Anna was selected as an instructor in the Educational and Vocational Training (EVT) programme. When a vacancy arose, she worked as a language teacher with the rank of acting sergeant in a number of bases, including back at South Cerney, then Watchfield (Oxford) and Beaulieu Heath (New Forest). She was expected to travel between RAF bases by train but the journey between Watchfield and Beaulieu was especially complicated. When the young flight crews in Watchfield heard of her predicament, they persuaded their commanding officer to give permission for Anna to be flown to Beaulieu in one of their smaller planes. Anna was demobilised in May 1946.

*Chapter 11*

# WAR CRIMES INVESTIGATIONS, INTELLIGENCE AND MILITARY GOVERNMENT

On 8 May 1945 the war in Europe was over, but the peace had yet to be won. A huge task faced the Allies in the denazification and reconstruction of Germany and the countries occupied by the Nazi regime. It was an undertaking which in hindsight could not have taken place without the German-speaking refugees who were drafted into every aspect of postwar work. The vast majority of the king's most loyal enemy aliens returned to the countries of their birth to carry out their final duties in British uniform, many setting foot on native soil for the first time in at least five years. At the Yalta Conference in February 1945 the Allied leaders met to set the agenda for postwar Germany, which included dividing the country into four zones administered by the United States, Britain, the USSR and France. An Allied Control Commission was set up in Berlin, and Austria was also divided into four zones. The German-speaking refugees were transferred in their thousands from the fighting regiments and the remaining alien Pioneer companies to the British Control Commission and British Army of the Rhine (BAOR). They were assigned to interrogation of POWs, engaged in the hunt for Nazi war criminals, gathering evidence for the War Crimes Investigation Unit, translation at the War Crimes Tribunals, and overseeing military government. Their fluency in German meant that they were an inestimable asset to the Allied Forces, not available in such circumstances at any other time.

Those with a legal background were given central roles within military government and the translation of new laws. Major Norvill, an Austrian lawyer who served with the Royal Armoured Corps, became an officer in military government at Lübeck. Major Lasky (Laszky) worked in the legal division of the British-Austrian Legal Unit and also the Legal Division of British Control Commission in Germany. Since the *Anschluss* of March 1938 Austria had been integrated into Germany (the Ostmark) and governed by German Nazi law. One of the key processes in the denazification of Austria as a newly 'liberated' country was to reinstate a system of democratic Austrian laws. This was not a matter of merely passing pre-1938 statutes. Each new law had to be approved in special sessions by the four occupying powers (Britain, the USSR, the United States and France). This required extensive and precise translations of the texts and drafts. Lasky was aided by five ex-Austrian refugees, who included Eric Sanders and Theo Neumann, both formerly of SOE.[1] They were recruited into the British Austrian Legal Unit (BALU) in Vienna to translate the laws into English. Translations were important and could take many hours. Eric recalls:

> When we had finished translating sections of the law, we would all meet at Lasky's flat in Vienna and read the translation word for word, sentence by sentence. Lasky would then take the translated laws to the next regular session of the four Elements where it was discussed and a final text eventually approved.[2]

Many Germans and Austrians in the British Forces were sent back to their place of birth to oversee key administrative duties. This was the case with Peter Perry (Peter Pinschewer) who returned to the Charlottenburg district of Berlin in charge of the redistribution of food as Food and Transport Officer.[3] For about a year Rolf Holden (Rolf Hirtz, born in Frankfurt-am-Main) was stationed at the printing works in Lübeck managing the staff and organising the resumption of printing. It was here that all the printing was carried out for BAOR and the Control Commission: forms, questionnaires, daily information sheets for the local population, and administrative forms for the

German authorities. Local Germans were employed on the staff, all of whom had to be screened as part of the denazification process, a job given to Rolf because of his fluency in the language. Stephen Freud also returned to Germany in British Army uniform to carry out duties under the denazification process. The eldest son of the eminent Berlin-émigré architect Ernst Freud, and elder brother of the artist Lucian Freud, he first joined the Rifle Brigade and then served in a self-propelled gun field regiment with the Royal Artillery in Italy from 1944. At the end of the war he was posted to the German Personnel Research Bureau, running examinations for important German civilians to ascertain whether they were suitable to work in the newly democratic state of Germany. He was demobilised with the rank of captain in 1946.[4] Little did John Langford (Erwin Lehmann, born in East Prussia) realise that after transferring from the alien Pioneer Corps to the 6th Airborne Division, he would return to Germany to guard Prime Ministers Winston Churchill and Clement Atlee at the Potsdam Conference in July 1945.[5] Edward Norton (born in Mannheim) was based at Babelsbergh in charge of security for Churchill and Atlee at Potsdam. The Mobile Intelligence Unit of the Field Security Service was headed by Major Calman and Major Kendal.

Others were engaged in the interrogation of POWs in camps across England and Germany. In October 1945 Viennese-born Eric Sanders (Ignaz Schwarz) returned from duties with SOE in Italy and became an interpreter at a camp for German POWs at Norton Fitzwarren, near Taunton in the south-west of England. The POWs, graded according to their Nazi sympathies, were all considered pro-Nazis and active Nazis. Eric comments:

I made a report to the PID (Political Intelligence Department) which questioned the grading of the POWs in the camp. The report caused a big fuss because it was thought it couldn't possibly be true. About 2–3 weeks later PID officers arrived and concluded that my assessment was in fact accurate. Subsequently the prisoners were all re-graded. It was an interesting time because I was also involved in re-educating the POWs in democratic ideals. Studying economics

I was able to talk on this subject. I was instrumental in starting various discussion and interest groups run by committees. When the company moved to a camp outside Evesham, the process began to separate the real Nazis from the others who were being prepared to run the camp by themselves until their repatriation.

About 80 British soldiers (originally refugees from Germany and Austria) had been transferred to the Intelligence Corps and were now serving in a specialist unit called CSDIC (Combined Services Detailed Interrogation Centre), a unit where the British intelligence officers and German POWs were from all three services of army, navy and air force. CSDIC consisted of two POW camps, one at Latimer House near Little Chalfont and Latimer in Buckinghamshire and the other at Wilton Park, east of Beaconsfield. Fritz Lustig, originally of the Pioneer Corps orchestra and then Southern Command, transferred to CSDIC in 1943 and worked at both camps. He was required to sign the Official Secrets Act because of the highly confidential nature of the work:

When I arrived at CSDIC, most of our prisoners were either shot-down Luftwaffe pilots or members of U-boat crews who had been rescued when their boat was sunk. There might have been a few army prisoners captured in North Africa, but a major influx of those only started after D-Day. The POWs cells were bugged. A microphone was concealed in the light fitting, and we had to listen to their conversations in the hope that they would discuss something that might interest our side. There were always two prisoners to a cell, as far as possible from different services or units in order to encourage them to talk to each other about their experiences. We had to identify which was which by their voices and accents. We operated in teams of about six, each team with a separate room and an officer in charge. We sat at tables which were fitted with record-cutting equipment – this was before electronic tapes were invented – and had a kind of old-fashioned telephone switchboard facing us, where we put plugs into numbered sockets in order to listen to the POWs through our headphones. Each operator usually had to monitor two or three cells, switching from one to the other to see whether something interesting was being discussed. As soon as we heard something which we thought might be valuable, we pushed a switch to start a turntable revolving, and pulled a small lever to lower the recording-head onto the record. We had to keep a log, noting what our 'charges' were doing or talking about, and indicating at what times and about what subjects we had recorded their conversations. As soon as a record had been cut, somebody else had to take over monitoring, and the operator went to a different room to transcribe what he had just recorded. Not every word that was spoken, of course, but only those bits of the conversation which were important. The transcript was then checked and edited by a more senior operator for any errors, omissions or superfluous material, and finally typed in a different section for distribution to various intelligence centres and ministries.

We worked in two shifts, early and late. The early shift started at 9 a.m. and ended at 4 p.m. The late shift started at 4 p.m. and finished whenever the prisoners had stopped talking or went to sleep. All prisoners were interrogated several times, always by officers not working in our monitoring section. We never dealt with any of them face-to-face. Their reaction to interrogation was often particularly fruitful. They would tell their cell-mate what they had been asked about, what they had managed to conceal from the interrogating officer and how much we (the British) already knew.[6]

## RADIO HAMBURG AND THE GERMAN NEWSPAPERS

One of the most important tools for the Allies in reconstructing Germany was to gain control of the media. A key task was to take radio stations and newspaper premises and begin transmitting news to the German public. Walter Eberstadt, who was wounded in action serving on the frontline in France with the Ox and Bucks Light Infantry (attached to the Worcestershire Regiment), was one of the ex-refugees assigned to Radio Hamburg. He writes:

We were 'Radio Hamburg', the military government station. We were on air a few hours each day. Our main job was to relay military government announcements, regulations and some news. We advised our listeners about food rationing, monetary regulations, curfew hours, anything to do with daily living under British military rule. We were the main information link between the British military, German civilians, the disintegrating German Army, released prisoners of war, and displaced persons from what had been German-occupied Europe. We took our first tentative steps to re-educate the Germans with programmes about their Nazi past. To attract an audience we broadcast lists of missing persons, which reunited many families.'[7]

Berlin-born Geoffrey Perry (Horst Pinschewer) was part of T Force the brief of which had been to take Radio Hamburg, which his unit successfully achieved in early May 1945. He read the first Allied broadcast from the same microphone which two days earlier Britain's most wanted traitor and Fascist William Joyce (aka Lord Haw-Haw) had used in his last message to the German people. Joyce had gone into hiding, but at the end of May a chance meeting in a forest north of Hamburg led to his arrest by Geoffrey and a colleague:

On 28 May, Bertie Lickorish and I ventured out into the nearby forest to collect some firewood for the cooking stove. There we saw a man walking around on his own looking a bit lost. Lickorish and I did not take any notice of him and busied ourselves picking up bits of firewood and putting them in the truck. The man approached us and asked: 'Would you like me to show you where there is some more firewood?' We said yes. Then Bertie said to me: 'That sounded remarkably like Lord Haw-Haw.' Having engaged the man in conversation, he began talking about deciduous trees. He spoke fluent English and clearly was very knowledgeable, but his voice sounded very much like that of the unmistakable William Joyce. So I said: 'You wouldn't be William Joyce by any chance, would you?' At that, his hand plunged into his pocket.

The war was only just over, and with all the armed Germans in Flensburg, I was very suspicious. Apart from the official army-issue revolver I was carrying, I had in my pocket the Walther police pistol I had confiscated in Hamburg. When Joyce went for his pocket, I pulled it out and fired. I aimed low for his pocket – or rather, his hand – and hit him in his buttocks. He clutched his backside and fell to the ground. As he lay on the ground, I asked him again: 'Are you William Joyce?'

He said, 'No, I'm Fritz Hansen.'

Suddenly I thought I was in a great deal of trouble. I was in a town I should not be in and had just wounded a German civilian. I imagined he was unarmed and simply reaching for his papers. I had visions of being court-martialled. By this time, Lickorish had approached the scene. While I stood over the wounded man, Lickorish rifled through his pockets and pulled out a German *wehrpass*, which is like a military passport, in the name of Hansen. He also had one in the name of William Joyce, which came as something of a relief.

I tried to apply an army-issue bandage pad, but the bullet had ripped through both cheeks of Joyce's buttocks, creating four holes in all. The field dressing simply had not been designed for such unlikely multiple wounds. As a German in British uniform, the irony of having captured this notorious 'traitor' had not escaped me. It was one of life's coincidences.[8]

Joyce was found guilty of treason and hanged on 3 January 1946.

## LIBERATING THE CONCENTRATION CAMPS

On 15 April 1945 British troops liberated Bergen-Belsen concentration camp. Nothing prepared them for the unspeakable horror. Army chaplains the Revds Leslie Hardman and Isaac Levy, both British-born Jews, began ministering to the needs of the desperately ill survivors and burying the thousands of emaciated bodies of the victims murdered in the gas chambers and those who had died of starvation. Garry Rogers (Gunter Baumgart), of the Royal Armoured Corps, was among those who entered Belsen:

We were advancing towards a town, Soltau, via the small German town of Bergen. We had come across mass graves before and we were not immune to the horrors of the Third Reich. The concentration camp of Bergen-Belsen opened our eyes to the real horror and atrocities Hitler and his henchmen had perpetrated. Much has been written about the horrors of the death camps and the Holocaust. At the time nothing was known to us while fighting was still in progress, although we had come across mass graves and other indications. Nothing could have prepared us for what we were about to see. Most of the guards had fled and all we found were the inmates in a condition which defies description. These are memories I have blocked out all my life. My own feelings at the time were that of shock rather than drawing any conclusions. Hate for the perpetrators, pity for the survivors, horror for the inhumanity of men, disbelief for the enormity of the crime, love for those I lost in the Holocaust. We tried to feed and comfort the inmates, but then had to pass them on to the medical staff and proceed with the war. Did it change me? Of course it did, and will always be a part of me.[9]

Herbert Landsberg, who served in Pioneer Corps Companies 93, 220 and 249, was also among the enemy aliens in British uniform who entered Belsen just days after its liberation. He came unexpectedly face-to-face with the past:

We arrived at Belsen and could not believe our eyes when we saw the survivors in the camp. They were walking skeletons, having been systematically starved by the SS guarding them. We had orders to find the medical officer who had performed operations in the camp on Jewish inmates without anaesthetic to find out how much pain a human body could withstand. By the time we arrived, he was hiding but we eventually found him. When I saw him, his face looked familiar. It suddenly came to me where we had met before. It was in 1931 when I was reading Law at Leipzig University. He was the medical officer there and I had to see him when I was suffering from an inflammation of the kidneys. He had looked at my papers then and shouted, 'Go away, you bloody Jew boy! All you suffer from is a disease typical of your race.' Here in Belsen, he stood before us, wanted for war crimes of unbelievable seriousness. At his trial in Nuremberg he was sentenced to death although he claimed what he did was in the interest of science.[10]

Landsberg was posted to the Psychological Warfare Branch of Montgomery's 21st Army Group, with the rank of staff sergeant. He was attached to the Guard's Armoured Division in a special mobile unit, travelling in an armoured scout-car equipped with sensitive listening equipment, gun and eight loud speakers. His work involved the interrogation of German military personnel, including a German general on Lüneburg Heath in the summer of 1945, when the German Army in the West surrendered to General Montgomery's 21st Army Group.

Rolf Holden (Rolf Hirtz), survivor of Buchenwald before coming to England, was among the first liberators into Belsen:

I was amongst the first British troops to enter Belsen, and from that moment, I was aware of exactly what had been going on in Germany since my departure. I had seen some horrible things in Buchenwald, but what I saw there . . . I'll never forget the first night of the liberation of Belsen. Six of us sharing a tent and we all had different religions. We talked about our beliefs all night. After what we had seen that day, we all asked the same question: how could God tolerate such things? We came to the same conclusion: that there can't be such a thing as God. From that moment, I was disillusioned with religion. Belsen profoundly affected every soldier who was there. We all had one priority – to try to alleviate the suffering of those who were still alive. For most of them, there was no hope. We caught many of the SS who ran the camp. Some of them dressed themselves as inmates, but they were too well-nourished. It became an important matter to us to bring these people to justice.[11]

### THE SEARCH FOR SURVIVORS

Among the utter devastation and knowledge that much of central-European Jewry had been murdered in Hitler's Final Solution, the German and Austrian contingent in the British Forces began the painful and uncertain search for surviving relatives. All too often confirmation came that their families and friends had perished in the Holocaust. George Rosney (Georg Jakob Rosenfeld) travelled over 2,000 miles from Kiel on the Baltic coast to Theresienstadt (Terezin, north of Prague in the Czech Republic) in search of his parents. Born in Karlsruhe, Germany in February 1921, he came to England in January 1939. After internment in 1940 he enlisted in the Pioneer Corps in Ilfracombe and served with 249 Company. Between 28 February and 30 September 1942, he was transferred to the Royal Army Service Corps (RASC) and then REME from 1 October 1942 until 27 October 1946. During 1944 and 1945 he was seconded to the Royal Horse Artillery (RHA) and trained in bayonet warfare at Buntingford in East Hertfordshire. On D-Day+8 he embarked at Newhaven and received his instructions ahead of landing in Normandy.

George served with the RHA through France, Belgium, Holland and into Germany where his primary duties involved the repair of vehicles damaged in the fighting. In early May 1945 he was granted permission to travel to Theresienstadt concentration camp, near Prague, in search of his parents whom he knew to be in the camp. By that time it was in the Russian Zone and he was given a motorbike, a Union Jack, revolver, map and an official letter in Russian requesting assistance. On 21 May he arrived at Theresienstadt where he was accommodated by the Russian commandant. The full nature of the camp was unknown to the outside world at that time, because it masqueraded as a town/haven for Jews. George travelled there in the full belief that he would be reunited with his parents. He was carrying food and supplies for them. In the camp he met Albert Steiner, his father's business partner, who had survived the war. Steiner broke the news to him that his parents had been sent east to Auschwitz. That terrible moment of truth was so unexpected and traumatic that it affected George for the rest of his life. Steiner kept a secret diary while in Theresienstadt in which he recorded George's visit:

Entry for May 21, 1945, Whit Monday:
Cleaning the park 7–11am. Afternoon off.
5pm: Georg Rosenfeld arrived here by motorbike as an English soldier from Kiel to look for (and meet) his parents. Great disappointment that he didn't find them (here). Together with him in the evening, tins of food, jam, rice, meat, bread, tea, coffee, biscuits and cigarettes. Since 1940 in the army. Very noble young man. Stays overnight in the house of the Russian Commandant.
May 22: morning, together with Georg Rosenfeld in the park. Left 10.30am.

Having left Theresienstadt, George spent several days in the forest of Bohemia grieving for the loss of his parents. He tried to make his way back to the British Zone, but was picked up by Russian soldiers who accused him of being a German spy in British uniform, especially since he spoke fluent German. George offered his cover story that his parents were Czech and he had lived in the Sudetenland and attended a German school. He was detained and interrogated for five days, always by a different interrogator, but fortunately released. He found his way back to his regiment and when he arrived at the canteen, his comrades fell silent because they thought he had been killed.

George's parents perished in Auschwitz. On 23 August 1942 both were sent on transports from Württemberg to Theresienstadt, where they survived for just over two years. On 6 October 1944 his father Karl was sent on transport number EO1505 to Auschwitz and his mother Elisabeth on transport number EO1506.[12] It is thought that they were murdered on arrival.

Harry Rossney (Helmuth Rosettenstein) was among the fortunate ones who eventually found his mother. He writes: 'It took the Red Cross several years to locate my mother who had left Berlin in March 1939 and returned to my home-town Koenigsberg. It was twelve years before we met again in London because at the end of the war, she was trapped in the east under Russian occupation. It was then that I learned that three of my cousins had been killed in Stalingrad.'

## THE WAR CEMETERIES IN NORMANDY

As British Forces advanced beyond Bayeux, the task of burying thousands of fallen Allied soldiers in Normandy began. The cost of war was a daily reality for Harry Rossney, a sign-writer by trade, who was transferred from 93 Company of the alien Pioneer Corps to 32 Graves Registration Unit in Bayeux. He was responsible for organising and training the labour force that would carry out the sign-writing on the temporary grave markers, later replaced by white stones erected by the Imperial War Graves Commission (subsequently the Commonwealth War Graves Commission). He also painted by hand every large signboard for the war cemeteries around Normandy, including Bayeux, Ranville and Hottot. He describes that period:

I was ordered to join 32 Graves Registration Unit (32 GRU) in Bayeux immediately. No argument, no requests, no alternatives. With heavy heart I left my old mates of 93 company – this oasis of fellow Jewish-German and Austrian refugees who understood and felt the same, had the same outlook, accents and humour. I felt shattered and very alone. When they told me what I had to do, my heart sank to my boots. Bury the dead. Create a workshop to paint white metal crosses and sign-write every dead soldier's name, number, regiment and religion. We came face-to-face with the price of war each and every day. But someone had to do it. The dead numbered in their thousands. Our unit which was responsible for about eighteen British war cemeteries, occupying a single-storey house with garage, garden and space behind. It consisted of a handful of selected specialists, local French labourers and a dozen German POWs. Tools were in short supply, so the POWs made their own brushes and rulers. Two other German refugees joined our unit, a non-Jewish artist Walter Nessler who had refused to toe the Nazi party line, and Jack Dalton, originally a paint-sprayer. I made it my business to hand-letter every big nameboard for each cemetery, white lettering on black, large enough to be seen from a clear distance.

One day whilst in Normandy, close to Hottot, one of our cemeteries, I stumbled across a hastily dug shallow grave with a small wooden cross, and a German helmet with a neat sniper's bullet hole in the temple. The name read 'Heinz Brand'. I was shocked. It was none other than my school friend from Berlin. He had been no Nazi, but had obviously fought in the German Army.

Harry has written a poem dedicated to his friend, part of which is quoted here:

Once we'd left school each went his way . . .
I left for England just in time, before war cut every line.
Time flew on wings to '44. Normandy lay dusty-red like a savage torn-up bed
Below a blazing July sky, I came upon a hasty cross deep in a narrow orchard lane,
It lay in hiding, airless, stilled
A German soldier had been killed . . .
The helmet bore a sniper's mark.

And as I knelt to read the name
Shock pierced the silence black and stark . . .
Of all the thousands left behind,
It had to be the very same . . .!

Harry remained with 32 Graves Registration Unit until 1946, working at the Allied cemeteries in Normandy.

THE SEARCH FOR NAZI WAR CRIMINALS

As Allied forces swept into Germany, the most wanted Nazi war criminals went into hiding and assumed false identities and disguises. One of the central tasks was to capture them alive and bring them to trial. Howard Alexander (Hans Alexander), originally of 93 Company of the Pioneer Corps, returned to Germany in British uniform as a captain:

> We were unloading disinfectant at Belsen. We had no idea what we were coming to. I was to work as an interpreter, which included an interview with Irma Grese, the infamous 'beast of Belsen'. I visited her in Celle prison where a British policeman interrogated her and I interpreted her responses. I told the policeman that it was a waste of time interrogating her – she was such a hardened woman who had committed horrendous crimes in Belsen. I would rather hunt for those who had not yet been captured.[13]

Irma Grese was eventually hanged for her crimes. Howard was then assigned to tracking down Rudolf Hoess, the notorious commandant of Auschwitz, responsible for the most horrendous crimes in the camp and the deaths of thousands of Jews. Hoess had fled and was believed to be living under the assumed name Fritz Lang in a remote farmhouse near Flensburg, a few miles north of Hamburg. A group of British soldiers including Howard Alexander, tracked down Hoess's wife and carried out surveillance of the area. Hoess was finally caught in early March 1946:

> One night after the 11 o'clock curfew, we went to a farmhouse about five miles from the Danish border where we were reasonably sure he was hiding. We were accompanied by a medical officer in case he took a cyanide pill. We took Hoess out of the building and he naturally protested that he was someone else. But we had photographs of him. He had put a lot of effort into changing his identity but he had kept his wedding ring with the date of his marriage inscribed on it. I interrogated him no end of times.

A copy of Hoess's sworn statement exists in the archives of the Imperial War Museum, donated by the family of Charles MacKay (Karl Krumbein).[14] An Austrian, he came to England on the Kindertransport in December 1938, working at Whittingehame Farm, Lord Balfour's estate in Scotland. He enlisted in the British Forces in

September 1944 and served for nearly two years in the Intelligence Corps. It is not known to what extent he was involved with Hoess but it would appear that he took the sworn statement with Karl Abrahams, another refugee in British uniform.

Captain Murdoch and Captain Eric Schweiger, both members of 12 Force of SOE, were to track down SS Obergruppenführer Oswald Pohl who had built up the Nazi administration during the 1930s. By the end of the war Pohl was responsible for the administration of the concentration camps and SS industrial enterprises. After months of tracking Pohl's last known movements under the name of Ludwig Gniss, Schweiger finally discovered that Pohl was living opposite the barracks of the Black Watch regiment in Verdun. The priority was to capture Pohl before he committed suicide using a cyanide pill:

He [Schweiger] set out in uniform, accompanied by a German policeman and a corporal in the Black Watch disguised as a Polish displaced person. On arrival, the policeman was sent into the village to ascertain that Pohl/Gniss was there, discovered him working in a garden. Schweiger then hid and the young corporal, who spoke broken German, went forward with the policeman and accused Pohl of having stolen his bicycle. Feigning anger, the corporal leapt at the unsuspecting Pohl and dived into his pockets – where two poison capsules were discovered.[15]

Pohl was arrested and taken to Verdun prison for a few hours before being transferred to 'Tomato', a small prison in Minden used by the War Crimes Investigation Unit. He was tried by an American military tribunal after the Nuremburg trials. Pohl was found guilty of war crimes and eventually hanged in 1951.

Garry Rogers (Gunter Baumgart) was involved in interrogation work and the hunt for war criminals. He comments on what it was like as a German Jew returning to Germany and coming into close contact with the perpetrators:

Most of the history of that time had not yet come to light until many years later. It is clear now that not just a few, but tens, maybe hundreds of thousands were actively involved in the extermination of six million Jews in Europe. At the time we were looking for just the top echelon of the Nazi Party; the SS, the concentration camp guards and commanders and the special *Einsatz Gruppen* (murder squads). My job was to find these and bring them to justice. I hope I did my job well and was instrumental in finding and sentencing many war criminals. Many thousands were never found and have lived out their lives in comfort, untroubled by their consciences. I have great regrets that I did not devote my life to weeding out these cancers of society.

My job was to interrogate prisoners and hope to get information from them. Rather an arduous task. Why would anyone admit guilt? We were not in the Gestapo or the KGB and our methods to extract information were strictly controlled. We were not allowed to handle any suspect physically, although the temptation was often great. British fair play had to come above everything else . . . I could not hate an entire population, having met some perfectly normal people. By entering Germany as a soldier, and being able to get to know people on a personal level, it was possible to sort out my feelings at the time.[16]

## THE WAR CRIMES INVESTIGATION UNIT AND TRIALS

The War Crimes Investigation Unit for the British sector was based at the headquarters of the British Army of the Rhine at Bad Oeynhausen. On 2 May 1945 British troops arrived at Neuengamme concentration camp outside Hamburg to find the camp virtually empty. The inmates had been evacuated towards the end of April, 9,000 of whom were believed to have been boarded onto three ships. Two of the ships, the *Cap Arcona* and *Thielbek*, were bombed in the bay of Lübeck in a British attack which had not expected the ships to be carrying survivors from a concentration camp. Neuengamme was not intended as a death camp, but thousands certainly died there. It had a crematorium and punishment cells. Of 106,000 prisoners, among whom were Dutch and French resistance fighters, homosexuals, Jehovah Witnesses, 500 gypsies and 13,000 Jews, only half survived. In 1943 the Nazis rounded up 2,000 of the Danish police force, all of whom were taken to Neuengamme. Medical experiments were carried out on children, and other inmates worked in harsh conditions in nearby factories. The SS guards of Neuengamme had fled, but once caught, were imprisoned in Hamburg. The camp commandant, Max Pauli and ten others, were sentenced in a British court in March 1946.

After the acceptance of the formal unconditional surrender of Germany on 8 May 1945, the area north of Hamburg became full of defeated German armies, displaced persons and forced labourers, presenting a huge task for the British Army. Neuengamme became an internment camp, run by British Forces. Dennis Goodman (Hermann Gutmann), in the uniform of the 8th Kings Royal Irish Hussars, was posted there in mid-September 1945. He explains:

The initial concern was not that individual activities might have been criminal but whether they were a danger to the security of the British Forces. I was allocated to the Review and Interrogation Staff at No. 6 Civilian Internment Camp at the former Neuengamme concentration camp near Bergedorf, a suburb of Hamburg. This was a small unit of around seven linguistically qualified personnel plus administrative staff under the command of Major Bateman and then Captain van Peborgh of the Intelligence Corps, quartered in Bergedorf with offices in a building near the entrance of the camp. Most individuals arrested in the Hamburg area fell into arrestable categories: members of the SS, senior officials of the Nazi apparatus and government, justices, court officials, senior army and naval officers (U-boat commanders) and members of the Hamburg *Abwehr* (Nazi intelligence). They were brought to Neuengamme where they completed an initial questionnaire and then it was our task to interrogate and assess them. We had to write-up a report on each of them. It was extremely hard work because we were always too few to cope with the number of people brought to the camp. Many of our evenings were spent discussing individual cases. It was also depressing to learn how it was possible for Nazism to dominate to such an extent as to eliminate civic courage amongst the vast majority, suppress opposition and abolish the rule of law as understood in a civilized world. It didn't take me long to realise that every German must have known what was happening but turned their heads because of fear or apathy.

Rudolf von Alvensleben was arrested and brought to Neuengamme where he was shown into my room practically on arrival. I knew only what was filled in on the questionnaire and it is possible that I had seen his name on a listing of suspected war criminals. He was a self-possessed man but with an ingratiating mien which conveyed to me a feeling that his rank and area of service combined with personality required thorough investigation and my assessment stated that he was a potential danger to security and likely to attempt an escape. I impressed on the officer in charge of the camp guards that the man should be held in the high security compound. This was disregarded. I went on leave and on return reported back at Hamburg Intelligence Headquarters to be greeted by the words, 'von Alvensleben has escaped'. Everyone knew how concerned I had been about the man who, it transpired, was not only a General of the SS Police but also a close associate of Himmler and responsible for the murder of many Jews, Russians and Poles. My investigation at the camp found that he had left in an ambulance in substitution for another 'ill' patient. I had heard of the existence of well-planned escape routes with safe houses and border crossings and was very keen to track him down, but at this point I had to hand over to Bad Oeyenhausen. It always irked me and when in my subsequent career I spent time in Buenos Aires in 1949, I was befriended by my dentist. He also worked at the University Dental Clinic at which many Germans were being treated. I had told him the von Alvensleben story and someone told me that he was living in the Province under an assumed name. It was common knowledge that Argentina's President Peron had offered asylum and made use of a number of Nazi war criminals. Although von Alvensleben was sentenced to death *in absentia* by a German Court, he died in Argentina in 1970. He was never brought to justice.[17]

Walter Freud, who was parachuted into the Styria region of Austria with SOE, worked on the Neuengamme war crimes investigations at the end of the war. He was based in Hamburg rather than Neuengamme, although he visited the camp on several occasions. He was also assigned to investigating the activities of the Hamburg-based company Tesch & Stabenow:

I was on the Stabenow case which was a firm which supplied Zyklon B to the concentration camp. It was a firm of fumigators for ships bringing grain to Europe. After each trip they were fumigated for rats, mice. . . . That firm specialised in fumigating the ships. They were asked by the SS to produce an expertise in fumigating. . . . And the man in charge said 'Yes, of course. I supplied so much Zyklon B to the concentration camps. He couldn't deny it because we found all the receipts, but they were for the clothes of the prisoners, they were full of mice. And I had no idea it was used for humans.' He was a dreadful person, not only from my point of view, but also his own employees, and they all came and they said 'There was a meeting between Dr Tesch and the SS, where he was told what it was for, and his technicians advised the SS on how to do it, because it is a dangerous powder, and you had to have the technique of introducing it into the chambers and so on.' It had to be studied. It was Dr Tesch's staff who advised the SS of how to do it. So there was no excuse and he was hanged. He was one of the very first German technicians who were actually hanged and not excused or let free after a few years. He was an absolute die-hard Nazi. An honorary SS man, and his books were only Nazi books. It's interesting for instance that when Hamburg was so badly bombed, Himmler wrote a letter to the Mayor of Hamburg saying please help Tesch to get up on his feet again. Only Stabenow was given that privileged treatment.[18]

Towards the end of the investigations, Walter discovered the appalling suffering inflicted by the Nazis on French Jewish boys. This was the last straw for him. The Nazis were experimenting by cutting off parts of the boys' bodies and freezing them. He could tolerate no more and left the War Crimes Investigation Unit. He later recalled to his family that the other distressing part about the investigations concerned the *Kapos* – the Jews who were put in charge of other Jews. He found that the *Kapos* were more brutal than the Nazis and this shocked him to the core. Freud was also assigned to the case of the German industrialist Krupp who was thought to have helped the Nazis at the highest level and supplied munitions. He found no evidence to convict Krupp and concluded that most of the documentation had already been destroyed. During a visit to Denmark in 1946 as part of the war crimes investigations, he met his future wife Annette Krarup and they married in a small church in Vallø on 20 August 1947.

Max Dickson (Max Dobriner) served originally in the Pioneer Corps and then 3 Troop of No. 10 Inter-Allied Commando, attached to 41 RM Commando. He was deployed as a commando later in the war and involved in front-line fighting in Belgium and Holland. At the end of the war he was engaged in the demobilisation of the German Army, assigned to interrogation work. He recalls: 'One day, one of our Jewish boys was interrogating a Gestapo man who had sent his parents to their deaths. We had to restrain him physically.' After interrogation work, Dickson was posted to 98 Field Security and sent to an outpost at Beckum, south of Osnabrück, in Westphalia.

> We had meetings once a week and were given a list of people to interrogate and write up a report. Our group covered the districts of Beckum, Tecklenburg and Münsterland. We had to flush out some of the Nazi war criminals. It was all top secret. Four of us went to Krupps factory in Essen. We had to go through all their papers. It was a huge factory which had employed over 50,000 workers. It was responsible for making guns, tanks, ammunitions and heavy armament. Krupp employed a lot of foreign labour and it was our task to investigate crimes committed against the people who had worked for him. By the time we visited, they were making pots and pans and machines for other factories. I was disgusted by the working conditions for the employees.[19]

In the autumn of 1945 Fred Warner, who had been parachuted behind enemy lines in an SOE mission, was given instructions to join the War Crimes Investigation Unit. He had no desire to return to Germany, but an order was an order. He had also received confirmation that his parents and young sister had perished in Auschwitz. This was his opportunity to catch some of the perpetrators who had a hand in his family's death. He joined one of the investigation teams first in Bünde near Bad Oeynhausen and then Hamburg, to arrest and interrogate suspected Nazi war criminals. If they had not yet been arrested, he was to find and interview witnesses to prepare the case for the legal section. In his unpublished memoirs, he gives an example: 'Another officer and I had to arrest the owner and the foreman of a quarry near Bad Eilsen. Inmates from the nearby Lahde-Weser concentration camp, who were forced to carry out extremely heavy work there in terrible conditions, had been ill-treated and a number had died there.' One of his responsibilities was, on occasion, to look after witnesses for the war crimes trials. He was responsible for one witness, Sylvia Salvesen, the wife of the Norwegian king's personal physician. She had been sent to Ravensbrück concentration camp by the Nazis. Warner also met another witness from the camp, Odette Churchill (née Samson). Not only was he responsible for witnesses, he was often called up to transport prisoners:

We also had to take suspects from 'Tomato' prison to other prisons and from interrogation centres to Hamburg, where they had to give evidence at trials. In the case of the *Höhere SS* and *Polizeiführer* von Bassewitz-Behr (a senior security official), whom I had to take to West Berlin, the British War Crimes Liaison Officer handed him over to the Russians. Prior to his posting to Hamburg he had been stationed in Russia where he had been responsible for mass shootings. On another occasion, my boss and I took the head of the Bremen Gestapo, Dr Schweder, to Hamburg where he was to give evidence at a war crimes trial. . . . During my time with XXX Corps at Lüneburg, I was ordered to interview a German ex-naval rating to get information to be used in the case against Admiral Raeder who was being tried in Nuremberg with the other top Nazi leaders.

The German was held at the time in prison in Schleswig-Holstein for a minor criminal offence. I was to bring his statement immediately to the British prosecution staff at Nuremberg.

Being down there in the American Zone of Germany, I was also given a brief for a short interrogation of one of the SS officers responsible for the most murders committed by the SS outside the concentration and extermination camps. He was *Obergruppenführer* Otto Ohlendorf, the head of the *Einsatzgruppen* (Action Groups) who arrested and shot thousands of Russian commissars and Jews in Russia. He had already been tried by the Americans and was awaiting his sentence in jail in Nuremberg. All that was wanted was the answer to one question, which could have helped one of his fellow SS officers on trial by the British. When I asked him what he did at the *ReichsSicherheitshauptamt*, the main security headquarters in Berlin, where he was a leading figure, he had the cheek to say that he looked out of the window all day long admiring the trees and flowers in the garden below. That was the end of the interrogation. Ohlendorf was sentenced to death by hanging.

Being in Nuremberg, I attended the main trial of the leading Nazis one whole day as an observer. I had seen some of these evil men before I left Germany, and Hess in Wales during the war. They looked a motley lot and, with the exception of Goering and Schacht, they appeared fairly downcast. Goering seemed to enjoy the proceedings. I was of course in uniform and sat in the visitors' gallery next to Air Commodore Fielden, the Captain of the King's Flight. During the break, he asked me rather incredulously if I really could understand German so well that I could listen to the original language. I told him that I could, but wondered if he believed me or thought that I was showing off.[20]

In early 1947 Warner was promoted to leader of the Investigation Team, during which time he handled many interesting cases and some of the most brutal Nazi figures were brought to justice. This included investigations into the Fuhlsbüttel Gestapo prison in Hamburg. The team arrested about 60 prison staff, most of the prison's personnel. They were eventually brought to trial in two separate groups. Warner's work occasionally overlapped with investigations of the atrocities at the Neuengamme concentration camp. He was finally demobilised in August 1948, and as such, was among the last of the enemy aliens to be discharged from the forces.

As the perpetrators of the atrocities were gradually brought to trial, German and Austrian refugees in British uniform were called upon to carry out translation work. Every town and city court needed interpreters and this is where the Germans and Austrians in the forces came to the fore. In October 1946 Peter Eden (Werner Engel, born in Breslau) was involved with the Essen War Crimes Trials of twenty-two Germans accused of murdering British pilots. At Nuremberg Captain Forest, an actor from Vienna, and Captain Palmer acted as court translators, with Captain W. Frank and Sergeant Hachenberg as the main interpreters at the trial. Viennese-born lawyer Stephen Stewart (Stephen Strauss) played a key role in the prosecuting teams in a number of the trials. He was considered a left-wing lawyer in Nazi terms and his life was at risk, so he had to leave Austria. He was smuggled into Poland after the *Anschluss* and came to Britain where he was eventually drafted into the alien Pioneer Corps. In 1940 he was appointed as a liaison officer with the Free French Forces and the Belgian Army. In 1945, with the rank of major, he was assigned to the Judge Advocate General's office of the 21st Army Group. In September 1945 he was appointed Assistant Prosecutor in the tribunal convened in Lüneburg for the trial of those involved in the atrocities at Belsen concentration camp. This included the trial of forty-four of the jailers. In 1946 Stewart was responsible for preparing the evidence against fourteen members of staff of the Neuengamme concentration camp and presided at their trial as Chief Prosecutor in Hamburg. He headed the legal team which investigated, and then prosecuted, those responsible for the torture and deaths of hundreds of thousands of women in the Ravensbrück concentration camp, gathering testimonies from the survivors of the camp. In his opening prosecution statement in Lüneburg he addressed the issue that the Allies were accused of exacting revenge as the victors. He firmly outlined that nothing could be further from the truth and such assertions were not only dangerous but also wrong in law. He went on to establish why the defendants were being prosecuted for war crimes and the nature of their guilt.

By the end of 1947 the vast majority of the King's Most Loyal Enemy Aliens had received their demobilisation papers. Returning to civilian life was far from easy. Most left the army with a small amount of money and a demob suit, and had to start a career from almost nothing. They tended to help each other to find their first jobs whenever possible. It was an uphill struggle because for many, their education had been disrupted by the Nazi regime and they lacked any formal training or trade. During 1946 and 1947 they applied to become British citizens and were granted British nationality – and their desire to become British was complete. Many went on to establish successful careers and make an invaluable contribution to the sciences, the arts and humanities, business, and public life.

# REFLECTIONS: THE CONTRIBUTION OF THE KING'S MOST LOYAL ENEMY ALIENS

The story of the King's Most Loyal Enemy Aliens is one of extraordinary survival against the odds but also one of unprecedented loss. All paid a heavy price in the fight to set Europe free from Nazism. The majority lost family and friends in the concentration camps as well as comrades on the battlefields of Europe. When they returned to Germany at the end of the war in British Army uniform, the full scale and horror of the Holocaust began to unfold. Six million of Europe's Jews and five million others had perished in the death camps. The camp survivors could barely speak of their experiences, so too those who fought in the British Forces. They remained silent for over fifty years. They did not wish to burden their children with the past. Now in their late eighties and early nineties, we stand on the threshold of losing their stories. Some have begun to record their experiences for their grandchildren, but there are many more that have yet to be told. Often they believe that theirs is not worth telling, but once they start doing so the pain of their sacrifice and immense selfless bravery comes to the fore.

Over half of those who enlisted in the British Forces had begun their army career in the unglamourous Pioneer Corps. Every one of them were volunteers. Most waited patiently for their chance to play an active role in the defeat of Hitler, not knowing whether that opportunity would be realised. As the stories in this book demonstrate, from 1942 and 1943 they went on to make an inestimable contribution to the successful defeat of Nazism, not only on the frontline but also in operations behind enemy lines. Their knowledge of, and fluency in, German was the single-most factor for the government permitting them into fighting regiments and special forces. And at the end of the war, as their stories show, they transferred in their thousands into the Intelligence Corps and BAOR for the reconstruction of postwar Europe. The decision to admit them into fighting units profoundly affected the course of the war. For those veterans who survived, they lived in the knowledge that they played their part in the downfall of Hitler. They were granted British nationality after the war and lived out their lives in total loyalty to the Crown and contributed in no small way to public life. Many have ensured continuity with the past and survival for the future through their children, grandchildren and great-grandchildren.

In spite of all that they have been through, these men and women have not harboured bitterness against the perpetrators. Scars remain deep within, but they have now found the strength to tell their story however painful. Most are philosophical about the need to forgive but never forget. All express a profound sense of gratitude to Britain for saving them from certain death in the Holocaust. Ernest Goodman (Ernst Guttmann) was one of the few Germans in the Coldstream Guards. His words are a permanent reminder of their selfless sacrifice:

What did (and do) the Germans think of us? Some say readily that we committed high treason. Of course, I don't mind that at all. We were not British subjects at that time and I have had many interesting conversations about that with German colleagues while on visiting professorships in Wuerzburg. We did what we thought we had to do. My conduct was deemed exemplary in the demob document as was that of others too. We tried to fight for the redemption of the human race and to give history another chance.

Lest we forget their contribution: the King's Most Loyal Enemy Aliens.

# SELECT BIBLIOGRAPHY

## PAPERS AND ARCHIVES

The Imperial War Museum; the Association of Jewish Ex-service Men and Women (AJEX); the Association of Jewish Refugees; the Wiener Library of Contemporary History and Holocaust; the Freud Museum, London; the Jewish Military Museum; the Library, Belsize Square Synagogue, London; the National Archives (Public Record Office), Kew; the Royal Logistics Corps Museum; the RAF Museum, Hendon; the National Army Museum; the Tank Museum; the Ilfracombe Museum and the North Devon Record Office.

## BOOKS AND MEMOIRS

Alexander, John, *A Measure of Time*, privately published, 2000, copy in Belsize Square Synagogue Library

Ambrose, Kenneth, *The Suitcase in the Garage: Letters and Photographs of a German Jewish Family, 1800–1950*, unpublished memoirs

Ambrose, Tom, *Hitler's Loss: What Britain and America Gained from Europe's Cultural Exiles*, Peter Owen, 2001

Behrendt, Gideon, *The Long Road Home*, privately published memoirs, Israel, 2005

Bellamy, Bill, *Troop Leader: A Tank Commander's Story*, Sutton, 2005

Bender, Edgar, *Reminiscences of the Pioneer Corps: 1940–1942*, unpublished

Bentwich, Norman, *I Understand the Risks: The Story of the Refugees from Nazi Oppression who Fought in the British Forces in the World War*, Victor Gollancz, 1950

Berghahn, Marion, *Continental Britons: German-Jewish Refugees from Nazi Germany*, Berg, 1988

Clare, George, *Last Waltz in Vienna: The Destruction of a Family 1842–1942*, Pan, 1990

Cresswell, Yvonne, *Living With the Wire: Civilian Internment in the Isle of Man during the Two World Wars*, Manx National Heritage, 1994

Dale, Stephen, *Spanglet or By Any Other Name*, privately published memoirs, 1993

Dear, Ian, *Ten Commando 1942–1945*, Leo Cooper, 1987

Eberstadt, Walter Albert, *Whence We Came, Where We Went*, WAE Books, 2002

Farringdon, Ava and Leicester City Museum Service, *A Life Divided: Johannes Matthaeus Koelz*, catalogue to accompany the exhibition

Fournier, Gérard and André Heintz, *Opération 'Aquatint' 12–13 September 1942. Le raid d'un commando britannique á Saint-Laurent-sur-Mer*, France, OREP Editions

Fournier, Gérard and André Heintz, *If I Must Die . . . From Postmaster to Aquatint*, France, OREP Editions, 2006

Frayling, Christopher, *Ken Adam: The Art of Production Design*, Faber & Faber, 2005

Freud, Anton Walter, *Before the Anticlimax: with Special Operations Executive in Austria*, unpublished memoirs, copies in the Freud Museum and the Imperial War Museum

Freud, Martin, *Glory Reflected. Sigmund Freud – Man and Father*, Angus & Robertson, 1957

Friedlander, Gerhart and Turner, Keith, *Rudi's Story: The Diary and Wartime Experiences of Rudolf Friedlander*, Jedburgh, 2006

Fry, Helen, *Jews in North Devon during the Second World War*, Halsgrove, 2005

Gillman, Peter and Gillman, Leni, *Collar the Lot: How Britain Interned and Expelled its Wartime Refugees*, Quartet Books, 1980

Goodman, Ernest, unpublished memoirs

Gottlieb, Amy Zahl, *Men of Vision: Anglo-Jewry's Aid to Victims of the Nazi Regime 1933–1945*, Weidenfeld & Nicolson, 1998

Grenville, Anthony, *Continental Britons: Jewish Refugees from Nazi Europe*, the Jewish Museum, London, 2002

Hampshire, A. Cecil, *Beachhead Commandos*, William Kimber, 1983

Holden, Rolf, *One of the Lucky Ones*, unpublished memoirs

Kemp, Anthony, *The Secret Hunters*, Michael O'Mara Books, 1986

Kemp, Anthony, *The SAS at War: The Special Air Service Regiment 1941–1945*, John Murray, 1991

Leighton-Langer, Peter, *X Steht für unbekannt: Deutsche und Österreicher in den Britischen Streitkräften im Zweiten Weltkrieg* ('X Means Unknown: Germans and Austrians in the British Fighting Forces in the Second World War'), Berlin, Verlag, 1999

Leighton-Langer, Peter, *The King's Own Loyal Enemy Aliens*, Vallentine Mitchell, 2006

Lindsay, Martin, *So Few Got Through*, Collins, 1946

Lustig, Fritz, unpublished memoirs

Masters, Peter, *Striking Back: A Jewish Commando's War Against the Nazis*, Presidio Press, 1997

Miles, Wilfred, *The Life of a Regiment: 1919–1945. The History of the Gordon Highlanders*, Frederick Warne, 1961

Mortimer, Gavin, *Stirling's Men: The Inside Story of the SAS in World War II*, Weidenfeld & Nicolson, 2004

Pelican, Fred, *From Dachau to Dunkirk*, Vallentine Mitchell, 1993

Perlès, Alfred, *Alien Corn*, George Allen & Unwin Ltd, 1944

Perry, Geoffrey, *When Life Becomes History*, White Mountain Press, 2002

Perry, Peter J., *An Extraordinary Commission: The Story of a Journey Through Europe's Disaster*, published by the author, 1997, distributed by T.J. Gillard Print Services, Bristol

Rogers, Garry, *Interesting Times*, privately published autobiography, 1998

Rossney, Harry, *Grey Dawns: Illustrated Poems about Life in Nazi Germany, Emigration, and Active Service in the British Army during the War*, privately published, 2003. Copy in the Imperial War Museum

Rossney, Harry, *Normandy 1944: Recollections*, privately published, copy in the author's possession. Copy in the Imperial War Museum

Rossney, Harry, *Personal Recollections during War-service Abroad 1944–46*, privately published, copy in author's possession

Stent, Ronald, *A Bespattered Page? The Internment of 'His Majesty's Most Loyal Enemy Aliens'*, Andre Deutsch, 1980

Streat, Norman (trans.), *The Sacrifice We Are Now Making . . . Letters from one of His Majesty's Most Loyal Enemy Aliens, July–November 1940*, unpublished, copy in the author's possession

Ward, Kenneth, *And then the Music Stopped Playing*, Braiswick, 2006

Warner, Fred, *Personal Account of SOE Period*, unpublished memoirs, copy in the Imperial War Museum and courtesy of Eric Sanders

Wright, Irene, B.M., *Looking Back*, privately published memoirs of Irene Bleichroeder Metzger Wright

Young, D., *Four Five*, Leo Cooper, 1972

## ARTICLES AND INTERVIEWS

Chamberlain, Lesley, 'Malice through the looking-glass', in *FT Magazine*, 28 February 2004, pp. 22–5

Hamilton, Paul, 'Good Show the Paratroops', in *Time & Tide*, 15 July 1944, pp. 614–16

Lewkowicz, Bea, *Conversations with Professor Julius Carlebach*, Centre for German-Jewish Studies, 2000

Lewkowicz, Bea, *Video Interview with Anton Freud*, copy in the Jewish Museum, London

Sugarman, Martin, *Jews at the Battle of Arnheim, September 1944*, copy sent to the author

Sugarman, Martin, *No. 3 (Jewish) Troop, No. 10 Commando*, copy given to the author

# NOTES

Introduction
1. Count Bernadotte (1895–1948), nephew of King Gustav V of Sweden, acted as mediator in both world wars.
2. Walter Eberstadt, *Whence We Came, Where We Went*, p. 340.

Chapter 1
1. Alfred Perlés, *Alien Corn*, pp. 54– 5.
2. Harry Rossney, *Grey Dawns*, privately published memoirs and poems.
3. Alfred Perlés, *Alien Corn*, pp. 60–1.
4. Edgar Bender, *Reminiscences of the Pioneer Corps: 1940–1942*, unpublished, p. 2.
5. Edgar Bender, *Reminiscences*, p. 4.
6. Harry Rossney, *Grey Dawns*.
7. William Howard, *They Shall Not Pass: Recollections from Private Horst Adolf Herzberg*.
8. *Before the Anticlimax*.
9. Interview with the author.
10. Interview and correspondence with the author.
11. Harry Rossney, *Grey Dawns*. For a fuller profile, see Helen Fry, *Jews in North Devon during the Second World War*, pp. 19–23.
12. See Peter Perry, *An Extraordinary Commission*; and Geoffrey Perry, *When Life Becomes History*.
13. *Glory Reflected*, p. 204.
14. Interview with the author during 2005 and 2006.
15. For a more detailed account of the entertainment in Ilfracombe, see chapter 5 of *Jews in North Devon during the Second World War*.
16. Fritz Lustig, unpublished memoirs.
17. *Ilfracombe Chronicle*, 28 March 1941.
18. *Ibid.*, 4 April 1941.
19. *Ibid.*, 1 August 1941.

20. Fritz Lustig, unpublished memoirs. After Ilfracombe he stayed with the Pioneer Corps Orchestra in Bulford until May 1943 when he volunteered to be transferred to the Intelligence Corps. He was subsequently stationed at two POW camps in Buckinghamshire until the end of the war.

21. Garry Rogers, *Interesting Times*, pp. 124–5.

22. Alfred Perlés, *Alien Corn*, p. 81.

23. Rolf Holden, *One of the Lucky Ones*, p. 42.

24. Harry Rossney, *Normandy 1944 Recollections*, privately published.


Chapter 2

1. The organisation of units in the Royal Armoured Corps differed prior to the Second World War.

2. The 1st Royal Tank Regiment was part of the 22nd Armoured Brigade, the main armoured element of the 7th Armoured Division. The 8th Kings Royal Irish Hussars was the Divisional reconnaissance regiment, directly under the 7th Armoured Division. I am very grateful to David Fletcher, historian at the Tank Museum, for his help with the material in this chapter.

3. Interview with the author.

4. Ken Ward, *And then the Music Stopped Playing*, pp. 87–8.

5. Interview with the author.

6. Ken Ward, *And then the Music Stopped Playing*, pp. 93–4.

7. Profile based on Ken Ward's autobiography *And then the Music Stopped Playing*, plus interview and correspondence with the author.

8. Ken Ward, *And then the Music Stopped Playing*, pp. 95–6.

9. The two main German Divisions operating in the area were 1st SS Panzer Corps which included 1st and 12th SS Panzer Divisions plus supporting units, and LXXXVI Corps which was not SS, but included 21st Panzer Division and 503 Heavy Panzer Battalion with substantial infantry, artillery and other units. I am grateful to David Fletcher, historian at the Tank Museum for his help in this respect.

10. Ken Ward, *And then the Music Stopped Playing*, pp. 105–7.

11. *Ibid.*, pp. 118–20.

12. This is confirmed in the official War Diaries for the 7th Armoured Division and 1st RTR and correspondence with David Fletcher of the Tank Museum, 27 September 2006.

13. Ken Ward, *And then the Music Stopped Playing*, p. 121.

14. Based on interviews with the author and correspondence.

15. His army number: 13118382.

16. Bill Bellamy, *Troop Leader: A Tank Commander's Story*.

17. Based on interviews and correspondence with the author.

18. His sister Dorothea also came to Britain and served with the ATS. They had an older sister, Betty, born in 1910 (died 1938) and an older brother Manfred, born 1917 who perished in the Hololcaust.
19. Based on extensive interviews with the author.
20. His regimental number was 13046415.
21. A photograph exists in official archives with Willy standing on his tank as King George inspects the tank and crew.
22. The official War Diaries show that some of C Squadron landed as late as 13 June 1944.
23. For a history of the Regiment, see Olivia Fitzroy, *Men of Valour: The Third Volume of the History of the VIII King's Royal Irish Hussars, 1927–1958.*
24. Copy of letter given to the author by Willy Field. On his demobilisation, Willy visited John Gardner's parents in London for what turned out to be an emotional meeting.
25. Bill Bellamy, *Troop Leader*, p. 162.

Chapter 3
1. See Ian Dear, *Ten Commando 1942–1945*, p. 20.
2. Richard Lehniger and Julia Dorfler were married in November 1939.
3. Army number: 13801849.
4. During her lifetime, Richard's wife always maintained that he had been involved in the Dieppe Raid. (3 Commando were there.) It is possible that they had discussed it during a private moment.
5. For official records, see The National Archives (Public Record Office) Kew, ref: ADM 179/227. For a detailed study of the raid, see Gérard Fournier and André Heintz, *Opération 'Aquatint' 12–13 Septembre 1942: Le raid d'un commando britannique á Saint-Laurent-sur-Mer*. See also the English translation entitled *If I Must Die . . . From Postmaster to Aquatint.*
6. *If I Must Die*, pp. 98–9.
7. In the family's possession are numerous letters written in German from Richard dating from 1940 to 12 September 1942. The last letter was written on the day that he died.
8. The three graves are next to each other with a standard headstone erected by the Commonwealth War Graves Commission.
9. *If I Must Die*, p. 123.
10. Extract used by kind permission of his daughter Irene Walters. Copyright resides with her.
11. I am grateful to Dr Gerhart Friedlaender, Keith Turner and Peter Oppenheimer for providing material for this profile.
12. Gerhart Friedlaender & Keith Turner, *Rudi's Story*, p. 11.
13. *Rudi's Story*, pp. 12–13.

14.  *Ibid.*, pp. 13–14.

15.  *Ibid.*, p. 38.

16.  *Ibid.*, pp. 57–8.

17.  Rudi's journal, reproduced in full in *Rudi's Story*, is a fascinating, revealing and touching account of his entire experience in the Italian campaign, including the weeks spent hiding in the cave.

18.  Extract from *Rudi's Story*, p. 129.

19.  See Gavin Mortimer, *Stirling's Men: The Inside History of the SAS in World War II*, London, Weidenfeld & Nicolson, 2004, pp. 258–9; and Tony Kemp, *The Secret Hunters*, pp. 25–35.

20.  *Evening Standard*, 27 March 1945.

21.  See also Gavin Mortimer, *Stirling's Men*, pp. 258–9.

22.  Anthony Kemp, *The Secret Hunters*, pp. 34–5.

Chapter 4

1.   This profile is based on extensive interviews with Colin Anson and also material in the Sound Archive at the Imperial War Museum, ref: 11883.

2.   Gustav Noske became the first *Reichswehrminister* of Germany.

3.   This is taken from St Paul's letter to the Romans 12:19 which is quoting Deuteronomy 32:35.

4.   Copy sent from the Ministry of Defence to his daughter, Sylvia Skinner.

5.   A small amount of information has been forthcoming from veterans of SOE and 3 Troop who knew him. Sources seem to suggest that he was probably part of SOE operations in Yugoslavia.

6.   Jasenovac, the infamous concentration camp of the Second World War, was situated in the Sava Valley, just 85km south-east of Zagreb.

7.   I am grateful to Sylvia Skinner for the information in this profile.

8.   Peter Masters, *Striking Back*, pp. 145–8.

9.   *Ibid.*, pp. 149–50, 153.

10.  *Ibid.*, pp. 157–8.

11.  It has been difficult to ascertain precise numbers of 3 Troop who landed at Walcheren.

12.  His army number: 13116420.

13.  Interview, 18 September 2005.

14.  Information in this profile is based on an interview in the Imperial War Museum, Sound Archive, ref: 13389.

15.  For the Commando action around Wesel, see D. Young, *Four Five*, p. 99ff.

16.  See also A. Cecil Hampshire, *Beachhead Commandos*, p. 357.

Chapter 5

1. Stephen Dale, *Spanglet or By Any Other Name*, p. 80.
2. *Ibid.*, p. 81.
3. The information here on Charles Kaiser and Harry Williams has been supplied by Dr Elisabeth Lebensaft and Christoph Mentschl from the Austrian Academy of Sciences in Vienna.
4. This profile is based on Walter Freud's unpublished memoirs *Before the Anticlimax* and interviews with members of his family.
5. Letter dated 30 January 1943, Anton Freud's papers, the Imperial War Museum.
6. Unpublished memoirs, Walter Freud, *Before the Anticlimax: With Special Operation Executive in Austria*, p. 32.
7. Freud, *Before the Anticlimax*, p. 43.
8. *Ibid.*, p. 52ff.
9. This profile uses extracts from Fred Warner's unpublished memoirs, *Personal Account of SOE Period*, pp. 59–80. Copy in the Imperial War Museum.
10. The details of Fred's movements and contacts during this period can be read in pp. 65–80 of his memoirs.
11. Sound Archive interview, IWM, ref: 14582 and also Stephen Dale, *Spanglet or By Any Other Name*, privately published memoirs, pp. 88–91.
12. Sound Archive interview, and Dale, *Spanglet*, p. 97.
13. Stephen Dale, *Spanglet or By Any Other Name*, p. 110.
14. Dale is referring to Pope John Paul II who died in 2005.
15. Sound Archive interview, IWM, ref: 14582.
16. There is no date on the article.
17. This profile is based entirely on an interview and correspondence with the author during August and September 2006.

Chapter 6

1. The Sound Archive at the Imperial War Museum, ref: 11481.
2. Information provided by Colin Anson of 3 Troop.
3. This profile is based on a number of interviews given to the author by Sir Ken Adam and also material in the Sound Archive at the Imperial War Museum.
4. His army number: 13803430. His eldest brother Peter also joined the Pioneer Corps in 1940, but enlisted at Westward Ho!
5. RAF number: 187137.
6. Christopher Frayling, *Ken Adam: The Art of Production Design*, pp. 37, 39.
7. Ken Adam to the author, October 2006.
8. Named after Ernest Bevan, Minister of Labour.
9. Interview with the author, September 2006.
10. RAF number: 1897060.

11. Interview with Ken Ambrose at the Sound Archive, Imperial War Museum, ref: 22682.

12. Ken Ambrose, *The Suitcase in the Garage*, p. 365.

13. He eventually escaped through France, and when Nazi forces swept through France he sailed to England as a stowaway on a ship.

14. Interview on 11 July 2005.

15. Profile based on correspondence with the author.

16. This profile is based on an interview with the author and Sound Archive interview at the Imperial War Museum, ref: 90002.

17. Sidney was demobilised in August 1946.

Chapter 7

1. This profile is based on interviews with his widow Myrna Carlebach and interviews carried out by Dr Bea Lewkowicz for the Centre for German-Jewish Studies at the University of Sussex, 2000.

2. Army number: 13807379.

3. Royal Navy number: CJX 611460.

Chapter 8

1. Ernest Goodman, unpublished memoirs, p. 11.

2. *Ibid.*, p. 29.

3. Extracts from pp. 87–92.

4. Letter to the author dated 27 August 2005.

5. Unpublished memoirs, pp. 92–4, 98.

6. *Ibid.*, pp. 98–9.

7. *Ibid.*, p. 100.

8. Army number: 14447083.

9. Details sent to the author, 29 August 2005.

10. Letters 7 July and 29 August 2005.

11. Diaries for the period 1944–6 lent to the author by his son Peter Lee. See also Wilfred Miles, *Life of a Regiment: 1919–1945. The History of the Gordon Highlanders*.

12. Martin Lindsay, *So Few Got Through*, p. 96.

13. *Ibid.*, p. 131.

14. Peter Lee, *The Long Dark Shadow*, section 3.

15. *Ibid.*, final page.

16. Based on an interview with the author and correspondence.

Chapter 9

1. 'Good Show the Paratroops', extract from an article written by Paul Hamilton in *Time & Tide*, 15 July 1944, pp. 614–16.

2. Sound Archive interview, Imperial War Museum, ref: 9243.

3.  Sound Archive, IWM, ref: 17973.

4.  For a profile see Helen Fry, *Jews in North Devon during the Second World War*.

5.  Norman Bentwich, *I Understand the Risks*, p. 98.

6.  See Martin Sugarman's article, 'Jews at the Battle of Arnhem', privately published, copy in the Jewish Military Museum, London.

7.  I am grateful to his son Nigel Hamilton for providing information for this profile.

8.  Service number: 13116470.

9.  Paul Hamilton, 'Good Show the Paratroops', *Time and Tide*, p. 614–16.

10. Army number: 13804250.

11. This profile is based on information provided by his niece Sally McNichol and his army record.

12. He changed his name once again when he emigrated to Israel. Gene O'Brian became Gideon Behrendt.

13. *The Long Road Home*, p. 68ff.

14. *Ibid.*, p. 81.

Chapter 10

1.  For more on the continental ATS girls in Ilfracombe, including photographs, see *Jews in North Devon during the Second World War*.

2.  For a full history of Milton Bryan, see Geoffrey Pidgeon, *The Secret Wireless War*, pp. 129– 48.

3.  Based on interviews with the author.

4.  Pidgeon, *The Secret Wireless War*, p. 143.

5.  Extract from unpublished memoirs.

6.  Correspondence with the author.

Chapter 11

1.  Eric served with BALU in Vienna first as a sergeant and then promoted to warrant officer II. He finished his military service in the rank of warrant officer I.

2.  Interview with the author, 25 August 2006.

3.  For his career in the British Forces, see his autobiography *An Extraordinary Commission*.

4.  Information based on correspondence with Stephen and Ann Freud, 2005.

5.  For a detailed profile on John Langford, see *Jews in North Devon during the Second World War*.

6.  Fritz Lustig, unpublished memoirs, pp. 82–3.

7.  Walter Eberstadt, *Whence We Came, Where We Went*, p. 332.

8.  Geoffrey Perry, *When Life Becomes History*, pp. 54–5, 57.

9.  Garry Rogers, *Interesting Times*, pp. 152–3.

10. Letter to the author 5 September 2006.

11. Rolf Holden, *One of the Lucky Ones*, p. 49.
12. Details taken from Auschwitz transport lists. Information traced by Mrs R. Rosney.
13. Based on interviews with the author.
14. Imperial War Museum, ref: 05/14/1.
15. Anthony Kemp, *The Secret Hunters*, p. 83.
16. Garry Rogers, *Interesting Times*, pp. 168, 170.
17. Interview and correspondence with the author.
18. Interview with Anton Freud by Bea Lewkowicz, the Jewish Museum, London.
19. Based on an interview with the author.
20. Fred Warner, unpublished memoirs, pp. 100–2.

# INDEX